Sor Juana

And Other Plays

Bilingual Press/Editorial Bilingüe

General Editor
Gary D. Keller

Managing Editor
Karen S. Van Hooft

Senior Editor
Mary M. Keller

Editorial Board
Juan Goytisolo
Francisco Jiménez
Eduardo Rivera
Severo Sarduy
Mario Vargas Llosa

Address
Bilingual Press
Department of Foreign Languages
and Bilingual Studies
EASTERN MICHIGAN UNIVERSITY
Ypsilanti, Michigan 48197
313-487-0042

Sor Juana

And Other Plays

Estela Portillo Trambley

Bilingual Press/Editorial Bilingüe
Ypsilanti, Michigan

All inquiries regarding performance rights to these plays should be addressed to the publisher: Bilingual Press, Dept. of Foreign Languages & Bilingual Studies, Eastern Michigan University, Ypsilanti, Michigan 48197. (313) 487-0042.

ISBN: 0-916950-33-6

Library of Congress Catalog Card Number: 82-73752

PRINTED IN THE UNITED STATES OF AMERICA

Cover design by Christopher J. Bidlack

Back cover photo by Achilles Studio

Acknowledgment

I have a friend, a dear and special friend, who found time in the midst of a multitude of commitments to advise me and guide me in the writing of these plays.

Thank you, Jorge Huerta, for inspiration, for your excellent suggestions, and for the minute scrutiny that helped me to improve my work, little by little.

I have become a considerably better playwright through his guidance, his generosity, and his great skill.

To my children:

Robert
Robbie
Tracey
Tina
Joyce
Naurene

CONTENTS

FOREWORD

The writing of plays has not been an easy task for me, for I have undergone a long apprenticeship; it has been above all a process of trial and error. I do believe that the art of good writing is rewriting, at least for me. I have tried my hand at most genres of writing: poetry, essay, short story, novel. I have found the writing of plays the most difficult, the most exciting, and the most rewarding. I have a long way to go before I can master this fragile craft. Yes, I believe the nature of a drama is fragile, built solely on emotional dynamics—the dynamics of human conflicts, the subtleties of feelings that make up the currents of movement, all dependent on words and responses in dialogue.

A well structured play is awesome. Unlike other genres, it does not have the backup of description, written detailed actions, or the force of proven ideas. A line of dialogue in drama can compress the quantum experience, revealing histories of the human soul or psyche. And because plays are not written to be read but to be produced, experienced by a living audience, they are never alive on paper. There is what William Carlos Williams might call "a beleaguered line of understanding" among writer, director, and audience. It is the most difficult of art forms, but the most rewarding: the life experience magnified for many to share—a living thing, theatre.

What drove me to write plays was not expertise in the art form but rather ignorance of it. I love theatre. I have acted in many plays. I put together a Chicano group while teaching drama at El Paso Community College. I decided to write plays. The members of the Chicano Theatre were novices too. There we were, innocents without funds, attempting a most demanding art form. We had one good thing in common—we loved putting a play together and had an instinctive love for the art. The members of the group were marvelous. They suffered through my first versions, heavy, verbose, dull. When a scene just wouldn't cut it, I rewrote, and they went along with it, discarding the lines they had learned for the rewrite, without any thought of lynching me. We worked—my, how we worked! We begged and borrowed material for sets, working long into the night hammering, cutting lumber, painting. We scrounged around for props, printed tickets, sold them, and consumed scripts. We were, in Shakespearian terms, a "household." The final productions, the talk sessions, all helped me to improve the play.

All the members of the Chicano Theatre were troupers and I thank them for sharing with me and giving so much of themselves. They included people like Alice Armendariz and Cindy Reyes, who inspired others to be as professional as they were, and Bert Salazar, who was the male lead in two of my productions and served so well in other capacities. In the New Lines Theatre at the University of Texas there was the tremendous support of professionals like Jo Mae George and Nick Kelemen. And there were my brothers, Frank Portillo and Dr. Robert Portillo, who never gave up on me.

And what have I learned from all this? I have learned that there are limitations imposed upon the art. The freedom of creativity is a myth. It is the expertise, knowledge of a given craft, that is free. All creative flow must be caught, carved, and curbed to be true to what is honest about life and people. When I first started writing drama I believed that the universal theme was the main concern. From there I could build an edifice. I was wrong. Honesty is the underlying structure that never fails. Serious literature is concerned with serious themes that touch human lives. You blow life into emotion and deeper needs with honesty—the simpler, the better. I also learned that the craft has basic techniques that cannot be ignored: the flow of movement, meaningful actions, levels of tension, the reality of characters are primary in bringing a play to life. The universal themes are then pleasant discoveries once the play is already written.

I have learned many things about my craft, but still not enough. And though I can voice with words how a good play comes into being, it is the most intricate of endeavors, where it is so easy to fail doing what you know should be done. It is truly a fragile and subtle craft. I still feel inadequate, but it will never stop me from trying to improve.

Puente Negro

CHARACTERS

(*In order of their appearance*)

OLD MAN   INOCENCIA
LA CHAPARRA   NARCISO
EL TOPO   TWO MEMBERS OF
MELITON   "LA MIGRA"
AMALIA

ACT ONE

ᒲᑊ ᒲᑊ ᒲᑊ

SCENE 1

The set is divided into three rooms. It is an old abandoned shack a few miles from the Rio Grande, which spans the border between El Paso, Texas, and Juárez, Mexico. The room stage right has a bed but no other furnishings. The center room is a kitchen; it has a table, two chairs. Upstage center is a door leading out to an open field. Next to the door is a rope hanging on a nail. The third room, stage left, has a bed, a broken-down dresser, and a small table holding a plaster saint, the VIRGIN MARY. *Around the statue are bottles and cans full of dusty paper flowers in an array of colors. In the center room, the door leads not only to the field of tall crabgrass, but beyond that to an area thick with cottonwoods, then a small wooden bridge. Beyond the bridge is a cleft between the hills that enclose the shack. It is an isolated hideaway out of sight of the highway or the old river path. Downstage, facing the audience, are imaginary windows in each of the rooms, looking out over the hills to the high outline of el Puente Negro that marks the border crossing. A tower stands on the center of the bridge.*

It is early afternoon on a Sunday, a hot day of heavy winds moaning sharply. In a corner (downstage) of the center room huddles a wizened old man, all carcass. He is wide awake, listening to the howling of the wind and the sound of approaching voices. His hands, deformed by rheumatism, are poised before him as if holding on to air. He does not move, but remains as if petrified by time, consumed by the moan of the wind.

The door bursts open. He immediately closes his eyes as the voices become people. LA CHAPARRA *stands outlined at the door. She walks in cautiously looking about her and goes from one room to another checking. She does not see the old man in the corner. She goes back to the doorway and beckons.* EL TOPO, MELITON, AMALIA, INOCENCIA, *and* NARCISO *enter.*

LA CHAPARRA *is a small-framed, fiery-eyed woman of indeterminable age. Her brown skin shines against an orange blouse snugly belted at the waist with a man's belt; a wide skirt comes down to her army boots, which seem incongruous with her long, dangling earrings. She wears a wide sombrero like* EL TOPO *and* MELITON. EL TOPO *is swarthy, strong, about forty-five. He wears a huge mustache on a face that indicates quick intelligence. He carries a guitar over a roll of blankets on his shoulders.* MELITON *is a man of the same age and similar build. He has Indian features, a face carved by the desert of his homeland, El Llano Grande. His body never seems at rest.* INOCENCIA *and* AMALIA *are not easily discernable at this time because they are bundled up in several layers of clothes and rebozos cover their faces.* NARCISO *is the possible reincarnation of the original Greek; he is astonishingly handsome, about twenty, lean and graceful. He is also carrying a pack on his shoulders. All their shoes are covered with mud.*

CHAPARRA: Everything—on the table.
> *All of them put their loads on the table.*

CHAPARRA: How you like it, eh?
> *Everyone looks around, but they offer no comment.*

CHAPARRA: Not a palace exactly. But it's safe. This is my way station. No one ever comes here except me—and my clients, of course. The hills hide it well and only I know the secret entrance.

EL TOPO: You make a good profit at five hundred pesos a head.

CHAPARRA: For that they get deluxe services. Don't dirty up my place with your muddy shoes.

AMALIA: It's dirty already.

CHAPARRA: Off! Off with your shoes!
> *Some lean on table, chairs, wall; they all take off their shoes.* CHAPARRA *sits on the floor and contemplates her muddy boots. She loosens her belt and sighs. She sniffs the air, turns her head and sniffs* MELITON, *who stands behind her.*

CHAPARRA: Manure—ugh!

MELITON: What you expect? We crawled through that cow pasture after we crossed the river.

CHAPARRA: You Indians are supposed to see at night.

MELITON: Allá! Look over there! (*Points to old man.*)

CHAPARRA: Who . . . (*She crawls on all fours to where the old man sits.*) Viejito—where you come from?
> *The old man stares vacantly into her eyes.*

CHAPARRA: I think he's dying. (*Crosses herself.*) Give him some tequila. (EL TOPO *rummages through sack on table, finds tequila, takes a swig, crosses to old man.*)

EL TOPO: Here, old man. (*The old man does not move, stares out into space.* EL TOPO *shrugs, takes a drink himself, crosses to table, sets down bottle.*)

CHAPARRA: Give him a chicken liver. (INOCENCIA, *full of compassion, rummages through sack, finds the plastic bag full of fried chicken livers, takes one, crosses to old man, squats, tries to make the old man eat.*)

INOCENCIA: Señor, coma, a little piece.

MELITON: (*To* CHAPARRA.) I thought no one knew about your place. What's he doing here?

CHAPARRA: Stumbled on it by accident. (*The old man's hand flutters to his stomach.* INOCENCIA *puts a piece of liver in his mouth. His jaws move, then he gulps with great difficulty.*)

EL TOPO: Pobre, he's forgotten how to swallow.

INOCENCIA: Let him be. He's done fine. Bueno, abuelito . . .

EL TOPO: Look, he wants more! (*The old man eagerly opens his mouth;* INOCENCIA *sits by him and feeds him with patience.* LA CHAPARRA *crawls back to center of room, leans back on hands.* EL TOPO *sits down beside her.*)

CHAPARRA: The old buzzard was starving.

EL TOPO: (*Sighs.*) So am I. (EL TOPO *leans against her, sighs deeply again, reaches for her hand. She pushes herself to her feet, kicks* EL TOPO *with the tip of her boot. He howls. She moves away.* EL TOPO *makes a grab for her, bringing her down to the floor again. They roll around, then he manages to stay on top of her, sitting on her stomach, grinning at her. She reaches out and slaps his face, curses.* TOPO *arches his back, expecting another slap, but it does not come. Instead, she wiggles from under him, pushing herself back to sit up and face him, knees bent, skirt gathered between her knees.*)

CHAPARRA: ¡Abusado! I warn you—keep your hands off . . .

EL TOPO: All I want is what's between your . . . (CHAPARRA *kicks forward, knocks him off balance, laughing lustily. She straightens out her leg, dangles her foot in front of his nose.*)

EL TOPO: Anything for you, querida. (*With a back-sweep pull,* EL TOPO *pulls one boot off, then the other. She picks up boots, hands them to him.*)

CHAPARRA: Now you take my boots and everybody's shoes and wash the mud off.

EL TOPO: Why me?

CHAPARRA: You know where the spring is.

EL TOPO: The river better.

CHAPARRA: Don't you dare go to the other side of the hills! La migra could spot you. Meliton, go with him.

MELITON: I did not pay good money to clean shoes.

CHAPARRA: Everybody helps. (*To* NARCISO.) Go, go with them, pretty boy.

> EL TOPO *and* MELITON *pick up shoes, grumbling. Exit through kitchen door.* CHAPARRA *motions to girls.* NARCISO *follows the men.*

CHAPARRA: Take the blankets to the bed. Leave one here for the men.

> INOCENCIA *does as she is told.* AMALIA *crosses to table, sits, watches as* CHAPARRA *empties sacks of contents.*

CHAPARRA: What's the matter with you? You work like everybody else.

AMALIA: I'm not doing anything with that mosca muerta.

CHAPARRA: Got your pretty little brother, eh?

AMALIA: That's what she thinks, the little hypocrite.

CHAPARRA: She is really a very nice girl.

AMALIA: Straight out of the farm, pink cheeks and all. He's known her three weeks! Only three weeks! And he thinks he's in love—the fool!

CHAPARRA: Don't blame me.

AMALIA: They met at your house.

CHAPARRA: So? All of you came to me so I could bring you across the river. I cannot help it if he got to her.

AMALIA: *She* got to him.

CHAPARRA: Awh . . . She's a virgin.

AMALIA: No more! They've been sleeping together.

CHAPARRA: How beautiful! He was a virgin too, eh? Oh, first love!

AMALIA: I'm going to break it up. (*Points bedroom left.*) That bedroom is for my brother and me.

CHAPARRA: The chicken's out of the henhouse. Leave them alone.

AMALIA: No. This is the time to break it up. He's dumb enough to want to take her with us.

CHAPARRA: You can't stop them.

AMALIA: I'm sure going to try. I can't let my brother be wasted on . . . on that country bumpkin. (INOCENCIA *returns from bedroom.* CHAPARRA *continues taking things out of the sack. She takes out a recorder.*)

CHAPARRA: Yours?

AMALIA: My most precious possession. My mother's music.

CHAPARRA: She made it up?

AMALIA: The most talented lady in the world. She composed it for Narciso and me.

INOCENCIA: Where shall I put my things?

CHAPARRA: You and I (*points bedroom right*) will sleep in there.

INOCENCIA: ¿Y el viejito? He's still just sitting there.

CHAPARRA: Maybe he can't get up anymore. He must be centuries old.

INOCENCIA: I'll give him a blanket for tonight.

CHAPARRA: Just leave him alone. As soon as the men return, I'll take Narciso with me to scout around. We'll go down to the watergate (*Takes out tequila bottles from sack.*) See, I provide my clients with the best.

AMALIA: Why do you want to take Narciso?

CHAPARRA: You think I'm after your precious little brother too, eh? We'll go to the other side of the hills through the mountain crack, up close to the highway. Your brother, he does not look like a mojado. The other two—¡ay, ay, ay, Jesucristo!

AMALIA: I'm going to take off all these clothes. They're hot and uncomfortable.

CHAPARRA: (*To* INOCENCIA.) You do the same. Take off your worldly possessions and fold them neatly for your journey tomorrow.

The girls look at each other, then walk in opposite directions, AMALIA *to the left bedroom,* INOCENCIA *to the right bedroom. The girls begin to remove the layers of clothes they are wearing. They're distinguishable now.* AMALIA *is a girl about twenty-five, very good-looking like her brother. She takes off several dresses; one of them is a costume, elaborate, satin, with flounces. It is a dancer's dress.* INOCENCIA *is about seventeen. She wears long braids down her back. She's very pretty. In the kitchen,* CHAPARRA *puts up her feet, opens a bottle of tequila, drinks and thinks. The girls busily fold their clothes, then* AMALIA *lights a cigarette and sits on bed looking at statue of the Virgin.* INOCENCIA *walks about restlessly, then lies down on bed. The men return with the assorted footwear.*

CHAPARRA: Water in the spring, eh?

EL TOPO: It runs into the mountain. I think there's fish.

CHAPARRA: You have to go to the river for fishing. Give me my boots. (*The men put footwear on table.* EL TOPO *takes boots to* CHAPARRA.)

EL TOPO: Can I put them on for you?

CHAPARRA: Why not. (*He helps her with the boots. She stands, he grabs her from behind and kisses her neck.*)

EL TOPO: You can be sweet to me tonight.

CHAPARRA: Get away, apestoso! (*To* NARCISO) You and me, we're going to look around.

EL TOPO: He's too beautiful for you.

CHAPARRA: Mind your business, baboso. (*To* NARCISCO.) Come on, come on. (*She pushes him toward door; they exit.* EL TOPO *and* MELITON *cross to old man, squat on each side of him.*)

MELITON: How old you think he is?

EL TOPO: A hundred at least.

MELITON: Hey, old man, how old are you? (*No answer.*)

EL TOPO: How many women you think he's had in his lifetime?

MELITON: What difference does it make to him now?

EL TOPO: And you? How many have you had?

MELITON: Here and there—not enough, I suppose.

EL TOPO: You married?

MELITON: Was married. Wife died. She just wore out. Gave me four sons.

EL TOPO: They're back home?

MELITON: El Llano Grande. I'll get them out of there. If I work hard, save my money in the United States . . .

EL TOPO: It'll never happen. What little you earn, they take away. No different than Mexico.

MELITON: But there's work.

EL TOPO: Slavery, you mean. It's a big country of big industry. All big industry needs slaves. That is the way they make profit—lots of profit. Mojados work hard because they're desperate, so the gringos stick them.

MELITON: Work is work.

EL TOPO: See what I mean—desperate!

MELITON: Why do you come to the United States?

EL TOPO: Not to work. I use the way of the gringos—deceit.

MELITON: How many times you cross that puente?

EL TOPO: Too many to count. Crossing's easy. (*Points to tower on bridge.*) Look up there, two guards. They can't handle us. We come like locusts. Big money gets slaves and the Big Power in Mexico avoids another revolution—for a little while. It's smart of them to make it easy for the hungry to come across. Can you imagine what would happen if Mexico didn't have a way to get rid of us?

MELITON: You sound like a Communist.

EL TOPO: Communists—shit! They're just as bad. It's not good to be political. Me—I'm a lover.

MELITON: Estás loco. Ever been caught?

EL TOPO: Couple of times. They throw you in a cow shed behind the coliseum. A week later, after a lot of talk and threats, they throw you back to the Juárez side. If you give them a hassle they beat the hell out of you. Some crazy guards shoot first, ask questions later.

MELITON: Same as everywhere.

The old man's head falls forward; he claws the air with open hands.

MELITON: He's still hungry. (EL TOPO *crosses to table, takes a chicken liver, crosses to old man, dangles it before him. The old man stares straight ahead.*)

EL TOPO: Eat! (*The old man takes the chicken liver with a trembling hand and chomps on it.*)

MELITON: No teeth.

EL TOPO: He's sure working those gums. Look at him go! (EL TOPO *crosses to table, picks up his guitar, begins tuning, sits on chair.* MELITON *joins him, sits, picks up bottle of tequila, drinks, watches* EL TOPO.)

MELITON: You play that thing?

EL TOPO: A little. (*Sings.*) "¿Quién sabe?—dolor, fortuna . . . ¿Quién sabe?—amor, desengaño. ¿Quién sabe?—Dirá la cuna. ¿Quién sabe?—el enterrador . . ."

MELITON: What do we know of love? life? death?

EL TOPO: We know very little, but that's good.

MELITON: Good?

EL TOPO: It's better not to know too much. (*Hums while strumming.*) You own property back in Mexico?

MELITON: Would I be here if I did?

EL TOPO: Ah, compadre, you know as well as I do, you can own property in Mexico and still starve to death. This was not the dream of Emiliano Zapata—the land free, free for all without overseer or masters. It never happened.

MELITON: I know what you mean. After the revolution, el delegado del estado went to my pueblo and gave my grandfather a deed for El Llano Grande, miles and miles of useless desert. My grandfather threw the deed in el delegado's face and demanded good land. It never happened. El latifundista kept all the good land. The rich stayed rich. There are no dogs in my village! And you?

EL TOPO: All I own is this guitar. That's the way I want it.(CHA-PARRA *and* NARCISO *return. She notices the old man eating.*)

CHAPARRA: Viejito! You've got some life in you.

EL TOPO: He's ready for a little fire in his veins.

> EL TOPO *crosses to table, then to old man with bottle of tequila. He puts the bottle to the old man's lips. The old man sucks it like a baby, gulps, coughs. He holds the bottle for another drink.*

EL TOPO: Look at him! Won't let go.

CHAPARRA: You'll kill him.

EL TOPO: This old guy still has a lot of life, cabrón!

MELITON: See anyone?

CHAPARRA: Picknickers down by the river, fishing.

EL TOPO: It's safe! We can go fishing. We get lost in the crowd.

CHAPARRA: You? They'll spot you, with your bigotón and your sombrero. Puro mojado.

EL TOPO: Nobody fishes in the river but Chicanos. They look like me.

CHAPARRA: And if I say no?

EL TOPO: No vieja tells me what to do.

CHAPARRA: This is the last time you cross with me.

EL TOPO: I'm your best customer.

CHAPARRA: I haven't seen your money for this trip.

EL TOPO: My credit's good.

CHAPARRA: You better keep out of sight.

NARCISO: I'm going with him.

MELITON: What do we fish with?

EL TOPO: I have a way of making fishing poles—you wait.

CHAPARRA: Men! (INOCENCIA *comes into room, crosses to* NAR-CISO.)

INOCENCIA: Stay with me.

EL TOPO: Look at the pretty boy, Melitón. He's not coming. (INO-CENCIA *takes* NARCISO *by the hand, leads him to bedroom. They sit on the bed, she kisses him, he holds her.* EL TOPO *and* MELITON *exit.* AMALIA *enters from bedroom left, recorder in her hand. She plays music—a tango—and dances a few steps, then turns music off.*)

CHAPARRA: First time I bring dancers across.

AMALIA: You think we'll make it to Chicago?

CHAPARRA: All things are possible.

AMALIA: We shall make lots of money and become famous.

CHAPARRA: That's talk. Dancers starve like anybody else.

AMALIA: We're special.

CHAPARRA: Does that guarantee success?

CHAPARRA: My mother was Esmeralda Topaz.

CHAPARRA: Never heard of her.

AMALIA: She was a famous dancer.

CHAPARRA: Was she ever on television?

AMALIA: No.

CHAPARRA: Famous—ha!

AMALIA: People loved her—everywhere we went.

CHAPARRA: Where was that?

AMALIA: San Domingo, Maranga, San José . . .

CHAPARRA: Never heard of those places. Big cities?

AMALIA: No. Little pueblos. We're gypsies. We travelled in a cara-van. We set up tents, sold tickets. I want to show you some-thing. (*Runs to bedroom, comes back with dance costume.*) She had a dream for Narciso and me. It's our dream now.

CHAPARRA: Dreams! Pitfalls, a luxury for the young and foolish.

AMALIA: It will happen. I feel it inside me.

CHAPARRA: You dance nice.

AMALIA: (*Turns on recorder. The tango has lyrics: "Dibujo mis días en mil colores, colores, colores. Encuentro mis sueños entre flores, mil flores, mis flores . . ." The tango continues without lyrics.*) This is the song of our dreams . . . (*The old man is fast asleep.* NARCISO *stands, takes* INOCENCIA *in his arms and dances, very slow.*)

INOCENCIA: I—I can't dance . . .

NARCISO: Shhhhhhh. . . . (CHAPARRA *takes a drink and sighs.*)

CHAPARRA: It would be nice for someone's dreams to come true. There are not many famous mojados in the United States. Come to think of it, I can't think of one . . . You have to make practical plans. You have no money to get to Chicago.

AMALIA: We mean to work hard and save our money until we can buy a ticket.

CHAPARRA: Chicago's a big city—cold and frightening, especially for the helpless.

AMALIA: We're not helpless. You've never been to Chicago!

CHAPARRA: No, I haven't, but a big city is a big city. You should not want too much. Look at Inocencia. She has a head on her shoulders. She will work as a housemaid, send her money to her family, then go back home where she belongs. That's sensible.

AMALIA: A maid! I would never be a maid! (NARCISO *and* INO-

CENCIA *come into kitchen.* NARCISO *holds* INOCENCIA *protectively.*)
INOCENCIA: I'm not going to work as a maid.
CHAPARRA: Huh?
INOCENCIA: I'm going to Chicago with Narciso.
AMALIA: I knew it! Did you hear her?
NARCISO: She's coming with me.
AMALIA: Shut up! I make the decisions in this family.
NARCISO: I can make my own decisions.
AMALIA: She's not going with us. (*To* INOCENCIA.) My brother doesn't really want you. You slut!
NARCISO: Don't you call her any names. She's better than you! If she doesn't go, I don't go with you.
AMALIA: You don't know what you're saying. Have you forgotten Mamá? You promised her. I don't believe you. You can't do it, you can't! (*She runs into bedroom crying, falls into bed.*)
INOCENCIA: Go after her.
NARCISO: I'm sick and tired of her running my life. I do what I want.
INOCENCIA: She doesn't want me. I can't come between you.
NARCISO: She'll just have to accept, that's all.
CHAPARRA: All of you—crazy! The only sane ones are that old man and me.

    CHAPARRA *watches as* NARCISO *kisses* INOCENCIA *to comfort her. She grins, takes a drink from bottle.*
CHAPARRA: Now, that makes sense!

SCENE 2

Sunset of the same day. INOCENCIA *and* NARCISO *are sitting on bed in right bedroom. He is unbraiding her hair, then he brushes it gently; playful gestures of love continue. In bedroom left,* AMALIA *sits on bed looking at her dance slippers. In kitchen,* CHAPARRA *is finishing off a bottle of tequila at the table. She stands, a little unsteadily, rummages through her sack, comes up with big, colorful paper flowers. She puts empty tequila bottle up to her eye, puts out tongue for last drop. The* OLD MAN *is still in his corner snoring. He awakens, opens one eye, sees* CHAPARRA *and closes eye again.* CHAPARRA *takes a full bottle of tequila, the empty bottle and the flowers, crosses to bedroom where* AMALIA *sits on bed. She sits opposite* AMALIA, *drinks from new bottle, hands it to* AMALIA, *who takes a sip and gives bottle back. In the kitchen, when* CHAPARRA *goes into bedroom, the* OLD MAN *manages to stand up with great effort. With wobbly legs he crosses to table, takes some food, bottle of tequila, then exits by kitchen door. In the bedroom,* CHAPARRA *arranges the paper flowers in the empty tequila bottle.*

CHAPARRA: I never forget the little Virgin.

AMALIA: (*Pointing to accumulation of dusty flowers.*) All those are from you?

CHAPARRA: Yes. She's my Virgencita. When I found the entrance to this place, I found her here. She sits here and waits for me. I count on her blessings. (*Takes flowers to* VIRGIN, *starts dusting, straightening flowers.*) Look at the dust. I'm sorry, Virgencita, that things are so messy. But here I am. Are you glad to see me? You won't be so lonely now.

AMALIA: (*Crosses to window.*) Look, the bridge looks so far, yet so near. It's frightening, isn't it?

CHAPARRA: You're just afraid of being in a strange land—in spite of your big talk. Tomorrow morning we meet El Gordo on the road above that hill. Then we part, each his own way.

AMALIA: Is El Paso a big city?

CHAPARRA: Not big enough to hide from la migra sometimes. Now, Chicago, that city could swallow you up.

AMALIA: You know Julio?

CHAPARRA: Everybody knows Julio.

AMALIA: He's going to give me a job—dancing.

CHAPARRA: Ha!

AMALIA: What's that supposed to mean?

CHAPARRA: Is that all you know about Julio?

AMALIA: This friend of mine said he hired dancers—that's where I got his address. Narciso and I are to meet him at San Jacinto Plaza.

CHAPARRA: You're in for a lot of trouble.

AMALIA Why?

CHAPARRA: Did you know Julio was a pimp?

AMALIA: A pimp?

CHAPARRA: The most successful one around. Wears a red vest and diamonds on his pink, fat hands. His place is on the southside. He hires dancers alright—if you don't mind dancing naked.

AMALIA: Naked?

CHAPARRA: His girls do not make their money dancing.
AMALIA: I didn't know. What are we going to do! We have to work to raise our fare to Chicago.
CHAPARRA: See what I meant—about practical plans?
AMALIA: Surely I can work at something else besides being a housemaid. And what is Narciso to do? I just thought Julio would hire both of us.
CHAPARRA: You know how to wait on tables?
AMALIA: Yes. Both Narciso and I worked in a restaurant in Chihuahua.
CHAPARRA: I will take you to Adela. She needs people in her restaurant.
AMALIA: You can find us jobs?
CHAPARRA: Yes, yes—you think I'm going to leave you at San Jacinto Park without any place to go? That's not the way I do business. That park has a pond with alligators, but the alligators are not the alligators. Poor little mojadas sit there and become prey to gringas looking for cheap workers, pimps, or old, dirty men who take them to cheap hotels.
AMALIA: Oh, thank you, Chaparra. I shall never forget your help when I'm rich and famous.
CHAPARRA: I won't hold my breath. I'm just helping you with one problem. So many will knock all that nonsense about riches and fame out of your head.
AMALIA: My dream is my passion. I must try!
CHAPARRA: I believe in trying.
AMALIA: I know I sound crazy sometimes, but there's a talent in Narciso and me, something beautiful. I'm not bragging—it's a truth inside me. Do you understand?
CHAPARRA: Oh, yes.
AMALIA: Then help me.
CHAPARRA: That's what I'm doing, no?
AMALIA: No, I mean . . . don't take Inocencia to Adela's. She has a job already. She has the name of her gringa on a piece of paper. She showed me. Please, don't help her come with us.
CHAPARRA: If I help you—I help her and Narciso.
AMALIA: She will ruin Narciso. His whole life is dancing as it is with me.
CHAPARRA: No time for love?
AMALIA: They're children! What do they know about love? They're all passion.

CHAPARRA: It is good.

AMALIA: I wouldn't know. You won't help me then?

CHAPARRA: I will not force things, that's all. Let them be.

AMALIA: We've worked so hard—for Mamá's dream, our dream. You just don't understand. (*She runs to the bedroom, crying.*) CHAPARRA *follows her, tries to comfort.* INOCENCIA, *in other bedroom, breaks free from Narciso, crosses to window.*)

INOCENCIA: I don't want Amalia to hate me.

NARCISO: She's unreasonable. Why should she tell me how to live? I'm not a child.

INOCENCIA: I'm not good enough.

NARCISO: That's dumb talk. You and I—we love each other, don't you understand?

INOCENCIA: Why doesn't she like me then?

NARCISO: To her, dancing is all. We've been partners since we were children. We are wandering gypsies who have danced all our life. It gets in your blood. With Amalia, it's an obsession. We were close to Mamá. In a way, it's all we know.

INOCENCIA: I'm not going to stop you from dancing. I just want to be near you—to take care of you. Why does she think I'm in the way?

NARCISO: Because to her there's just music and her and me before a public. Nothing else matters. But you see—it's different now. I don't care about fame and fortune. Just you—that's all I care about.

INOCENCIA: I have no talent—except the way I feel.

NARCISO: I love you.

INOCENCIA: But Amalia . . .

NARCISO: Forget about my sister. (NARCISO *kisses her.* EL TOPO *and* MELITON *come through kitchen door.* EL TOPO *has a string of fish.*)

EL TOPO: (*Whistles.*) Where's everybody?

MELITON: You think maybe . . .

EL TOPO: Nah—this place is safe.

CHAPARRA *enters from* AMALIA's *bedroom.*

EL TOPO: Ah, Chaparrita de mi corazón, look what I got for you! (*Hands her the fish.*)

CHAPARRA: Take the smelly things away. You clean them, cook them yourself.

EL TOPO: That's a woman's job.

CHAPARRA: Who sez?

MELITON: (*Notices the old man gone.*) The old man—he's not there.

CHAPARRA: What? I didn't notice! I was here a little while ago—but I don't remember . . . Amalia!

>AMALIA *comes from the bedroom.* INOCENCIA *and* NARCISO *come into kitchen also.*

CHAPARRA: (*To* AMALIA, *pointing at corner where old man was huddled before.*) Look! He's gone. Was he here when you and I were talking?

AMALIA: I didn't notice. El viejito was like part of the wall.

EL TOPO: Took off—ha! Had more life than I thought.

CHAPARRA: He knows about it.

EL TOPO: About what?

CHAPARRA: The entrance to this place. He must have stumbled on the cleft between the two hills.

EL TOPO: So what?

CHAPARRA: ¡Estúpido! I know the likes of him.

EL TOPO: He's just an old man.

CHAPARRA: Now you tell me—what's wrong in that old man's life?

MELITON: Starving to death. He's so old.

CHAPARRA: That's not the worst thing.

EL TOPO: What are you talking about?

CHAPARRA: Amalia said it. He was like part of the wall. A discard!

MELITON: So?

CHAPARRA: So la migra picks him up—or the police—for vagrancy. I'm sure it's happened before—an old scarecrow tottering along the highway.

EL TOPO: So he gets a bed for the night, and food.

CHAPARRA: No. He gets something better. He knows about us and this place—something la migra doesn't know. He tells them. He'll get attention. He's going to talk.

MELITON: Maybe he didn't make it to the entrance. He could be asleep by the watergate.

EL TOPO: You're right. How fast can he walk?

MELITON: Let's go.

NARCISO: I'll go all the way to the highway.

EL TOPO: I'll go toward the cottonwoods.

CHAPARRA: I'll go with you.

EL TOPO: Oh, but I'm so hungry for my fish. You should stay here and clean the fish. (CHAPARRA *gives him a push toward the door.* NARCISO *and* MELITON *follow.* AMALIA *and* INOCENCIA *sit across from each other at the kitchen table. As soon as the*

others leave, they begin to feel uncomfortable with each other,
AMALIA *angry,* INOCENCIA, *shy, embarrassed.*)
INOCENCIA: We could clean the fish.
AMALIA: I'm sick of this place. I wish Narciso and I were already in Chicago.
INOCENCIA: It's getting dark. The sun's almost down. Look, the bridge looks black against the red sky.
AMALIA: ¡Maldito puente! I hate the sight of it. I hate hiding and sneaking through darkness and mud. I hate the uncertainty of of it all.
INOCENCIA: They may find us—la migra, I mean.
AMALIA: It's possible.
INOCENCIA: What will they do?
AMALIA: They'll send us back.
INOCENCIA: Would you try again?
AMALIA: Yes, yes, yes. Nothing can stop me and what I want! Mamá used to tell us that our future, Narciso's and mine, had been planned by the gods, but that I should push the gods a little.
INOCENCIA: You scared?
AMALIA: Scared of what?
INOCENCIA: What you said—uncertainty, going to a strange country, being alone.
AMALIA: I'm not alone. I have my brother. Where are you from?
INOCENCIA: Tabasco.
AMALIA: It's near the ocean, isn't it?
INOCENCIA: Yes.
AMALIA: I love the ocean—Guaymas, Acapulco!
INOCENCIA: You've been to Acapulco?
AMALIA: Yes. Two years back. Narciso and I worked in a big rich hotel. But Guaymas . . .
INOCENCIA: When were you there last?
AMALIA: Nine years ago.
INOCENCIA: That's a long time ago.
AMALIA: My mother died there.
INOCENCIA: I'm sorry.
AMALIA: It's not a sad memory.
INOCENCIA: Narciso told me your mother was a very special person.
AMALIA: She was. The summer she died the gypsies camped on the beach after a long tour. My mother, although very ill, danced to the very last. Once music played, her illness disappeared—the horrible cough. She drew from some energy inside her. She

never feared life, so she never feared death. It was a beautiful death . . .

INOCENCIA: A beautiful death?

AMALIA: Yes. Narciso and I had set up our tent on the beach that morning. My mother watched the seagulls with such excitement. I had peeled an orange and we shared it together talking about the strength of the ocean, the seething excitement of its life. The three of us walked out to the water—my mother, barefooted, hair flying free, her face flushed with the heat of the day. She played and sang our song, the one she composed for Narciso and me. Right there, she closed her eyes and fell asleep, pillowing the sand. She never woke up.

INOCENCIA: You loved her so much.

AMALIA: I loved what she was—brave, free. She danced like that. If we worked hard and loved what we were, she said, her dream for us would come true. But we had to make it come true. She made me promise never to give it up, that I would never let Narciso give it up. We have lived with that dream for a long time. Inocencia, please don't take Narciso from me.

INOCENCIA: You think I'm taking him away because we love each other?

AMALIA: No, because you have interfered with the dream already. He doesn't practice enough or plan enough any more. You would tie him down. Don't you see?

INOCENCIA: How?

AMALIA: When you're in love, you forget the reality of things. What do you want out of life? What were you taught to want out of life? Back in your papa's little farm, did you dream about a home, a husband, babies?

INOCENCIA: What's wrong with wanting that?

AMALIA: That's for ordinary people. Not my brother.

INOCENCIA: I don't believe you.

AMALIA: He has a God-given talent. Few people have that. He can't give it up.

INOCENCIA: He doesn't have to give anything up. I make no demands.

AMALIA: Oh, you'll make demands, alright! What if you get pregnant, have a baby? He'll want to take care of you. He can't do that if he's to dance. Dancing means sacrifice—total commitment. It means your time consumed by practice, by trying to make the right time, the right place to be seen. You would put him in a cage. He could very well learn to hate you because the dream never came to be.

INOCENCIA: No!

AMALIA: Yes!

INOCENCIA: Don't you know about love? You loved a man once— he told me.

AMALIA: Loved? No. It wasn't like that. I pretended to love this man for Narciso's sake, my sake—for the sake of our dream. We had jobs that barely kept us alive, that would consume all our time. There was no time or money for dance lessons, for practice—until this man came along. He was much older, kind. I lived with him to buy time, to have money to make plans. It wasn't love.

INOCENCIA: You left him?

AMALIA: Yes. I had planned it that way. When there was enough money to come north. The dream had to be kept alive—that's all that mattered.

INOCENCIA: Then you know nothing about how we feel—how it matters more than anything.

AMALIA: Not more than his talent! Never more than his talent! Listen, you know what real love is? It's letting a person belong to himself. If you really love him, you will let him go.

INOCENCIA: You're confusing me.

AMALIA: Think on it. I think tonight we'll have a celebration!

INOCENCIA: Celebration? Are you mad? What if they don't find the old man? What if he leads la migra to this place?

AMALIA: Why think of only the terrible things? Whatever happens, we shall celebrate tonight. Narciso and I shall dance for all of you. Inocencia, when you see us dance, you'll know what I mean—how special, the gift we have. You will know then that you can't really be a part of us.

INOCENCIA: You're cruel.

AMALIA: I don't want to be. I really think you're a good person— that's why I'm asking you to do as I ask. I'm going to clean the fish, cook it over an open fire outside. (*Notices* INOCENCIA *crying*.) Stop crying! You might think we dance badly. Then I say you should keep my brother.

INOCENCIA: I don't understand you.

AMALIA: Don't try now. Just help me with the fish.

INOCENCIA: We might be discovered any minute and you want to build a fire and cook fish!

AMALIA: Why not? It's as good as any time.

ACT TWO

⊒⅃: ⊒⅃: ⊒⅃:

SCENE 1

Late the same evening. The group is finishing a meal of fish and tequila. The room is lighted by candles placed here and there. Bedroom stage left is dark; the one to the right is in half-light. The flickering lights of candles give the place a sense of dreams, fantasy. CHAPARRA *is sitting next to* EL TOPO *on the floor.* EL TOPO *is playing a love ballad on his guitar.* AMALIA *hums along and at times harmonizes with* EL TOPO. MELITON *sits at the table listening. In the shadows,* NARCISO *and* INOCENCIA *are whispering to each other, she against the wall, he leaning over her.*

EL TOPO: (*Sings.*)

> A la madrugada
> Cuando el sol asoma la cara
> Siento tu suspiro entre sueño
> Y en silencio puro,
> Estoy yo tan seguro
> Que de tu amor yo soy el dueño.
>
> Despierta mi amiga, mi consuelo,
> Y mi vida
> Necesito que me digas, necesito
> que me digas
> Que las lágrimas d'este payaso
> d'este mundano de mal paso
> Te hablaron de mi pena
> De la vida que envenena—
> Y que solo soy.
>
> Despierta—asegúrame el día—asegúrame
> que eres mía
> Despierta ya . . .

AMALIA: It's beautiful. Yours?

EL TOPO: I play around with words and my guitar.

AMALIA: You have a talent!

EL TOPO: Enough to get along.

CHAPARRA: Why are we celebrating? We never found the old man.

EL TOPO: Let's not ruin this beautiful evening. Let's just say he's gone—that's all.

CHAPARRA: So Amalia builds a fire and cooks fish out in the open like a fool.

MELITON: It was very good.

CHAPARRA: We sit here like pigeons, eating, singing, drinking . . .

EL TOPO: Relax—enjoy.

CHAPARRA: Estúpido—maybe we should camp out among the cottonwoods, just in case.

EL TOPO: ¡Estás loca! You want us to freeze to death? Let's just take things as they come. Stop playing general. Take off your boots.

CHAPARRA: Fool, what do you know?

EL TOPO: I know under that thick skin and that foul mouth there is a woman, a warm, beautiful woman.

CHAPARRA: Cabrón, cállate el hocico.

EL TOPO: Shall I tell them?

CHAPARRA: All you say is lies. There's nothing to tell.

EL TOPO: I remember a very special Chaparrita. You see, everybody, for many years we worked together at the city market in El Paso, unloading produce. She was a good worker—better than any man.

CHAPARRA: Too bad I can't say the same thing for you.

EL TOPO: And she has a good heart. The owners would give her sacks full of discarded fruits and vegetables and she would haul them, on foot, across the border to distribute among the poor and hungry. Now is this a human being?

MELITON: Una santa.

EL TOPO: Oh, she was that too. Very devout. She went to early Mass at Sacred Heart every morning, our Chaparrita . . .

CHAPARRA: You can stop right there.

EL TOPO: I haven't gotten to the good stuff.

CHAPARRA: I warn you . . .

EL TOPO: What's the matter with you? This is not the Chaparrita I know. Don't you remember? I would wait for you outside the church door, burning with love.

CHAPARRA: I remember the times I kicked you down the steps.

EL TOPO: Oh, you are a good Christian. You would yell at me "Not

before communion, desgraciado!" But I waited until you came
out of the church. Ay, ay, ay—it was worth waiting for!
> CHAPARRA *tries to slap him, but* EL TOPO *grabs her hand,
> then tries to hold her in his arms. They struggle, fall to the
> floor. He holds her down, kisses her fully on mouth. She
> kisses back.*

EL TOPO: That's the Chaparra I know!

AMALIA: It is time.

MELITON: Time for what?

AMALIA: (*Claps hands.*) Listen everybody! Tonight for the first
time and for our friends—a special performance by Los Topaz!
The next time all of you hear about us, Narciso and I shall be
performing in a huge theatre in Chicago where thousands of
people will go to see us dance!

EL TOPO: Ay, ay, ay, ay ay!

AMALIA: Our names—Narciso y Amalia— will be up in lights and
a huge orchestra will play for us!

EL TOPO: Are you that good? If you are good, it will happen!

CHAPARRA: Don't tell her things like that! Her head never comes
down from the clouds. (AMALIA *crosses to her brother, extends
her hand to him.*)

AMALIA: Come—let's put on our costumes. Tonight we dance
for our friends!

NARCISO: No.

AMALIA: Little brother—all those years, Mamá's dream—come!

NARCISO: I don't feel like dancing.

AMALIA: You think you can fool me? Your blood is my blood—oh!
the pure joy that runs through our bodies when we dance! You
want to dance!

INOCENCIA: Dance, Narciso. I want to see you dance.

NARCISO: Are you sure?

INOCENCIA: Yes. (NARCISO *takes* AMALIA's *extended hand, they
both cross to bedroom left to change.* INOCENCIA *stands by
doorway of bedroom right, watching the others, but not sharing in their anticipation. She's waiting for something to be
proved.*)

CHAPARRA: Hombres! Move! Let's make room for our dancers.
Let us see what their dream is all about. (MELITON *and* EL TOPO
move table and chairs back to make room. Then MELITON, EL
TOPO, *and* CHAPARRA *find places on top of table, on chairs,
to wait for the dancers.* EL TOPO *is full of excitement. He jumps
down from the table where he's sitting and crosses down center.*)

EL TOPO: Dreams! That's what the United States is made of. Gringos are not happy about mojados, but they love dreams—fairy tales. They really love them! They believe them to be true. Dreams—how you say it—are a valuable commodity.

CHAPARRA: What do you mean by "com . . . com . . . ?"

EL TOPO: Commodity? That means they are good for selling, for buying, for promising . . .

MELITON: What do you mean?

EL TOPO: Politicians use them to get elected. And big business, ah! They wheel and deal with dreams. There's a big city called New York and an avenue called Madison where many people have created empires selling dreams in newspapers, television, magazines! They sell dreams of youth, beauty, love, success.

CHAPARRA: And the gringos buy them. I buy them too.

EL TOPO: You don't know how to read.

CHAPARRA: That's what you think.

EL TOPO: Every time I cross el Puente Negro and put my foot on American soil, I become a different man.

MELITON: You, mendigo?

EL TOPO: I feel the magic of their dreaming, and I take advantage! There's a whole town in California dedicated to dreams—fairy tales. It's called Disneyland.

MELITON: And what is that?

EL TOPO: A whole pueblo put together with dreams and stories of funny little animals.

MELITON: You mean they did not use cement, nails, lumber?

EL TOPO: Well, I imagine so. But, what makes it stick together is animals that act like people and cotton candy and little strange planets.

CHAPARRA: He's lying again.

EL TOPO: I saw it with my own eyes. I was there! And people, thousands of people come on a pilgrimage to this pueblo—just like we Mejicanos go to see la Virgen de Guadalupe in San Miguel. They have this shrine to a little mouse.

MELITON: You make jest—no?

EL TOPO: I swear it—on the head of my mother—a mouse called Mickey—Mickey Mouse. (*He hums the Mickey Mouse song.*)

MELITON: What's that?

EL TOPO: That is the song they all sing to him.

MELITON: You don't go to pick lettuce like the rest of us mojados, eh?

EL TOPO: No. Not any more. I like gringos. They taught me something very important. It doesn't pay to work with your hands. It pays much better to work with your—cunning. It's part of their magic.

MELITON: How do you do that, eh?

EL TOPO: I play the game. Everybody plays it in America. For instance, tomorrow when El Gordo comes, he will take me to the Star Dust Bar in El Paso. It's a Chicano bar, so I'm safe. Also, la Watusi works there.

MELITON: Who's la Watusi?

EL TOPO: It is a woman who waits for me with eager arms . . .

CHAPARRA: I bet!

EL TOPO: Well, she saves this Charro suit for me. I will put it on after I make my beautiful Watusi happy. Mama mia, what a girl!

CHAPARRA: If you like six-foot giants with frizzy hair and sausage lips.

EL TOPO: Don't be jealous, corazón . . .

EL TOPO *tries to embrace* CHAPARRA; *she pushes him away.*

EL TOPO: As I was saying—I put this Charro suit on. I look handsome. Then, la Watusi stakes me for bus fare to San Antonio. Well, I get on this bus wearing my Charro suit—very impressive. I throw back my shoulders, hold up my chin and behave like I'm famous.

CHAPARRA: You?

EL TOPO: The people believe me because they're used to believing in dreams. I take out my guitar and I play and sing a love song. I don't do that bad, eh? Then someone will ask me where I'm going. I say New Orleans.

CHAPARRA: Why New Orleans?

EL TOPO: Because that's where I'm going this time. Well, I tell this friend on the bus my sad, sad story—in a very loud voice.

MELITON: What sad story?

EL TOPO: That someone stole my wallet. That my partners, Los Panchos, the famous singers, are waiting for me. But alas! I do not have the money to get there. Then, I take a bottle of tequila and pass it around. It makes everybody warm and they start dreaming. I take off my sombrero and pass it around. I say in a loud, grateful voice, "I know my American friends will help me." Then I sing a sad song, and what do you know! There will be enough money in my hat to get to New Orleans.

MELITON: You know that much English?

EL TOPO: Enough.

MELITON: What if they don't give you enough money?

EL TOPO: I take a bus to wherever the money takes me—then I create the dream again. I'll get there.

CHAPARRA: What's in New Orleans?

EL TOPO: The biggest dream of all. Fat Tuesday—that's what they call it—the day before Ash Wednesday. They have this big carnival where everybody enjoys—like the one in Buenos Aires—where everybody has an orgy. (*Hums, dances samba.*)

CHAPARRA: You never been to Buenos Aires.

EL TOPO: I go to the movies like everybody else.

CHAPARRA: Lent's six months away . . .

EL TOPO: I go, I wait. Time does not matter. Everybody disguises himself as someone they would like to be, everybody kisses their enemies, the rich drink with the poor, there's dancing in the street—then they crown the King of Tequila.

CHAPARRA: They have tequila in New Orleans?

EL TOPO: They have everything.

MELITON: Tell me compadre, all those dreams—what do they do for you? You don't have anything.

EL TOPO: Sure—I don't make the "big bucks," but I have life! people!

CHAPARRA: "Beeg bugs"—Mejicanos don't use that gringo talk.

EL TOPO: But I'm more than a Mejicano—I'm part of everyone who's happy, free. (AMALIA *and* NARCISO *enter wearing their beautiful dance costumes.* AMALIA *turns on their music.* NARCISO *looks toward* INOCENCIA *in the shadows of the doorway; he is still a little bit hesitant about dancing, but* AMALIA *leads him to the center of the floor and they dance, with effortless grace. It is obvious they are exceptional dancers. At the end of the music, there is silence, a silence of awe. Then* CHAPARRA, EL TOPO, MELITON *cross to where the dancers stand, hug them, kiss them, etc.*)

CHAPARRA: Never have I seen such dancing!

MELITON: It was very nice—more than nice.

EL TOPO: I could feel what you were feeling. Oh, you are great dancers. After the Star Dust Bar and my big Watusi—after New Orleans—I shall go to Chicago. I will sell your dream for you. I will be your manager. The three of us will be rich and famous! (*Everybody laughs.* INOCENCIA *has not joined in the excitement. She is crying quietly. When* AMALIA *crosses to her, she wipes her tears away.*)

AMALIA: (*Very softly.*) Well? (INOCENCIA *looks at her with pain in her eyes, but does not answer. She turns and goes into the bedroom, falls on bed crying.*)

SCENE 2

A few hours before dawn. CHAPARRA *and* AMALIA *are putting things together in preparation for the journey.* NARCISO *is asleep, bundled on the floor.* EL TOPO *sits at the table.* MELITON *is on watch outside the shack.* INOCENCIA *is still on the bed, wide awake.*

EL TOPO: (*Looking at the sleeping* NARCISO.) That pretty brother of yours looks like an angel asleep.
AMALIA: He's no angel.
EL TOPO: That's to his credit. Are you an angel?
AMALIA: Nobody's an angel.
EL TOPO: You're a smart girl.
AMALIA: It's been a long evening. I think I lie down before it's time to go.
CHAPARRA: Sure, sure—I'll wake you.
AMALIA: Good night—it's almost morning, isn't it?
CHAPARRRA: You can still sleep a couple of hours. El Gordo will be here around four.
    AMALIA *crosses to bedroom, lies down.* CHAPARRA *stops her work, stretches, yawns.*
CHAPARRA: My old bones tell me to go to bed.
EL TOPO: You? Get tired, like ordinary people?
CHAPARRA: Stop your joking, bigotón. You know something—I've really enjoyed this crossing.
EL TOPO: Me too.
CHAPARRA: Good night.
EL TOPO: May you be blessed with dreams of me. (CHAPARRA *ignores his comment, crosses to bedroom where* INOCENCIA *is lying down, sits on edge of the bed.*)
CHAPARRA: You asleep, chiquita?
INOCENCIA: No.
CHAPARRA: Hey, you've been crying—Amalia, eh?
INOCENCIA: It's not her fault.
CHAPARRA: I've decided that tomorrow I will find another job for you. At Adela's. That gringa would probably work you to death. Some gringas are O.K. But many think we are animals of burden.
INOCENCIA: Adela's?
CHAPARRA: Where I'm taking Amalia and Narciso. You can work with them and help earn the fare to Chicago.
INOCENCIA: I'm not going with them.

CHAPARRA: You love Narciso?

INOCENCIA: Yes.

CHAPARRA: He wants you to go with him to Chicago?

INOCENCIA: Yes.

CHAPARRA: Then go.

INOCENCIA: I can't.

CHAPARRA: Why you change your mind, eh? Because you want to marry Narciso and he hasn't asked? Your mama told you to be a good girl all your life—you feel guilty, no? You want to be married.

INOCENCIA: I don't care if he doesn't ask me. I just want to be with him.

CHAPARRA: It's because Amalia doesn't want you. That's it!

INOCENCIA: Tomorrow I go to San Jacinto Plaza and meet the gringa I'm supposed to work for. I will be a maid and save my money. I will go back home in a year.

CHAPARRA: Never mind Amalia. Listen to your heart.

INOCENCIA: That's the problem. I'm listening . . .

CHAPARRA: What you talking about?

INOCENCIA: Tonight, when I watched them dance, I knew I shouldn't go with him.

CHAPARRA: Because you don't dance?

INOCENCIA: They were so beautiful. They were in a world belonging only to them. He doesn't need me.

CHAPARRA: You silly girl, you think he's going to do nothing but dance for the rest of his life—day and night, night and day?

INOCENCIA: That should come first, dancing. Amalia is right. It is part of his very soul.

CHAPARRA: He loves you. He needs you. Dancing is not enough.

INOCENCIA: For them it is, because they're so special.

CHAPARRA: Now you talk nonsense.

INOCENCIA: When I go back home, I'll marry someone eventually.

CHAPARRA: And have a dozen children and grow old before your time? Could anyone back home be a Narciso?

INOCENCIA: No.

CHAPARRA: Narcisos happen seldom in a woman's life.

INOCENCIA: I know. (*Begins to cry.*)

CHAPARRA: Now stop that. Crying will not make things right. You cannot give up love. It's the most beautiful thing you have when you're young.

INOCENCIA: Did you fall in love when you were young?

CHAPARRA: Oh, yes. It is something that must be, for all young girls—like the measles. It comes like lightning and goes like lightning. After that, when you're no longer young, you become practical about being with a man. Believe me—it's not the same!

INOCENCIA: I can't interfere with their dream. It's *their* dream.

CHAPARRA: You're never going to forgive yourself if you give him up.

INOCENCIA: I know that. (INOCENCIA *begins to cry as if her heart is breaking. She turns away from* CHAPARRA, *who gathers her up in her arms to console her.*)

CHAPARRA: There, there, chiquita. Tomorrow maybe the cobwebs will go away . . . (MELITON *enters. He has a bottle of tequila which he is hugging.*)

MELITON: Brrrr—that wind! If it hadn't been for this (*holds up bottle*) I would be frozen out there.

EL TOPO: See anything?

MELITON: An occasional coyote.

EL TOPO: (*Looking down at* NARCISO.) Hate to wake up pretty boy, but it's his turn to keep watch.
    He nudges NARCISO *with his toe.* NARCISO *stirs, then turns away.*

EL TOPO: Look at that—he's dreaming of Inocencia. (*Nudges him again.*) Hey, wake up, Chulito. (NARCISO *sits up, half-asleep. He stands, pulls blanket around shoulders.*)

MELITON: Here, take this with you. (*Hands him a bottle from table.*) It's freezin' out.

NARCISO: What?

EL TOPO: Wake up. Your turn to stand guard.

NARCISO: Is it morning?

EL TOPO: Almost.

MELITON: There's some bushes by the side of the entrance up against the hills. The wind doesn't hit you so hard there.

NARCISO: O.K. (*Exits taking blanket and bottle with him.* EL TOPO *takes up his guitar, picks softly.* MELITON *listens.*)

MELITON: You telling the truth about Nu Orlins?

EL TOPO: Come with me.

MELITON: (*Laughs.*) I don't have a Charro suit. I don't sing. (*Serious.*) You know Los Siete Pasos al Infierno?

EL TOPO: Sure. Tenement on the south side.

MELITON: My coyote said I had to be there at seven tomorrow morning to board the truck.

EL TOPO: Where you going?

MELITON: San Fernando Valley.

EL TOPO: Hijo—that's beautiful.

MELITON: Green land.

EL TOPO: Yeah. The land's something to look forward to. But there's nothing for you, friend. All you get will be a choza with a dirt floor—no water, no electricity, and the smell of a ditch carrying shit outside your window.

MELITON: Where's the land of opportunity?

EL TOPO: Not for the likes of you, man. For one thing, you're illegal. Even if you had papers, all you are is a bonded slave.

MELITON: ¡Cabrones! Everywhere in the world the rich have us by the balls. If only the poor of the world banded together and cut off the heads of all the rich, like they did long ago. Why don't we do something!

EL TOPO: There's César Chávez in California.

MELITON: He's going to start a revolution?

EL TOPO: Mojados and Chicanos by themselves? You must be crazy. They use reason.

MELITON: How's that?

EL TOPO: Strikes—marches—take it to the courts.

MELITON: They might as well wait for hell to freeze over.

EL TOPO: Yeah . . . What we need is another Zapata.

MELITON: When I was young, my friends and me—we had horses and carbines. One day we got fed up with our condition so we went after the latifundista—put a gun to his mouth . . .

EL TOPO: I hope you pulled the trigger.

MELITON: We couldn't. Scared the shit out of him though.

EL TOPO: They set the federales after you. I know the story.

MELITON: They took our guns, our horses. No one in the village is allowed to have horses anymore.

EL TOPO: The rich are smart. They know slaves have to be kept hungry and helpless so they can squeeze the life out of them. (Sings.) "Arroyito revoltoso, ¿qué te dice aquel clavel? Dice que ya vuelve el jefe, que Zapata ha de volver . . ."

MELITON: Ah, we could use many Zapatas—every man a Zapata. No—eh?

EL TOPO: We're too ignorant. We always talk of the enemy in some far off place. The enemy's on top of us, hombre. We can't see beyond our noses.

MELITON: People's heads are full of rocks.

EL TOPO: What would happen if a Zapata took over? He would become rich with power—forget about the poor. Another bastard would have us in his power.

MELITON: Zapata did not betray the poor.

EL TOPO: Because he was shot. You know what the problem is?

MELITON: What?

EL TOPO: The human race is so dumb—it still doesn't know how to handle power or to beware of too much.

MELITON: There's no way out for people like us.

EL TOPO: Oh, yes there is. I have a secret . . .

MELITON: What's your secret?

EL TOPO: I can only take care of one person—*me*. So I must think big, I must hustle the dream. That way they won't put the make on me because I put it on them first.

MELITON: When I get to California, I'd like to meet this leader you mentioned.

EL TOPO: César Chávez.

MELITON: Yeah . . .

EL TOPO: You're going his way. (*Sings.*) "Arroyito revoltoso, ¿qué te dice aquel clavel . . ."

MELITON: SHHHHHHHHHHHH.

EL TOPO: Eh?

MELITON: Listen . . .

EL TOPO: Someone . . . running. (MELITON *and* EL TOPO *run to door.* MELITON *opens it cautiously, looks out.*)

MELITON: It's Narciso.

EL TOPO: Something's wrong. (NARCISO *bursts into room out of breath.*)

NARCISO: They're coming.

MELITON: Who's coming?

EL TOPO: La migra, I bet!

NARCISO: (*Nodding head vigorously.*) Two of them.

EL TOPO: You sure? Only two?

NARCISO: I'm sure. I waited and watched out for more. But there's only two.

EL TOPO: ¡Pendejos!

MELITON: (*Takes knife from pocket.*) We'll be ready for them.

EL TOPO: Put that thing away.

MELITON: They have guns.

EL TOPO: Doesn't matter what they have—there's only two of them. If we use our heads . . .

MELITON: You have a plan.

EL TOPO: Yeah . . . Wake the girls, Narciso. (NARCISO *crosses to bedroom stage right, shakes* CHAPARRA.)

CHAPARRA: (*Waking.*) Aaaa . . ¿qué quieres?

NARCISO: La migra. (CHAPARRA *jumps out of bed;* INOCENCIA *sits up in bed.*)

CHAPARRA: Chingones.

INOCENCIA: What do we do?

NARCISO: (*Sits by side of bed, takes her in his arms.*) Don't be scared. No one's going to hurt you. Just go into the other room with the others. (*They all go into kitchen;* NARCISO *crosses to bedroom left, wakes* AMALIA.)

AMALIA: What is it?

NARCISO: La migra.

AMALIA: Oh, no!

NARCISO: Come on, El Topo has a plan.

AMALIA: A plan? (NARCISO *and* AMALIA *join the others in the kitchen.* MELITON *is keeping watch through crack in door. Everybody's whispering.*)

EL TOPO: Listen to me . . .

CHAPARRA: You have a plan?

EL TOPO: Yes . . . Amalia, get your music.

AMALIA: My music?

EL TOPO: Yes, your mama's song.

AMALIA: Now?

EL TOPO: Get it! (AMALIA *goes for recorder.*)

CHAPARRA: I think you're out of your mind, loco.

EL TOPO: Be quiet, corazón. I want you and Inocencia to take the chairs, put them facing the door, and sit on them.

CHAPARRA: What?

EL TOPO: Do as I say. You and Inocencia are going to watch Amalia and Narciso dance.

CHAPARRA: I don't believe this!

NARCISO: This is no time for dancing.

EL TOPO: Oh yes, it is! it is!

MELITON: They're by the cottonwoods . . .

EL TOPO: Hurry everybody!

CHAPARRA: Not until you explain what you're doing, baboso.

EL TOPO: Trust me!

CHAPARRA: That will be the day!

AMALIA: There's no time to fight, you two.

EL TOPO: Don't you see, querida—the element of surprise! The unexpected!

CHAPARRA: What? I give up! No, no—I don't give up! Let's make a run for it everybody! (*Everybody starts to make a run for it.*)

EL TOPO: Stop!

MELITON: They're by the watergate . . .

EL TOPO: Don't you see? That's what they expect us to do—run like scared rabbits! But we're smarter than they think. You see, they don't expect to find the two most beautiful dancers in the world in this shack. It'll throw them off guard. If they knock at the door, we ignore. If they bust the door in, we ignore. We're too involved in watching the beautiful dancers.

CHAPARRA: Makes good sense, bigotón! Yes, I like it! Amalia, Narciso—hurry, start your music—dance.

EL TOPO: Now, Meliton and me, we stand by the door in the shadows. Even if they see us, we just stand and watch the dancers and ignore them. You know what will happen? Ha! they'll be so confused . . .

CHAPARRA: Stop your talking, baboso, and do it!

MELITON: What do we do besides watch?

EL TOPO: We'll jump them when they don't know what's happening.

MELITON: And after that?

EL TOPO: One thing at a time.

MELITON: (*Looking through crack.*) They're by the tall grass. . . . (AMALIA *starts music. She and* NARCISO *begin to dance.*)

EL TOPO: Good! They'll hear the music. (CHAPARRA *and* INOCENCIA *sit down to watch after putting the chairs in place. They try to look calm, casual.* MELITON *and* EL TOPO *stand by door. There's a loud knock at the door. No one budges.*)

MIGRA I: What you think?

MIGRA II: Is that music?

MIGRA I: Yeah . . . I hear it too. Probably a bunch of marijuanos—stoned.

> MIGRA I *kicks the door open; both of them rush in with guns drawn. The group is oblivious to them.* AMALIA *and* NARCISO *dance elegantly without stopping or looking toward them.* MIGRA I *and* MIGRA II *are bewildered.*

MIGRA I: They don't look like marijuanos . . .

CHAPARRA: (*Puts finger to lips.*) Shhhhhh . . .

MIGRA II: Could be a trick . . .

MIGRA I: The old man said they were mojados . . . They sure don't look like mojados. They sure can dance!

MIGRA II: Yeah . . . they are good . . . (MIGRA II *watches, then realizes he is off guard; he turns suddenly, but* MELITON *and* EL TOPO *jump them both before they know what's happening. They put up a fight, but are soon overcome by* MELITON *and* EL TOPO.)

EL TOPO: (*Pinning one down.*) Chingados, you don't know the game? It takes six of you to catch one of us.

MELITON: Poor guys have bad odds, eh? (*Has hammerlock on other* MIGRA.) What do we do with them?

EL TOPO: Take their clothes off.

MIGRA II: You won't get away with this!

MIGRA I: It'll go bad for you . . .

EL TOPO: Wanna bet? (EL TOPO, MELITON, *and* NARCISO *undress* MIGRA I *and* MIGRA II, *who holler and bellow threats through out the process.* CHAPARRA *takes a swig of tequila and watches with great amusement.*)

CHAPARRA: This is a new experience. I've never seen la migra naked.

EL TOPO: (*To* NARCISO.) Get that rope on the wall.

NARCISO *crosses to wall, takes rope, brings it to* EL TOPO. MELITON *takes his knife and cuts it in two.*

EL TOPO: Now we tie them up, stuff their mouths, and throw their uniforms in the pit by the watergate.

MELITON: (*Busy tying up* MIGRA.) And them?

EL TOPO: Throw them on the bed. By the time they get loose, we'll be far away.

AMALIA: It's light outside. Look at the bridge! It looks like a sleeping beetle.

CHAPARRA: Pobrecitos. Let's put them in the room with my Virgencita. They won't be lonely. Also, they can contemplate their sins. (EL TOPO *and* MELITON *take the struggling* MIGRA *to bedroom left, throw them on bed, tie them down some more. In the meantime, everybody gathers up their things, ready to depart.* LA MIGRA *are hollering for help.*)

EL TOPO: We better shut them up. Stuff their mouths. (*Looks around for something, can't find anything, calls out to other room.*) Got anything to stuff their mouths?

CHAPARRA: Lot of chicken livers!

EL TOPO: (*Touches scarf around his neck, is thoughtful for a moment, then takes it off.*) I am making you a gift. (*Stuffs scarf in one* MIGRA's *mouth.*) I have no hard feelings. I know you are just trying to do your job. Believe me, it's hard . . .

MELITON: What do I use? (*Has finished tying up his* MIGRA.)

EL TOPO: Got anything?

MELITON A dirty handkerchief—what with the dust storm and my sinuses . . .

MIGRA II: (*Starts screaming.*) No . . . no . . . it's inhuman!

EL TOPO: There, there, no time to be squeamish.

MELITON *stuffs handkerchief in mouth of screaming* MIGRA, *then he and* EL TOPO *contemplate their work.*

EL TOPO: Don't they look beautiful!

CHAPARRA: (*Calling out from kitchen.*) You two hurry up! El Gordo's up on the road by now. (MELITON *joins the others, but* EL TOPO *sits on the edge of the bed and looks at* LA MIGRA *sympathetically.*)

EL TOPO: Are you comfortable? I hate to go and leave you here by yourselves. (*Gets idea—rushes out to kitchen.*) Give me a bottle of tequila.

CHAPARRA: It's too early to drink. We have to hurry.

EL TOPO: It's not for me. It's for my friends in there—a little gift.

CHAPARRA: Good tequila for the likes of them?

EL TOPO: They're people like us, querida. They get thirsty—for sure after they work off the ropes.

CHAPARRA: Alright, alright.

CHAPARRA *takes bottle from sack, gives it to* EL TOPO, *who rushes back to bedroom left.* CHAPARRA *checks everybody's load, looks around for anything left behind. When all are about to leave, she takes piece of paper from bosom.*

CHAPARRA: Let's check our destinations. Narciso, Amalia, you go with me to Adela's. Inocencia, have you changed your mind?

INOCENCIA: No.

CHAPARRA: Then, you're meeting your gringa at San Jacinto Plaza. You have her name, address, and phone number?

INOCENCIA: (*Voice breaking.*) Yes.

NARCISO: I'm not going to let you do that . . .

CHAPARRA: Melitón, let's see, you go with El Gordo to second ward—Los Siete Pasos al Infierno . . .

MELITON: That's right.

CHAPARRA: Where's that imbecile?

MELITON: In the bedroom still.

AMALIA: Chaparra . . .

CHAPARRA: What?

AMALIA: Inocencia goes with us.

CHAPARRA: You listen to your heart, eh?

INOCENCIA: (*To* AMALIA.) You really want me?

AMALIA: Yes, little sister. (*They embrace.* NARCISO *kisses both of them.*)

CHAPARRA: There's no time for that—let's go! (EL TOPO *rushes in*

from bedroom. CHAPARRA *tries to push him out door. He grabs her and kisses her. She pushes him away.*)
EL TOPO: Go ahead! I catch up with you!
CHAPARRA: You are one big crazy man! (*They all exit except* EL TOPO, *who goes back to bedroom after taking up his pack and guitar. He crosses to* LA MIGRA, *sits on edge of bed again, and contemplates them with a fond grin.*)
EL TOPO: I wish I didn't have to leave you like this. We really like you, you know. It's just the way the cards fall. (LA MIGRA *struggle against ropes as he talks.*) Believe you me, I wouldn't like it either. (*He crosses to window, looks out toward El Puente Negro.*) That puente out there—it is a symbol of the great United States of America (*salutes*), symbol of the courageous BORDER PATROL! (*Takes bottle of tequila that is to be the gift for them.*) I leave you this present. (*Opens bottle, takes a swig, savours loudly.*) Ah, that hit the spot! I leave the rest for you, right here by the side of la Virgencita. (*Puts bottle down on table.*) That puente out there is the symbol of the most noble IMMIGRATION SERVICE, the vigilantes of America! You are brave soldiers. I really believe that. But what are you to do? We mojados—we grow out of the earth and multiply. An impossible game for you. But I understand that you must play it for your presidente. What my dream is—why bother with a border at all? Why not just one big happy country, México and the United States—one country, eh? That would be nice, eh? Mojados and gringos, true brothers. Listen, I'll have to leave soon, but La Virgencita over there will keep you company. She's the mother of us all! Now, I will sing you a farewell . . . (LA MIGRA *struggle as if they're being tortured.*) I know you will like it. Looks like you can hardly wait. I shall sing a little song about a great man, EMILIANO ZAPATA! (*Gives out a great yell.* LA MIGRA *sort of cower, confused.*) He was a man of love, you know, a man of the people like you and me. And you know something—he's coming back soon. (*Sings.*)

> Arroyito revoltoso
> ¿Qué te dice aquel clavel?
> Dice que ya vuelve el jefe,
> Que Zapata ha de volver . . .

CURTAIN

Autumn Gold

Oh, frabjous day!
Callooh Callay!
Callooh Callay!

—The Jabberwock
Alice in Wonderland

CHARACTERS

(In order of their appearance)

HELEN SCRIMER	RICHARD TALISMAN
ESTHER FORBES	ATTILA
SUSAN	AGNES SCRIMER
MIKE ALMAN	DR. SCRIMER
LOLLY GOLDMAN	SERGEANT BACON
LEONARD ETHANS	HARRY

ACT ONE

SCENE 1

Esther Forbes' living room. Downstage center—couch, chairs, coffee table. Upstage left—bar, stereo. Upstage right—plant area, chair, Kirlian camera. Next to couch, small table with telephone. Upstage left leads to kitchen; downstage right to bedroom. Center right—desk, typewriter, chair. HELEN, *Esther's daughter, is pacing floor. Calls out to* ESTHER *in bedroom.*

HELEN: You're not listening.

ESTHER: (*From bedroom.*) Of course, I'm listening.

HELEN: Mother! Come out here. This is serious. (ESTHER *comes from bedroom, crosses to front of coffee table.*)

ESTHER: Where did the time go? I'm late. Let's see, got to check on costumes, photos. Oh yes, flowers. For sweet Sister Superior. She provided the nuns' habits, you know. Oh dear, have I forgotten anything . . .

HELEN: Sit down.

ESTHER: What dear?

HELEN: Sit down. I can't believe what I heard. I have to talk to you.

ESTHER: Will it take long?

HELEN: That is not the question.

ESTHER: What question?

HELEN: Did you do what you did?

ESTHER: You're not making sense, Lambkin.

HELEN: Stop calling me that. I'm not a child.

ESTHER: You'll always be my little girl.

HELEN: Is it true?

ESTHER: Whatever it is, you seem to think so . . .

HELEN: I knew it! Lolly just came out with it. Cornered me at the supermarket. Everybody heard—about your weekend party.

ESTHER: Such a lovely party . . .

HELEN: I don't believe you! How could you? You're a mother.

ESTHER: Is that bad?

HELEN: You know what I mean. Lolly's spreading the news.

ESTHER: Stop being paranoid. It was just a party.

HELEN: The four of you, naked, in a jacuzzi, drinking.

ESTHER: One doesn't go into the water with clothes on, dear.

HELEN: You were with Leonard and Richard.

ESTHER: And Lolly. The Autumn Gold Society.

HELEN: Have you no shame?

ESTHER: What about? It was the most intellectually stimulating affair . . .

HELEN: Affair!

ESTHER: My, you do jump to conclusions. You must do something about airing out that mind of yours.

HELEN: You got drunk.

ESTHER: Lolly got drunk. I had one glass of Tokaji Aszu.

HELEN: Of what?

ESTHER: Tokaji Aszu. Lovely Hungarian wine. Very sweet. Of course, Tokaji Aszu is supposed to make you passionate . . .

HELEN: I'm not hearing right. You used to be so stable—so motherly.

ESTHER: (*Sighs.*) I wish I could stay around for your scolding, but I'm late.

HELEN: You're not leaving until you explain, in a clear, rational way, what in the hell you were doing.

ESTHER: Wonderful!

HELEN: What?

ESTHER: Hell.

HELEN: Hell?

ESTHER: That's a nice, healthy word. You've been so stuffy since you took up with those Baptists.

HELEN: Don't start that! At your age, you could use a little religion.

ESTHER: The Autumn Gold Society could be the beginning of a new religion.

HELEN: I bet. That was a prayer meeting you all had in the jacuzzi.

ESTHER: Bedpartners.

HELEN: Bedpart . . .

ESTHER: Religion and philosophy.

HELEN: Blasphemy.

ESTHER: Fire and brimstone.

HELEN: You're making fun.

ESTHER: Don't take things so seriously, darling.

HELEN: That ridiculous society! It's changed you. It's all Leonard's fault. He started the whole thing. He did, didn't he?

ESTHER: Let's see . . . Ah, yes, Leonard's third wife. Don't you remember? They had just moved next door—newlyweds. Two years ago exactly, before you got married. Such a pretty woman. Wore that funny, floppy white hat when she trimmed the hedges —trimmed with a vengeance . . .

HELEN: You're rambling.

ESTHER: No, I'm not. That's the way it started, the day she got up and went. Just went—and left poor Leonard. Took a taxi wearing that silly hat of hers. Never came back.

HELEN: Good for her. His two other wives did the same.

ESTHER: Poor Leonard.

HELEN: Living with him is no bed of roses for any woman. He's insane.

ESTHER: He's not insane. He's brilliant. Way ahead of his time.

HELEN: Oh, Mother, you're so naive.

ESTHER: After she left, Leonard was so helpless, so lost. He would fill up his cart with TV dinners at the supermarket. So I cooked hot meals for him. Don't you remember? That's when I heard about the book he was writing and how he needed people for the experiment. You used to think he was a genius. You were so impressed when you found out he was the author of that book, the Mac . . . Mac . . .

HELEN: *The Machiavellian Malaise.* He should have stuck with Machiavelli. Why did he pick on you, my mother?

ESTHER: He needed me for the experiment—people my age—because people our age are full of—autumn gold. That's the basis of his premise.

HELEN: Which is Greek to you. You don't understand it. You don't know what you're doing. That Svengali has you mesmerized. You're susceptible to people like him. I can imagine what he has you doing—besides jumping into a jacuzzi, naked, with strangers.

ESTHER: They're not strangers. They're my dearest friends.

HELEN: What kinky things does he have you do in the jacuzzi?

ESTHER: Float.

HELEN: Float?

ESTHER: Let go.

HELEN: Let go of what?

ESTHER: Don't be dense. Weight, tensions.

HELEN: Did you get high on something?

ESTHER: We got high on Leonard.

HELEN: I mean pills, marijuana.

ESTHER: Maybe that's what you do in a jacuzzi. *We* listened to Leonard explain immortality.

HELEN: Who does he think he is, God?

ESTHER: He's a philosopher.

HELEN: You're going to jump into the jacuzzi every time you have a meeting?

ESTHER: Not necessarily. We may meet on a mountaintop by the light of the moon. Or right here. Place doesn't matter.

HELEN: Can I talk you out of this insanity?

ESTHER: You can't.

HELEN: Mother, when Bob's parents were about your age, they were making plans for retiring. You should do the same.

ESTHER: Me? Retire?

HELEN: Why not. You spent your life in that drama department or writing silly plays. Now that ridiculous society. Look, I have a brochure at home about Sun City. Bob's parents love it there.

ESTHER: How gruesome—a problemless world.

HELEN: Bob's parents love Sun City. They're really happy living there.

ESTHER: You think they're happy. On the other hand, why shouldn't they be happy?

HELEN: Marvelous place for retirement.

ESTHER: Will you stop talking about retiring? Don't try to sweep me under the rug. I'm not old, Helen. You should look as young as I feel.

HELEN: Yes, Mother.

ESTHER: Don't you "yes Mother" me. So I'm a category, eh? I'm a person, full of plans, energy, hopes, ambition. These are my best years. I've found the gravitation of my nature. I'm learning to be free.

HELEN: Free?

ESTHER: Yes, free. You're still so sticky with life, with ego. Your chemistry—explosive. Your opinions—hot and narrow . . .

HELEN: Mother!

ESTHER: I'm not condemning. It's just that you're young—in the middle of the arena, you might say. But the arena's full of dust and it blinds you, chokes you. I've been there. In this time of my life—well, I'm on the sideline, free—or trying to be.

HELEN: I know you're not really old—not that way. But I don't know you any more. I'm afraid for you.

ESTHER: Why? 'Cause I don't fit a pattern?

HELEN: People have to conform.

ESTHER: I'd much rather celebrate.

HELEN: Celebrate what?

ESTHER: Life, death.

HELEN: Celebrate death?

ESTHER: Yes.

HELEN: Is that what it's all about, your outrageous society?

ESTHER: Partly. It's not something new. You've heard about the good old Irish wakes.

HELEN: What are you talking about?

ESTHER: We don't really die.

HELEN: Oh, Mother.

ESTHER: Celebrating the death of our loved ones. That's a good idea, you know. During the revolution in Mexico, Pancho Villa would gather his dead after a battle, clean them up, sit them around the campfire, tell them stories, eat, drink, cry. And in the darkness of the night, the dead were lost among the living. You couldn't tell them apart.

HELEN: Be serious.

ESTHER: Oh, but I am. Deadly serious. Have you ever seen a funeral down in New Orleans? When a jazz musician dies, there's a parade, dancing, singing—"Oh, when the saints, go marching in . . ."

HELEN: Stop that.

ESTHER: Why?

HELEN: This is a ridiculous conversation, all this talk about bandits, musicians. Leonard's to blame with that theory he's concocted out of thin air.

ESTHER: He didn't concoct it. It's very ancient. The concept has survived the ages. As old as the Tao, as modern as Jung, the Big Bang theory. Philosophers have played around with it for centuries. Life, they say, cannot be annihilated. Energy cannot be destroyed. The galaxies grow and grow.

HELEN: Mother, you're talking out of your element.

ESTHER: Perhaps. But I'm a fast learner.

HELEN: What's the use!

ESTHER: Don't look so stricken, my darling.

HELEN: Promise me . . .

ESTHER: Within reason . . .

HELEN: Bob's parents are coming to meet us and I want you to behave.

ESTHER: I'll try. (*Glances at watch.*) Oh, I'm late, I'm late, for a very important date. (*Kisses* HELEN, *exits to bedroom.*)

HELEN: You're absolutely mad, Mother. (*Doorbell rings.* HELEN *opens door to* SUSAN, *one of Esther's students.*)

SUSAN: Hi, she's still here?

HELEN: Bedroom. I held her up a bit.

SUSAN: I better get to work. Script changes.

HELEN: Changes! Her play opens in a few days! What is she thinking of? I can imagine how the cast reacted.

SUSAN: I heard talk of a lynching.

HELEN: That would teach her.

SUSAN: Not Esther. She plies them with wine and talk about the glories of art. She's catching.

HELEN: That's my mom. Well, I better not keep my husband waiting. He's taking me to lunch.

SUSAN: Run along, married lady.

HELEN: See you. (*Exits.*)

ESTHER *enters from bedroom.*

ESTHER: Hello, dear. Where's Helen?

SUSAN: Went to meet Bob for lunch.

ESTHER: That's nice.

SUSAN: Well, I'll get started.

ESTHER: (*Looks at watch.*) Darn it. I won't be back in time.

SUSAN: In time for what?

ESTHER: For Mike. If a Mr. Alman shows up before I do, keep him here 'til I get back. Don't let him intimidate you. He's all bark.

SUSAN: Mr. Alman—keep him here—O.K.

ESTHER: I just remembered. Lolly's coming over too. I'll try to hurry back. (*Kisses* SUSAN.) Thank you. (*Exits.*)

SUSAN *goes to desk, stacks papers neatly, starts typing.*

SCENE 2

Later. SUSAN *is still typing, stops to correct error, puts eraser between teeth, retypes. Doorbell rings; she takes look at correction before going to door, eraser still between teeth. Opens door to* MIKE ALMAN.

MIKE: Well, hello! Who are you?

SUSAN: (*Removes eraser.*) Susan.

MIKE: Susan—very nice.

SUSAN: Nice?

MIKE: To the eye. In fact, you're quite yummy. Aren't you going to let me in?

SUSAN: Are you Mr. Alman?

MIKE: One and the same. I'm expected.

SUSAN: You're to wait. She's going to be a little bit late.

MIKE: Sounds like Esther. (*Crosses over to plant area, pokes earth, inspects plants, looks at watch.*) I shall wait exactly fifteen minutes. Then, I'm gone. (*Crosses to* SUSAN, *walks around her, looking at her appreciatively.*) You can entertain me until she comes.

SUSAN: I have to finish . . .

MIKE: Her latest atrocity, I presume.

SUSAN: Her new play.

MIKE: How futile.

SUSAN: I really have to finish. (*Crosses to desk, anxious to get away from* MIKE.)

MIKE: Very well. I'll just play with myself.

SUSAN *does a double take, looks at him suspiciously.* MIKE *takes out a piece of string from pocket, begins to play cat's cradle, holds it up for her to see. She walks back to desk, flustered.*

MIKE: What did I say? (*Crosses to couch, sits, continues to play cat's cradle.* SUSAN *begins to type furiously. After a while,* MIKE *turns to her and shouts over typewriter.*)

MIKE: You know any other tune? (SUSAN *types more furiously. Doorbell rings.* SUSAN *runs to door, opens it to* LOLLY GOLD-MAN, *a very sexy lady.*)

LOLLY: Susan. Is she home?

SUSAN: Not yet.

LOLLY: (*Heads for bar.*) I'll make myself a drink. (*Notices* MIKE.) What are *you* doing here?

MIKE: That should be obvious. (*Playing cat's cradle.*) I am exploring the topological permutations and combinations of the geometric patterns formed by ten digits.

LOLLY *does not answer him, concentrates on making drink.* SUSAN *hurries back to desk,* MIKE *watching the movement of her derrière. He sighs loudly, then goes back to cat's cradle.*

MIKE: There. The multitudinous arrangement of a closed circuit of string—thus in quantum effected.

LOLLY: (*Crosses behind him, looks at cat's cradle.*) Is *that* all.

SUSAN *drops some papers, bends over to pick them up.*

MIKE *points to Susan's derrière, shapes roundness with hands.*

MIKE: I have computed *that* body of data, randomly composed. (*Sighs.*) Foci that were within the capability of my intuitive judgment. Two whole minutes worth—know what I mean?

LOLLY: I know what you mean and I think you're gross. What's so great about it, anyway . . . (SUSAN *crosses to kitchen,* MIKE *follows with eyes.*)

MIKE: Miraculous vibrations.

LOLLY: Chief Brittle Bones with Tongue Hanging Out, shut up.

MIKE: (*Ignoring her.*) Of course, the possibilities will require consultation with the computer center at Harvard.

LOLLY: It's easy to see what kind of senility you're headed for. You're so goddamned transparent.

MIKE: I hope so. (*Leans back, closes eyes.*)

LOLLY: Well?

MIKE: You still here?

LOLLY: You're as bad as Jake the Snake.

MIKE: Thank you. I did admire your husband—that is, your ex-husband, in retrospect. Fill me in. Did he divorce you, or did he let you divorce him?

LOLLY: I had perfectly good cause.

MIKE: Ah! Your love affair. He could never cope with infidelity.

LOLLY: My love affair! He was running around. It's documented.

MIKE: I was speaking of the love affair between you and you, my dear.

LOLLY: A few minutes with you (*heads for bar*) and already you're driving me to drink. Why don't you swallow the acid in your mouth, darlin'. Would you like a chaser?

MIKE: No, thank you.

> MIKE *stretches out on couch.* LOLLY *mixes drink, then crosses to couch, peeks at* MIKE, *tiptoes to chair, drinks.* SUSAN *comes from kitchen.* MIKE *comes to life, watches* SUSAN *as she makes her way back to desk, turning on his stomach for a better view.* SUSAN *gives her back to them as she sorts papers.*

MIKE: Marvels!

LOLLY: You're disgusting.

MIKE: Perfect! (*Calls out to* SUSAN.) I compliment you on your beautiful butt, Susan.

> SUSAN *fumbles for her things nervously, picks them up, hurries to door.* MIKE *jumps up and follows her.*

MIKE: Where are you going?

SUSAN *exits without a word.*

MIKE: There goes the view and the neighborhood with it.

LOLLY: You frightened the poor girl. Madman!

MIKE: My expert eye was just relishing the swivel, the roundness, the muscle tone, the youthful spring . . .

LOLLY· You're not speaking of a sunset.

MIKE: What's with a sunset? I'm speaking of something within reach, something tangible, warm, alive . . .

LOLLY: I'd hate to let you loose in a girls' gym.

MIKE: I was just making a simple biological observation. Take the mandril . . .

LOLLY: Dare I ask? What's a mandril?

MIKE: A baboon.

LOLLY: I knew you'd come around to yourself.

MIKE: Shut up and learn something.

LOLLY: By all means—do tell.

MIKE: Among the mandrils, it's the male who lures the female. Has the stuff to do it with. What a sight! He carries his biological history behind him. And what's marvelous about it, it's the old males who have the beautiful butts. Bright orange! Royal purple! The open book of their lives. Young males don't stand a chance. All the lovely, young females stand in line for an appointment with the old guys.

LOLLY: I see where you're coming from. You fantasize that your butt is deep purple by now.

MIKE: Good thinking! Let's find out. (*Starts to unbuckle pants.*)

LOLLY: (*Jumps up.*) Stop, you pervert! Don't you dare drop your pants! I'll call the police. (*Crosses to bar.*) I need another drink.

MIKE: You're already smashed, and it's only . . . (*Looks at watch.*) Oops! My time's up. I'm leaving. (*Crosses to door as* ESTHER *appears.*)

ESTHER: Mike! (*Crosses to him, hugs him.*) How wonderful! You're here.

MIKE: No, I'm not. 'Bye . . .

ESTHER: Wait . . . We haven't . . .

MIKE: Call me. (*Exits.*)

ESTHER: Well, I never! That man . . .

LOLLY: Same old obnoxious Mike. How come he materialized in your living room?

ESTHER: I need his help. I haven't seen him in two years.

LOLLY: I thought your last fight had really gotten rid of him.

ESTHER: I called him.

LOLLY: You were well rid of him.

ESTHER: One doesn't get rid of Mike. He gets rid of you.

LOLLY: What do you need him for?

ESTHER: My bishop left me. We open in a few days and there's pages and pages of script. Who else could do the job?

LOLLY: Hate his foul mouth, but you're right. He can do it. I have to admit, he does add class to your productions. (*Crosses to plant area.*) All these are from him, aren't they.

ESTHER: Never forgets my birthday.

LOLLY: What does Dottie say about all this?

ESTHER: Never asked. (*Remembers.*) Oh, I know why I called you.

LOLLY: My maid said "urgent."

ESTHER: Richard went and did it. (*Points to Kirlian camera.*) Over there.

LOLLY: The Kirlian camera!

ESTHER: Took it from the university.

LOLLY: Took it? What do you mean, "took it"? Did he borrow it from his nephew?

ESTHER: His nephew's at some conference in Europe.

LOLLY: He just took it.

ESTHER: Just took it.

LOLLY: You mean stole it.

ESTHER: Borrowed it—without his nephew's permission.

LOLLY: No one stopped him?

ESTHER: Uh uh. Took it in broad daylight.

LOLLY: That's what I like about our university president. Runs a tight ship. Wait 'til Leonard hears about it!

ESTHER: Exactly what I told Richard.

LOLLY: Why didn't you make him take it back?

ESTHER: That will be difficult.

LOLLY: Melon balls! Hiding stolen property is a felony.

ESTHER: He's going to take it back—eventually.

LOLLY: When?

ESTHER: Soon.

LOLLY: How does it work? (*Goes and inspects camera.*)

ESTHER: (*Following her, points here and there to parts of camera.*) Let's see. First you plug it in, push these levers, turn the knobs . . .

LOLLY: Why did I ask?

ESTHER: I, for one, am not going to worry about it.

LOLLY: You're right.

ESTHER: Well?

LOLLY: Well what?

ESTHER: What did you think of our celebration?

LOLLY: The jacuzzi was great.

ESTHER: I mean Leonard's theory.

LOLLY: Don't understand it.

ESTHER: But you'd hoot and holler every time he made a point.

LOLLY: Hoot and holler?

ESTHER: Don't you remember?

LOLLY: No. My mind is suddenly blank. I remember one martini. Takes about four before your wonderful ideas come into focus.

ESTHER: They're not my wonderful ideas.

LOLLY: O.K., Leonard's wonderful ideas.

ESTHER: You had more than one martini. You finished off all the gin. You were konked out of your skull.

LOLLY: Me?

ESTHER: You went under the water and half-drowned poor Richard. His nachito got all soggy.

LOLLY: I remember the nachitos.

ESTHER: Then you came up for air, hollerin' away, "Hell, wouldn't that make the whole world cross-eyed!"

LOLLY: What would make the world cross-eyed?

ESTHER: Leonard's concept. Don't you remember?

LOLLY: Bits and pieces are coming together. I saw some strange things under the water.

ESTHER: Really, Lolly, it was a serious occasion.

LOLLY: Prodigious, I would say.

ESTHER: What was?

LOLLY: What I saw under the water—belonging to Leonard and Richard.

ESTHER: You're vulgar.

LOLLY: Pure observation. That Leonard of yours is sexy. I mean, when he talks, he's kind of electric. And, what I saw under the water wasn't bad either.

ESTHER: The way he looks at life and death is stupendous. He's changing my life.

LOLLY: If people believed what he said in that jacuzzi, it would knock the shit out of religion.

ESTHER: True.

LOLLY: Some party! Food, drink, music, our naked warlock re-defining existence while he scratched his belly . . .

ESTHER: Felt so good.

LOLLY: There's nothing like scratching your belly button.

ESTHER: I mean, the way he talked about our autumn gold, this special time in our lives . . .

LOLLY: True. We are at the peak of our sexuality.

ESTHER: That's not what I'm talking about.

LOLLY: That's the good stuff.

ESTHER: Don't be flippant.

LOLLY: There's something fuzzy I seem to remember—didn't he plan to celebrate the death of a "loved one?" Something about needing a dead body?

ESTHER: He didn't put it that way.

LOLLY: That's what he meant. Where's he going to get a dead body? He could advertise in the newspaper: "Wanted—one agonizing person at death's door to join in celebration."

ESTHER: There is a possible prospect—Leonard's ninety-three-year-old aunt. Of course, she keeps on rallying.

LOLLY: Holy Humus! Leonard might do her in—for the sake of the experiment.

ESTHER: Don't be silly.

LOLLY: I can't celebrate the death of an old lady I don't even know.

ESTHER: Leonard will share her with us, remembering the good things, the sad things, the wonderful memories . . .

LOLLY: Like when the old lady dropped her teeth in the john.

ESTHER: She never did that.

LOLLY: All ninety-three-year-old ladies drop their teeth in the john.

ESTHER: We have to wait.

LOLLY: What if she lives to be a hundred and ten?

ESTHER: Leonard will find someone. He's resourceful.

LOLLY: He could steal a stiff . . .

ESTHER: That's dumb.

LOLLY: I wouldn't put it past him.

ESTHER: Has to be someone we know. (*In accusing voice.*) You told Helen about the jacuzzi.

LOLLY: I thought it would brighten up her life.

ESTHER: She was furious.

LOLLY: That girl used to be such fun—until she married into that Baptist family.

ESTHER: Bob's a good boy.

LOLLY: That's what's wrong. Helen's going through a terrible phase. I hate to be pessimistic, but most people never can kick religion once they're hooked.

ESTHER: We kicked it.

LOLLY: Ah, but we're special.

ESTHER: I doubt it. Something else—Helen's in-laws are coming in from Sun City.

LOLLY: About time.

ESTHER: You know they couldn't make it to the wedding 'cause Dr. Scrimer was ill.

LOLLY: Hey, a prospect for Leonard!

ESTHER: He only has asthma.

LOLLY: They're coming to disapprove of you.

ESTHER: I'm sure they will.

LOLLY: Listen, I got to run. Attila's waiting for me at the local bistro.

ESTHER: How is Attila?

LOLLY: Deliriously happy. Why shouldn't he be—he has me. And we're both at the peak of our sex . . .

ESTHER: Don't start that again.

LOLLY: You need a young lover too. Very therapeutic.

ESTHER: That's your way.

LOLLY: La-di-da . . . You're just chicken.

ESTHER: Yep.

LOLLY: But you're restless and waiting.

ESTHER: You're imagining things.

LOLLY: How long have you been without Eddie?

ESTHER: Five years.

LOLLY: That's too long to remain a widow. It's bad for your body chemistry. Marry Leonard.

ESTHER: For my body chemistry?

LOLLY: Very good reason. I see signs . . .

ESTHER: Stop psychoanalyzing me and get out of here. I have to call Mike.

LOLLY: Mike! Is it Mike? No, it couldn't be Mike . . .

ESTHER: He's a married man. Go meet Attila and let me do my business.

LOLLY: Some business. (*Exits.*)

ESTHER: (*Crosses to phone, dials.*) Mike? *You* forgive me? I know your time is valuable. Yes, I want you to come over. I'll get your favorite wine and cheese. O.K., O.K., I won't get the wine and cheese. We could talk about old times. Alright, I'll forget the old times. I promise not to bore you. What do you mean, I never keep my promises? Don't scream in my ear. Alright—no wine, no cheese, no old times, no promises. Yes, I need you. Get yourself over here, will you?

SCENE 3

Half an hour later, ESTHER, *wearing garden gloves, is caring for plants. Bell rings. She crosses to door as she removes gloves. It's* MIKE, *who kisses her cheek and hands her a new plant.*

ESTHER: It's beautiful. What is it?
MIKE: It's a Sorcerer's Ear.
ESTHER: Yes, the leaves look like ears, pointed ears.
MIKE: Sorcerers have pointed ears—and elves, artists, bartenders, poets, mountain climbers. They all have pointed ears.
ESTHER: Why?
MIKE: All tuned in to wonderland.
ESTHER: Are your ears pointed?
MIKE: Of course. (*Shows ear.*) See . . .
ESTHER: They *are* pointed.
MIKE: I'm an elf.
ESTHER: Some elf.
MIKE: Look at this. (*Shows her plant leaves.*)
ESTHER: All different colors. How strange. Saw a snake like that once. It looked black from a distance, but close up it just glistened in the sun.
MIKE: I like that about you—your primitive feel for things.
ESTHER: That's comforting, since you find so few things in me to like.
MIKE: Stop fishing. This plant's very rare.
ESTHER: It's not my birthday.
MIKE: Why do you insist on being a dumb creature of habit?
ESTHER: I'm not.
MIKE: Yes, you are. But, you're a good mother to my plants.
ESTHER: If it's so rare, why don't you keep it?
MIKE: It's for you. Now—what do you want from me?
ESTHER: I want you to play a bishop. The actor dropped out and it's pages and pages that you can pick up in no time at all. It's historical.
MIKE: Historical—hysterical. Me play a bishop? Not even in jest. Hate bishops.
ESTHER: My play won't open if you don't help me.
MIKE: I'm not so full of vim and vigor these days.
ESTHER: What are you talking about?
MIKE: I'm a dying man.

ESTHER: You're joking. You? Dying?

MIKE: *You* are dying. Everybody's dying.

ESTHER: Who said you were dying?

MIKE: My body sez.

ESTHER: What about your doctor?

MIKE: Doctors be damned. They're like bishops—useless and expensive.

ESTHER: Your gout . . .

MIKE: And high blood pressure and two heart attacks.

ESTHER: Heart attacks! I never knew.

MIKE: Don't like to spread good tidings.

ESTHER: And Dottie?

MIKE: What about Dottie?

ESTHER: It must be terrible for her.

MIKE: Took it in stride.

ESTHER: But . . .

MIKE: Anyway, she's too busy with a new boyfriend.

ESTHER: Now I know you're making up the whole thing.

MIKE: Think what you want to think—who cares?

ESTHER: I care.

MIKE: Do you?

ESTHER: Of course.

MIKE: You should have said that twenty years ago.

ESTHER: I did.

MIKE: You married Eddie.

ESTHER: I loved you both, but *he* offered marriage.

MIKE: You miss him, don't you.

ESTHER: It's getting better these days.

MIKE: *I'm* still here.

ESTHER: Yes, you are. (*Touches his cheek.*) Your skin—moist, warm . . .

MIKE: Shit! What are you into, anyway?

ESTHER: Never mind.

MIKE: What do you mean—never mind?

ESTHER: Do you mind that Dottie doesn't mind?

MIKE: What's there to mind? I'm relieved.

ESTHER: Relieved!

MIKE: Why not? She's never at the house, no wagging tongue. Let her enjoy. I have Ming Ming and Mimi. Dogs are wonderful. They really love you. Then, there are the days when you call.

ESTHER: That hasn't been often. And, if you're really dying—what can I do?

MIKE: Do?

ESTHER: For you.

MIKE: This conversation's upside down.

ESTHER: You like it when I call?

MIKE: You're good memories.

ESTHER: I married Eddie because you never asked.

MIKE: I asked you to go away with me. You wouldn't budge. You just wanted marriage.

ESTHER: Doesn't every woman?

MIKE: Eddie gave you what you wanted.

ESTHER: Yes. And you? You always felt marriage was a trap, but you fell right into it.

MIKE: Not until my life was going under. Dottie used to make such good spaghetti. She doesn't cook anymore.

ESTHER: Poor Mike.

MIKE: Poor Esther.

ESTHER: Did we miss something?

MIKE: Hell, doesn't everyone?

ESTHER: I suppose so. I think it's wonderful the way you're taking it.

MIKE: Taking what?

ESTHER: Dottie's boyfriend—if he really exists.

MIKE: He exists.

ESTHER: You're so understanding, to give her her "space." Allowing her to search for a meaningful experience, for her own self . . .

MIKE: Stop parroting all that crud. I'm just letting her have her last roll in the hay. Let him have the full benefit of her menopause.

ESTHER: You're crude.

MIKE: And you're a prude. (*Begins to chuckle.*) It's funny . . .

ESTHER: What's funny?

MIKE: The whole bit. Her lover is a young kid with a pregnant wife. Dottie tells me he's starved for cultural sustenance, so they neck out in the car.

ESTHER: I'm sorry.

MIKE: Stop shaking your little curly head like that. Anyway, it's cheaper than a divorce. You can't erase the facts. I watch them, you know.

ESTHER: Watch them?

MIKE: Through the kitchen window—when there's nothing good on TV. Last night they drove off into the desert to watch the eclipse. (*Laughs.*) A rattlesnake snuggled up to them.

ESTHER: You.

MIKE: What do you mean, "me"? A real rattlesnake. She told me about it this morning, sitting across from me, bleary-eyed, sipping her Sanka with that little special slurp of hers.

ESTHER: You *do* mind. I can tell you're hurting.

MIKE: Don't get sloppy.

ESTHER: You *are* hurting.

MIKE: If it makes you happy.

ESTHER: Oh Mike, I want to share this with you. Let me in . . .

MIKE: You're at it again, Esther.

ESTHER: Don't you see? You're a little mouse running the circle of your little cage. And I—I too am running the circle of my little cage.

MIKE: Mickey Mouse and Minnie Mouse.

ESTHER: There are no doors, Mike. Where are the doors? No doors . . .

MIKE: "Oh, thou, who didst with pitfall and with gin . . ."

ESTHER: Isn't it kind of early for gin? You really shouldn't, you know. It might cheer you up. Half a jigger . . .

MIKE: Goddamn—stop trying to ply me with drink.

ESTHER: You said "gin."

MIKE: Don't you ever read your Omar Khayyam? "Gin" means trap, you blasted woman, trap! trap! Not booze . . .

ESTHER: Shhh—take it easy. Your face is getting red. (*Leads him to couch.*)

MIKE: What are you doing?

ESTHER: We want to take care of you. Never mind the play. So we bomb. It isn't the first time. The important thing is you. We must see that you are taken care of.

MIKE: Who's "we"?

ESTHER: I am. Lie down. (*Sits on couch, pulls him down, his head on her lap.*) That's better. (*Rubs his temples.*) Relax, relax— I'm thinking good thoughts about you. Try to pick up my vibes. Do you feel them? Let go . . . new positive energy running through you, rivers and rivers flowing, carrying you like a huge wave . . . Do you feel my good thoughts? (*Puts ear to his face.*) You're purring.

MIKE: It's the death rattle.

ESTHER: Don't even joke like that. (*Kisses his forehead.*) I'm think- ing wonderful things.

MIKE: Never did the most wonderful thing of all.

ESTHER: One track mind.

MIKE: Come on. Doesn't it cross your mind—how it might have been between you and me? Maybe when you called . . .

ESTHER: Don't be ridiculous. I needed your help.

MIKF: That's what I mean.

ESTHER: Not like that! (*Pushes him away.*) I have other kinds of fulfillment. I'm too immersed in my creative efforts.

MIKE: Who're you kidding? Creative efforts, my eye! Those dumb words you put on paper. What about you? Your needs?

ESTHER: Everybody wants to play psychiatrist!

MIKE: I'm a dying man, Esther. Time's running out for me. You know why I'm here?

ESTHER: Because I called you.

MIKE: It's much more than that. I'm like a dying elephant looking for his burial ground. I have this urge to go "home." Everything in me says *you're* "home."

ESTHER: Oh, Mike . . .

MIKE: Will you go to bed with me?

ESTHER: Just like that.

MIKE: Just like that.

ESTHER: Why, because I'm the one that got away?

MIKE: Don't be dumb. I just told you why.

ESTHER: Two ships that passed in the night . . .

MIKE: Can the corn. I just want to go to bed with you.

ESTHER: Do you love me?

MIKE: Hell—don't get sentimental. I want to tidy up the loose ends in my life. You're "home." Remember that crazy song we used to dance to? It's always in my head. (*Sings.*) "Oh, it's a long, long time, from May to December, and the days grow short, when you reach September." (*Grabs her, begins dancing, humming song.*)

ESTHER: Frank Sinatra.

MIKE: To hell with that. It was our song, wasn't it?

ESTHER: Yes.

MIKE: You have it?

ESTHER: Yes, with my tapes over there.

MIKE: Aha! I knew it. Put it on, and get the wine and cheese.

ESTHER: You told me not to get the wine and cheese.

MIKE: Goddamn woman, you believe everything you hear?

ESTHER *crosses to stereo, looks for tape, finds it, inserts in stereo.* MIKE *crosses behind her, kisses her neck; arms a-round her waist, he begins to sway back and forth. Turns her around and sings as they dance.*

MIKE: "Oh, it's a long, long time, from May to December, and the days grow short, when you reach September . . ." It might have been an interesting experiment.

ESTHER: What . . .

MIKE: You, Eddie and me. They do it in Tibet.

ESTHER: Now you tell me.

MIKE: You feel so good.

ESTHER: (*Breaks away.*) The nudes . . .

MIKE: Nudes?

ESTHER: The ones you used to sculpt, remember?

MIKE: So . . . (*Brings her back to him, very close.*)

ESTHER: Bookshelves full. I never wanted to be one of them.

MIKE: You *were* one of them.

ESTHER: From your filthy imagination.

MIKE: From my clean thoughts.

ESTHER: Eddie was safe.

MIKE: (*Starting to lead her to bedroom door.*) You want safe? Don't get out of bed in the mornings.

ESTHER: I feel safe now.

MIKE: Maybe I'll strangle you. (*Dips her, kisses her on the mouth.*)

ESTHER: I don't believe you're dying.

MIKE: Not at this moment. You're right about those vibes. You're a miracle.

ESTHER: Flattery might get you everywhere.

MIKE: Exactly where I want to go.

ESTHER: Where?

MIKE: Your bedroom. (*They're by bedroom door.*)

ESTHER: Wait . . .

MIKE: Why? The world keeps turning—seconds, minutes, hours, years, eons, just whizzing by. No time to waste, little girl, now that I'm home. (*They kiss. Doorbell rings.* MIKE *puts finger to his lips, strides quietly to stereo, turns it off. Doorbell rings again. Voices are heard outside the door as* MIKE *puts his arms around* ESTHER.)

RICHARD: She's not home.

LEONARD: We'll wait. She always leaves the door open.

> Door opens. RICHARD *and* LEONARD *walk into room.* ESTHER *breaks away from* MIKE, *but not before* LEONARD *sees them embracing.*

LEONARD: Good thing you leave the door open.

ESTHER: Really, you two!

LEONARD: Who's he? (*To* MIKE.) Who are you?

MIKE: I don't know you either.

ESTHER: Mike, this is Leonard, my next-door neighbor.

MIKE: You're in the wrong house.

ESTHER: Mike!

LEONARD: Mike . . . Mike . . . Oh, *that* Mike!

MIKE: She never mentioned *you*.

LEONARD: That's a pity.

RICHARD: I'm Richard. (*They ignore him.*)

ESTHER: Whatever happened to privacy?

LEONARD: Privacy!

ESTHER: Yes, privacy.

LEONARD: What did we interrupt?

RICHARD: (*To no one in general.*) No one cares, but I'm Richard.

MIKE: (*To* ESTHER.) Where's the script?

ESTHER: You sure?

MIKE: Goddamn it, give me the script. I'll be at rehearsal tonight.

ESTHER: Oh, thank you.

MIKE: Get it. (ESTHER *crosses to desk, comes back with script, hands it to* MIKE.)

ESTHER: I'm sorry about . . .

MIKE: The story of my life. (*Exits.*)

LEONARD: (*Looking after him.*) Rude fellow. So that's your Mike. I'm not impressed. What were you two up to?

ESTHER: We were going to make love.

LEONARD: You and that . . . that . . .

ESTHER: That what?

RICHARD: I'll go see what's in the fridge (*crosses to kitchen*) while you two fight it out.

ESTHER: You ruined everything.

LEONARD: I saved you is more like it. I can't believe—I can't believe . . .

ESTHER: You better believe.

LEONARD: There's a wife somewhere, isn't there?

ESTHER: That doesn't have anything to do with it.

LEONARD: I can't believe what you're saying. Where are your principles?

ESTHER: That's trite, Leonard.

LEONARD: After all we've been to each other!

ESTHER: We've never been anything to each other, Leonard.

LEONARD: We're going to be.

ESTHER: We are the best of friends, that's all.

LEONARD: Just give me a little time.

ESTHER: I'm a subject for your experiment.

LEONARD: I had much more in mind, and you know it. I'm not going to let you make a fool of yourself.

ESTHER: You're not my keeper. What are you doing here anyway?

LEONARD: That goddamned camera! You aided and abetted . . .

ESTHER: I had nothing to do with it.

LEONARD: It's here, isn't it? It's in the papers this morning.

ESTHER: In the papers?

LEONARD: Front page headline—"Valuable camera stolen from university."

ESTHER: Oh, dear—oh, my . . .

LEONARD: You'd think Richard had more sense. (RICHARD *returns from kitchen chewing on a chicken leg. He shakes the chicken leg at* LEONARD.)

RICHARD: I heard that.

LEONARD: (*Looking around.*) That's it? (*Nods toward camera.*)

ESTHER: Yes.

LEONARD: (*Crosses to camera, inspects it.*) No one saw you take it?

RICHARD: No one stopped me.

LEONARD: You better take it back.

RICHARD: I went to all that trouble for nothing?

LEONARD: I told you I didn't need it.

RICHARD: But it photographs auras when people die. When your old aunt kicks off . . .

LEONARD: We're not looking for proof, you Philistine. I'm a philosopher. We don't need machines to prove anything.

RICHARD: I want to see the energy you've been gabbing about all this time.

LEONARD: Don't be a simpleton.

RICHARD: Don't get huffy. I think it's a good idea.

LEONARD: It goes back!

RICHARD: (*To* ESTHER.) What are you cooking for tomorrow night? I love your spiced meat balls.

LEONARD: Did you hear me?

RICHARD: How could I help it, the way you yelp. (*To* ESTHER.) I'm bringing smoked shrimp. Maybe I'll make some crab almondine . . .

LEONARD: Never mind the food. I want that thing out of here before tomorrow night.

RICHARD: Not tomorrow night. I've got all that cooking to do for our orgy.

ESTHER: It's not an orgy. It's a celebration. Tomorrow night we celebrate our autumn gold.

LEONARD: That's right, my darling. Tomorrow night we shall bring with us golden thoughts, rich experiences, mellow passions . . .

RICHARD: And good food. I still say it's an orgy or the beginning of a wild, wanton debauch . . . You bringing the champagne, Leonard?

LEONARD: Never mind the champagne.

RICHARD: Don't get hyper.

ESTHER: You must think of our celebration as a spiritual revelry, Richard.

LEONARD: I would prefer that our celebration remain undefined until our experiment has reached full scope. I venture to say that little by little all our inhibitions will fall to our feet. We shall learn to "radiate."

RICHARD: "Radiate?" That's tacky, Leonard, real tacky.

LEONARD: You could call the university and tell them you took the contraption by mistake.

RICHARD: Not me. I'll think of a better way. (*To* ESTHER.) Is that tuna fish salad I saw in the Tupperware?

ESTHER: I think it is. (RICHARD *exits to kitchen.*)

LEONARD: Why do I appeal to his childlike nature?

ESTHER: He doesn't understand, Leonard.

LEONARD: Doesn't understand what?

ESTHER: Your whole concept. It's still a game with him—and Lolly too.

LEONARD: And you? Do you understand my concept?

ESTHER: Some of it, when you don't get poetic and hammy . . .

LEONARD: Hammy!

ESTHER: You *do* get carried away. You're not an easy man to understand.

LEONARD: Very well. I shall explain it to you one more time.

ESTHER: Now?

LEONARD: Now.

ESTHER: I have a million things to do before rehearsal tonight.

LEONARD: A parable perhaps.

ESTHER: A parable?

LEONARD: No, no, no, no—that won't do. I have it! I shall create a new myth for you—a spanking new myth to explain the autumn gold in all beings and what happens to it after death—ugh! I hate that word! Let us look at the options . . .

ESTHER: What options?

LEONARD: The guesses made about life after death—that stupid word! It's ruining my digestion. Do you know what comes after death?

ESTHER: No.

LEONARD: That's a realistic, intelligent answer. O.K., here are the options: When one dies, there's the old myth about heaven and hell. Old, but childishly fantastic. Do you believe in heaven and hell?

ESTHER: I used to when I was a child.

LEONARD: You didn't know any better. You believe in it now?

ESTHER: I don't think so.

LEONARD: Good girl. The soul—what is it exactly? You think your soul has a personality, the personality of Esther Forbes?

ESTHER: Doesn't it?

LEONARD: Infantile thinking. Why should the "soul" be cramped by our silly little personalities?

ESTHER: Then what is it?

LEONARD: Something we feel but cannot explain. Another option: reincarnation. Stick the little personality into another body. That's messy, illogical, putting a square peg in a round hole. You believe that?

ESTHER: Of course not.

LEONARD: What's left then? Those who believe only what they see. The old body dies after its short life span. Gradual decay. They put the body in the ground and that's the end—fini—poof! You believe that?

ESTHER: No.

LEONARD: Well, then, do you believe there is such a thing as death?

ESTHER: According to you, there isn't.

LEONARD: When did I say that?

ESTHER: When you were pouring eucalyptus oil in the jacuzzi last week.

LEONARD: Did I say that?

ESTHER: Yes.

LEONARD: Well, it's true. Our limited thinking has created ambiguities—spirits, souls, wheel of Karma, Nirvana, all guesses.

ESTHER: You're guessing too.

LEONARD: Of course. There is our intuition, our instincts telling us there's something special in each of us. Autumn gold.

ESTHER: That's the soul and those other things?

LEONARD: Yes, with one difference. I can explain it logically.

ESTHER: How?

LEONARD: With my myth. Here it is: Once upon a time there was this great energy composed of elements we have not discovered yet. We'll call it ONE GUY, capital O, capital N, capital E, capital G, capital U, capital Y. Now ONE GUY fills the universe.

ESTHER: That's the story of Creation from the Bible.

LEONARD: No, no, no, no, no, no, no! Forget that medieval thinking. It's not your fault. We are communicating with an old language that explains old myths. That's part of the problem. My concept needs a new language. But I don't have the time to create a new language right now.

ESTHER: I still don't understand . . .

LEONARD: For Heaven's sake—Oops! I mean for Clarity's sake, don't interrupt.

ESTHER: I'm listening . . .

LEONARD: Well, all this strange energy, ONE GUY, is not made of bones, muscles, organs, skin, heart—in short it's not a being. It's sort of fluid, shapes and reshapes itself like an ocean in the air, mixing with known elements. But its main catalyst is—guess what?

ESTHER: What?

LEONARD: Human experiences! Whoa—I'm getting ahead of myself. You see, there is ONE GUY floating in light and air filtering through the light. A long time ago, ONE GUY was looking down at a little planet called Earth before anyone called it anything. It saw all this organic life scurrying about, looking for food, shelter, multiplying. ONE GUY was fascinated by some funny little creatures that once had walked on all fours but were soon running around on their hind legs. He was drawn, you might say, to their rather large heads. Lo and behold, one day ONE GUY flowed right into the empty little head of one of these funny creatures. The little head had some sticky force that just ripped a piece of ONE GUY away. It stayed in the little head. Pretty soon, the little heads were like magnets, sucking in chunks of ONE GUY like a strawberry soda. They were even absorbing ONE GUY through the pores. It wasn't long before ONE GUY heard all this jabbering—yakkity-yak, yakkity-yak. The little rascals were talking. Get me a drink.

ESTHER: Now?

LEONARD: Gets better after a scotch and soda.

    ESTHER *hurries to bar, mixes a drink, brings it back to LEONARD. He takes a long, leisurely sip.*

LEONARD: Ahhhhh . . . thank you.

ESTHER: Go on . . .

LEONARD: Got you, eh? Noisy creatures, those little 'uns. The more of ONE GUY they sucked in, the noisier they got. They were eating ONE GUY up like caviar. And inside those little heads, which the little 'uns called "brain," was that chunk of ONE GUY. Guess what it was doing . . .

ESTHER: You know I don't know.

LEONARD: That chunk was creating systems, theories, labels, ideas. In turn that changed the body chemistry, creating feelings, emotions. Complex situation. The little 'uns called it "consciousness." Now the little creatures lived a lifetime experiencing the outer world, struggling for survival. It was pure ambrosia for the chunk in the little heads. Experiences were literally food for thought, a banquet, you might say. But the little 'uns had a short life span. They eventually withered up and died like all other organic life. Guess what happened to the piece of ONE GUY in their heads . . .

ESTHER: Oh, you're infuriating!

LEONARD: It was freed. ONE GUY simply absorbed it. But when it came back to ONE GUY it was not the same. It was full of the experiences sorted out into definitions and systems and ideas. So ONE GUY got fatter and fatter, obese, you might say.

ESTHER: Was that good?

LEONARD: It was good and it is good! Very impressive—the chunks sucked in by new generations were rich with past experiences. But it was very sad too! The little 'uns really didn't know and still don't know how to use all that experience. I mean, things have gotten metallic—pyramids, skyscrapers, superhighways, nuclear bombs! Through time, the little creatures were identifying with ONE GUY , thinking they were all important. They became the sum total of a runty personality with a junky ego and refused to consider other life forms equal to themselves. So the little body becomes very important, as if that were the total of life. But you see, life is that energy still unidentified by the little creatures. It is ONE GUY, eternal, always flowing, growing, like the cosmos. That's our immortality. The rich experiences that we gather as little 'uns is our Autumn Gold. And that in us which is senses, feelings, knowledge really belongs to ONE GUY. That's all we know of immortality and all we need to know . . .

ESTHER: Oh, that's so beautiful, Leonard! And it makes sense, real sense!

LEONARD: ONE GUY is forever, that's why we must celebrate the freeing of the little chunk contained in the bodies of the living.

ESTHER: So the little personalities, the egos, don't matter, they're like, like . . .

LEONARD: The shells we throw away when we eat seafood.

ESTHER: No one's going to believe you. They'll put you away.

LEONARD: Do you believe it?

ESTHER: Yes, oh, yes!

LEONARD: Others will believe.

ESTHER: Oh, darn it!

LEONARD: What?

ESTHER: I'm running late. Get out of here. Take Richard with you. (LEONARD *kisses her lightly, crosses to kitchen.* RICHARD *pokes head out of kitchen.*)

RICHARD: Tell Lolly to bring curried lamb. Don't forget the meatballs! Your tuna was a little stale . . . (LEONARD *reaches out and grabs* RICHARD; *they exit from kitchen, assumedly through back door.*)

ACT TWO

ⵞⵙⵉ ⵞⵙⵉ ⵞⵙⵉ

SCENE 1

The next evening. Buffet table is set up. ESTHER *comes from bedroom wearing a cocktail dress, adjusting an earring as doorbell rings. She opens the door.* LOLLY *enters.*

LOLLY: I'm the first. (*Crosses to buffet table with covered dish.*) Curried lamb for the likes of Richard. (*Picks up champagne from bucket.*) 1942—was that a good year? Who cares.

ESTHER: You know Leonard—only the best.

LOLLY: All this for "radiating." Where on earth did he pick up that word?

ESTHER: It's the best he could do with our present language.

LOLLY: Whatever. (*Picks up book from coffee table as she walks around.*) Omar Khayyam. You're into Omar, I see.

ESTHER: Mike's favorite.

LOLLY: Oho! Mike. How did rehearsals go last night?

ESTHER: Wonderful. He's such a fine actor. Did marvels for the cast's morale.

LOLLY: Lousy human being. No—I'll be fair. I've only experienced the vampire side of him.

ESTHER: True.

LOLLY: (*Goes to window.*) Look at that moon! I feel sixteen tonight. You know something—the moon has always had something to do with my undoing.

ESTHER: Your vampire side.

LOLLY: Touché. But look at it! Tonight the four of us singing in the wilderness. Where's our guru? (*Doorbell rings. Before* ESTHER *opens door,* LEONARD *and* RICHARD *walk in, both handsomely decked out.* RICHARD *crosses to buffet balancing two dishes, dancing along. At the table he starts tasting food.*)

RICHARD: Heavenly!

LEONARD: Get away from the table. *That* feast comes later.

LOLLY: There will be music, won't there?

LEONARD: Of course. I brought it over this afternoon.

LOLLY: Not Debussy again?

LEONARD: Debussy was fine for the jacuzzi, but for tonight—the Rites of Spring!

LOLLY: Leonard, haven't you ever heard of New Wave, punk rock, even disco?

LEONARD: In time, we'll get to everything.

LOLLY: The Rites of Spring?

LEONARD: There's reason to my madness. It's music that frees us, brings out the wildness from our depths.

RICHARD: I told you it was going to be an orgy.

LEONARD: Now, when you listen to the music, I want you to feel it here (*touches head*), here (*touches heart*), and here (*touches stomach*).

ESTHER: I'll put it on . . .

LEONARD: Not yet. Everybody—sit!

> *Everybody scatters to couch, chairs, except* LEONARD, *who walks around as he speaks, going from person to person from behind.*

LEONARD: Your minds cannot fully grasp the truth coded in the clear fabric of your deeper self. But believe! There is no death— there is no death—there is no death. A daring thought! A thought for those who dare. Do you hear the voice inside you? It's saying: There is no death—there is no death—there is no death. The thought rises—nimble, fluid, flowing, circling: there is no death . . .

ALL: There is no death.

LEONARD: Relax—tell me what you feel, Lolly.

LOLLY: (*Sexy moan.*) Mmmmmmmmmmmm.

LEONARD: Interesting. Tell me again.

LOLLY: Mmmmmmmmmmmm.

LEONARD: Esther?

ESTHER: Relaxed.

LEONARD: Good enough. Richard . . .

RICHARD: Hungry.

LEONARD: Go to the mind now. Tell me what you think. Lolly . . .

LOLLY: My mind is absolutely blank.

ESTHER: Same here.

RICHARD: Food's getting cold.

LEONARD: I shall give you words to fill the mind. But remember, all words are inadequate. What we feel is much greater than what we understand. The beating of your heart, your breathing, is more eloquent than words. You're alive! You'll always be alive, and in our autumn years, the gold of experience is burning bright in us. We are harvest, full, rich—the senses know there is no death . . .

ALL: There is no death.

LEONARD: Champagne!

> LEONARD *crosses to bar,* RICHARD *follwing. They open champagne, pour it into wine glasses.* ESTHER *crosses to stereo, puts on the* RITES OF SPRING *very low. All meet down-center with raised champagne glasses.*

LEONARD: Prosit!

ESTHER: To Life!

RICHARD: Cheerio-chin-chin!

LOLLY: Bottoms up!

LEONARD: To the deeper experience, beyond the limits of the mind. Catch the fire of the music. Touch the person next to you. Catch his fire. Warm flesh breathing. Feel your blood soar, your heart beat. Do you feel beautiful and strong? Do you feel the flame of limb and loin?

ALL: CALLOOH CALLAY! CALLOOH CALLAY!

LEONARD: Now, take your space. Make yourselves comfortable.

> *Each person returns to his or her place.*

LEONARD: (*Before sitting.*) Now—to memories, experiences . . .

RICHARD: I remember something.

ESTHER: Tell us.

RICHARD: In the fifties—God! that was long ago. I used to go to North Beach in San Francisco. I was into Marlon Brando then, a real beatnik. There was a bar where Jack Kerouac hung out. He looked a little bit like James Dean. He would sit there . . . we would all gather round to hear him recite his stuff. I remember something he said . . .

ALL: CALLOOH CALLAY! CALLOOH CALLAY!

RICHARD: The only people for me, he said, are the mad ones, the ones who burn, burn, burn, like fabulous Roman candles exploding like spiders across the sky—something like that.

ESTHER: How beautiful! Spider Stars!

LEONARD: Oh, frabjous day! Fires—spider fires—golden fires—swollen fires—all our feelings exploding across the sky. Life! Splash! Bang! Boom!

ALL: CALLOOH CALLAY! CALLOOH CALLAY!

LOLLY: Oh, I love this music! Makes me want to dance naked in the moonlight.

ESTHER: It *is* sensuous . . .

LEONARD: You feel it, Esther? May I kiss you?

ESTHER: Why not? (*They kiss.*)

RICHARD: It's time to eat.

LOLLY: The music's turning sour.

LEONARD: A vague sense of discord, the heavy fear of youth.

LOLLY: Now it's getting savage, brutal—I love it!

LEONARD: At this particular point in the ballet, a Sage comes on stage, the oldest man in the clan. He kisses the ground, the Great Mother of us all—a benediction . . .

RICHARD: Meatballs, curried lamb, smoked shrimp, crab almondine—all—over there—and nobody cares! I care! I care! (*Crosses to buffet table, piles food on plate, crosses back to chair, eating.*)

LOLLY: (*Stretches out on couch.*) I feel—I feel like biting into Life.

RICHARD: Try the food; it's better.

LOLLY: (*Jumps up restlessly, crosses to window.*) That moon! It's too much for me. I wish Attila had come along.

RICHARD: What? Let a mere child into our holy temple?

LOLLY: He is young, so young. His skin is firm and sweet.

RICHARD: She's been tasting.

LOLLY: A little bite once in a while. Such perfection! Takes it for granted too. You know what I read the other day . . .

RICHARD: Tell us.

LOLLY: A long time ago, Grecian women used to count their age from their marriage, not their birth. That would make me twenty-one. Just right for Attila.

RICHARD: Is he complaining?

LOLLY: Of course not! He's crazy about me. But sometimes, I feel the heavy fear of his youth.

RICHARD: I think he's lucky—making it with a nice, sexy lady like you.

LOLLY: How sweet. Thank you, Richard. (*Crosses to him, kisses him on head.*)

RICHARD: (*Reaches up with fork full of food.*) Here, try my crab almondine.

LOLLY: Not now, Richard. Do you know how it happened?

RICHARD: Yes—I took two pounds of crab, marinated them overnight . . .

LOLLY: I don't mean that. I mean, Attila and me.

RICHARD: How did you meet?

LOLLY: That trip I made to New York last year. I saw him in Central Park, alone, helpless. He had jumped ship—bought some ridic-

ulous passport from some sailor. There I was, thousands of
miles away from home. There he was, oceans away from his
land. Our eyes met. He smiled that wonderful smile of his. So, I
brought him home with me. I really don't want to get too fond
of him.

RICHARD: Why not?

LOLLY: I like him too much for that.

RICHARD: Why do you want to be twenty-one?

LOLLY: Youth belongs to youth. I think it would please him more.
(*Hands her glass to* RICHARD.) Be a dear and get me another
drink. Oh, the music's wild, wild, wild!

RICHARD: It's coming—the wanton debauch.

LOLLY: I want to dance, dance, dance, dance, dance . . .

RICHARD: The Mad Hatter's tea party.

LOLLY: Get me my drink. (RICHARD *crosses to bar and* LEONARD
to stereo. He increases the volume of the music slightly. LOLLY
begins to dance.)

LEONARD: Bravo, Lolly! Dance the part of the old woman.

LOLLY: What?

LEONARD: No offense, my love. In the ballet, the old woman repre-
sents eternal life. She's ageless. In her are all the secrets of Nature.

LOLLY: That's better. Secrets, eh? Aha! (*Dances.*)

LEONARD: Young men dance around her, with her, following her.
Come on, Richard.

    RICHARD *and* LEONARD *follow* LOLLY *around the room
as she dances, awkwardly doing what she's doing.*

LEONARD: The Augurs of Spring love her. Love her! She is woman—animal—the most desirable of beings . . .

LOLLY: That I am!

    RICHARD *stops dancing, crosses to his chair and plate of
food, eats.* LOLLY *dances towards his chair, kicks off one
shoe.*

LOLLY: I shall share all my secrets with my young men! (*Kicks off
the other shoe.*)

RICHARD: Take it easy with your secrets!

ESTHER: "Come fill the cup, and in the fire of spring, your winter
garment of repentance fling . . ."

LEONARD: I've heard that before.

ESTHER: It's from the book.

LOLLY: Mike gave her a copy of Omar Khayyam.

LEONARD: Lout!

LOLLY: I think he's trying to seduce her.

LEONARD: I know he is.

ESTHER: Leonard, let's bring Mike into the group.

LEONARD: That gouty skeptic would ruin everything.

ESTHER: Who told you he was a gouty skeptic?

LEONARD: You did—in one of your better days.

ESTHER: Please, Leonard, let him be part of the Autumn Gold Society.

LEONARD: To control the experiment successfully, I must limit the number of people involved.

ESTHER: One more wouldn't make that much difference.

LEONARD: *He* would.

ESTHER: Please . . .

LEONARD: Well . . . maybe . . . under certain conditions . . . later . . . much later . . . of course, if I don't change my mind . . . and I probably will.

LOLLY: He's jealous, Esther.

ESTHER: Are you jealous?

LEONARD: Naturally. (LOLLY *dances, using the back of* RICHARD's *chair to pose.*)

RICHARD: Stop giving me your secrets, woman. (LOLLY *dances over to stereo, puts volume full blast, and dances passionately.*)

LOLLY: CALLOOH CALLAY! CALLOOH CALLAY! (LOLLY *begins to peel off her clothes in utter abandon.*)

LEONARD: Ah, secrets! (ESTHER *goes to stereo, turns it off.* LOLLY *is down to her slip.*)

ESTHER: Stop!
> Everybody stares at ESTHER. *As she speaks,* LEONARD *and* RICHARD *help* LOLLY *put clothes back on.*

ESTHER: (*To* LEONARD.) What did I tell you? You and your fancy words! Look at Lolly. Look at Richard. They're just having a good time.

LOLLY: Just?

LEONARD: That's part of it.

ESTHER: You know there's more. You haven't explained it to them. Tell them . . .

LEONARD: What?

ESTHER: About ONE GUY.

LEONARD: You're so wise, Esther. She's right. Let's go beyond the good times. Let's roll with the BIG GUY, the ONE GUY. The whole kit and caboodle belongs to us . . .

ESTHER: Shut up and tell them.

LEONARD: Richard, Lolly, my children, you have followed your

Pied Piper blindly long enough—for food, for fun. Now—for faith! Listen carefully: Once upon a time, there was this ONE GUY —capital O, capital N, capital E, capital G, capital U, capital Y; he was so big, I can't tell you how big . . .

SCENE 2

A week later. ESTHER *is cutting a review from the newspaper. She prepares to paste it in her scrap book.* LOLLY *and* ATTILA *come in from kitchen, having crossed the lawn between the two houses.*

ESTHER: Where did the two of you come from?
LOLLY: Came in through the kitchen door. We were all waiting for you at Leonard's so Attila and I decided to come get you. Well, look at you! You look gorgeous. New gown.
ESTHER: (*Modeling.*) I picked it up at Fraser's.
LOLLY: Doesn't she look nice, Attila? (ATTILA, *who does not speak English, nods and smiles.*)
ESTHER: Hello, Attila. Thank you, Attila. (*To* LOLLY.) You think it's too seductive?
LOLLY: Definitely. But you can't go to Leonard's luncheon in a lounging gown, seductive as it might be.
ESTHER: I forgot!
LOLLY: About Leonard's luncheon? He won't take that lightly.
ESTHER: I can't go.
LOLLY: Of course you can. Go change. We'll wait for you.
ESTHER: But I haven't finished pasting.
LOLLY: (*Picks up cut review.*) It's that terrible review of your play. You paste your bad reviews?
ESTHER: That's the only way I can fill the scrapbook.
LOLLY: Forget it. Go get dressed.
ESTHER: I can't. I'm waiting for someone.
LOLLY: Don't tell me—Mike! It must be him, if you're dressed like that.
ESTHER: I'm wearing this to pick up my spirits after the bad review. That's why I bought it. I didn't even know he was coming. When I came in from shopping, the phone was ringing.
LOLLY: Fate pieces our destiny. The stage is set.

ESTHER: You watch too many soap operas.

LOLLY: How could I do that (*crosses to* ATTILA, *takes his arm*) when I have Attila? We're living one right now.

ESTHER: Mike's not feeling well.

LOLLY: What's the matter with him?

ESTHER: Went mountain climbing—would you believe it? Sounded all out of breath. He just wants to stop by.

LOLLY: "Yesterday this day's madness did prepare"—Omar. So, you're going to give him comfort and aid.

ESTHER: I am "home" to him.

LOLLY: I have to admit, that's good. He's got you with that one.

ESTHER: Don't be silly! He's an old and dear friend.

LOLLY: I'll keep Leonard away from the window so he won't notice Mike coming up your walk.

ESTHER: Will you?

LOLLY: What are friends for? We'll tell him you have a migraine. (*Exits with* ATTILA. ESTHER *goes back to pasting the review, finishes, closes scrapbook, takes it to desk. Doorbell rings. She opens the door to* MIKE.)

MIKE: (*Making his way to couch.*) Esther—Esther—Esther . . . (*Flops down, face down.*)

ESTHER: You look awful.

MIKE: I feel awful.

ESTHER: Can I do anything?

MIKE *answers with a moan.* ESTHER *sits by him on couch, touches his forehead.*

ESTHER: You're sweating cold.

MIKE: My blood is cold.

ESTHER: You carry some medicine with you?

MIKE: Don't believe in it.

ESTHER: Don't you believe in anything?

MIKE: You.

ESTHER: I'll get a towel . . .

MIKE: Stay where you are. I feel better when you're near.

ESTHER: Tea, perhaps?

MIKE: My heart's on a roller coaster and you want to give me a stimulant, woman?

ESTHER: I'm sorry.

MIKE: Just sit here close to me. That's the miracle cure.

ESTHER *begins to rub his neck and shoulder muscles gently.*

MIKE: You could kill me with that too, but it feels wonderful. Use

both hands. That's it. Ahhhhhhhhhh—a little further down . . .
Ahhhhhhhhhh—now, go back to my neck.

ESTHER *massages for a while.* MIKE *turns over, facing her,
touches her face.*

MIKE: Esther is "home."

ESTHER: (*Leans over, puts her cheek against his.*) I'm glad.

MIKE: I climbed and climbed and climbed.

ESTHER: That wasn't good for you.

MIKE: Who cares—it was wonderful up on that mountain. I saw
the sunrise and found, guess what . . .

ESTHER: What?

MIKE: (*Takes a flower out of his pocket, all withered.*) A Mariposa
lily.

ESTHER: Mike, it's a spring flower.

MIKE: And it's autumn.

ESTHER: Yes. Where on earth did you find it?

MIKE: Right on top of the mountain, just waiting for me.

ESTHER: Strange. I've never seen one in autumn. You should have
left it there. It's all wilted now.

MIKE: I couldn't help taking it. I knew it was the last Mariposa
lily I would ever see.

ESTHER: Don't say that.

MIKE: But I know it is.

ESTHER: Maybe it'll live a little longer. I'll put it in water.

MIKE: Your touch is already reviving it—like you revived me.

ESTHER: Not really . . .

MIKE: You're magic.

ESTHER: You *are* feeling better, aren't you?

MIKE: Infinitely.

ESTHER: You're grinning like the Cheshire cat.

MIKE: And I'm sitting on this tree, and I have more teeth than I
can count, and you're Alice . . .

ESTHER: "Would you tell me please which way I ought to go from
here?"

MIKE: "That depends a great deal on where you want to get to . . ."

ESTHER: "I don't much care where . . ."

MIKE: "Then it doesn't matter which way you go . . ."

ESTHER: "As long as I get *somewhere*." (*Touches tip of* MIKE's *nose.*)
You're a good pussy cat.

MIKE: Go put your lily in water.

ESTHER *exits to kitchen.* MIKE *sits up, leans back, obviously has gotten second wind.* ESTHER *returns;* MIKE *observes her intently.*

MIKE: Same color as your dress.

ESTHER: What?

MIKE: The Mariposa lily. Same color you're wearing.

ESTHER: It is, isn't it? You *are* feeling better.

MIKE: (*Beckoning her to his side.*) Sit here.

ESTHER: Are you sure I can't get you anything?

MIKE: Not now. Put your head on my shoulder.

ESTHER: (*Puts head on his shoulder.*) Mike . . .

MIKE: Uh-huh.

ESTHER: Remember the Crescent Pavilion on Saturday nights when we were young?

MIKE: Of course I do. We used to dance and I'd hold you close— so close, I could feel your very pores wanting me.

ESTHER: That's true.

MIKE: But you were one scared little kid.

ESTHER: I was eighteen.

MIKE: Alright—an eighteen-year-old scared little kid.

ESTHER: Maybe I'm still that scared little kid.

MIKE: Are you?

ESTHER: Right now, I don't want to be.

MIKE: "Fill the cup that clears Today of Past regrets and Future Fears . . ."

ESTHER: Oh, I do have regrets!

MIKE: Let's fill the cup—got any wine?

ESTHER: Your favorite. There's still the future fears. You come and go out of my life. (*Assumes Alice's voice.*) "I wish you wouldn't keep appearing and vanishing so suddenly. You make me quite giddy."

MIKE: I'll promise you, then, that even if I vanish, I shall still be here—even if you can't see me.

ESTHER: Oh, Mike . . .

MIKE: The night at the Crescent Pavilion—when I asked you to go away with me—you were wearing a dress that color.

ESTHER: You remember.

MIKE: Let's go "home," Esther. (*Embracing, they walk toward the bedroom together.*)

SCENE 3

Some hours later. The room is dark with afternoon shadows. There's a piercing scream, then sobbing. ESTHER *comes out of the bedroom crying. Crosses to couch, still crying desperately, reaches for phone, dials* LEONARD's *number.*

ESTHER: Is Lolly there? (*Cries while waiting.*) Lolly? (*Sobs loudly.*) It's me. Something terrible happened. Alright—I'll try to be coherent. Lolly . . . Mike's dead—on my bed. Died in his sleep after . . . after . . . Yes, yes, I went and done it. Stop congratulating me. This is no time for joking. Yes, I'm sure he's dead. I checked. You think if I wasn't sure I wouldn't be calling an ambulance? He's dead, I tell you. I can tell. I touched him. He was already cold. What am I going to do? No, no, don't tell Leonard. Just you, please come. He's gone, Lolly. I want to die too. Alright, alright, I'll stop. We've got to do something. Hurry, and don't bring Leonard.

> *Puts down receiver, makes attempt at self-control, resorts to sobbing in great pain. She stands and paces, still moaning, wiping tears away. Her eyes fall on the plant* MIKE *gave her. the Sorcerer's Ear. She picks it up, holds it close to her, takes it to coffee table, sits and stares at it.*

ESTHER: Rare, you said. Rare like you, my darling. I love you. We never really said it. (*She begins to sob again.*)

> LOLLY *rushes in through kitchen door; following her are* LEONARD, RICHARD, *and* ATTILA.

ESTHER: What are *they* doing here?

LOLLY: (*Points at* LEONARD.) He eavesdropped.

LEONARD: How could you, Esther! (*Crosses to bedroom.*) I'll go make sure. Come on, Richard. (RICHARD *follows* LEONARD *into bedroom.* ATTILA *crosses to* ESTHER, *clicks heels, kisses her hand, smiles broadly, then follows men into bedroom.*)

ESTHER: (*Calls out.*) He's dead, I tell you, dead!

LEONARD: (*Runs from bedroom.*) Just making sure. (*Runs back in.*)

ESTHER: Oh, Lolly, he's dead.

LOLLY: There, there, don't think about it.

LEONARD: (*Comes out of bedroom, very dramatically.*) There's a smile on his face. Did you hear me, Esther—a smile! How

could you, Esther! (*Runs back into bedroom screaming.*) There's
a smile on his face!

RICHARD: (*Comes out of bedroom.*) Dead as a doornail. (ATTILA
*comes out of bedroom, thoroughly confused. Flops down on
chair. Doesn't quite understand anything.* LEONARD *comes
from bedroom suspiciously composed.*)

LEONARD: Are you thinking what I'm thinking?

RICHARD: Mike's Esther's "loved one"! We don't have to wait
for your old aunt . . .

LEONARD: Exactly.

ESTHER: No! You can't!

LOLLY: Have you no feelings?

LEONARD: I know how you feel at this moment.

ESTHER: No, you don't.

LEONARD: Now use your head. He's not gone, Esther. He's here,
all around us—free and more alive than any of us.

RICHARD: He's above us—behind us—to our right—to our left. A
little chunk of ONE GUY.

ESTHER: He's lying on my bed, dead.

LEONARD: That's only the body—a mere shell. Esther, this can be
the test for your beliefs, for all of us. Do you believe in ONE GUY?

ESTHER: I think so.

LEONARD: Mike will be absorbed by ONE GUY, but he's still here
with us, milling around, floating in the air.

ESTHER: Mike! Mike! Are you here? I don't think I can go through
with it, Leonard.

LEONARD: Yes, you can. Leave everything to me. We'll bring him
out here so we can celebrate his freedom. He'll like that.

ESTHER: The body?

LEONARD: That's not Mike. That's just flesh, blood, sinew, cell . . .

ESTHER: You sound like Dracula. You're enjoying all this—just
because Mike and I . . . Mike and I . . .

LOLLY: What you need is a good stiff drink. (*Motions to* ATTILA.)
Attila, some wine—vino—sake—vin—vein . . . hell, just make it
vodka!

ATTILA: (*Understanding.*) Ah! Vodka! (*Crosses to bar, fixes drink,
comes back to* ESTHER, *hands it to her with a click of his heels.*)

LOLLY: Drink it. (ESTHER *hesitates.*) Damn it, drink it! You'll feel
much better. (ESTHER *downs it in one gulp.*)

RICHARD: I'll go in the kitchen and rustle up some food. (*Starts
toward kitchen.*)

LEONARD: (*Grabs* RICHARD, *turns him around.*) Never mind food.

LOLLY: (*Hands glass to* ATTILA.) Get her another one—vodka!

ATTILA Vodka! (*Goes to fix drink.*)

LEONARD: Now you take hold of yourself, Esther. We're going to bring the Mike we knew out here.

ESTHER: I don't think I can go through with it. I don't know if we should . . . (ATTILA *comes with drink.* ESTHER *downs it like water.*)

LOLLY: You're looking better already.

LEONARD: Remember, the real Mike is floating, waiting for ONE GUY to suck him in, to make him a part of immortality. Once he's back with ONE GUY, he will become the experiences of millions of people.

LOLLY: The Big Blender in the sky.

RICHARD: A little piece of this and a little piece of that, one little chunk, two little chunks, three little chunks . . .

LEONARD: He's watching us hesitate—especially you, Esther, who should be the joyous one because he's free. Soon he'll be mixing with the oceans of the universe—air, light, earth, water, unknown elements, seething with the experiences of every being. Imagine the sounds, the vibrations, the voices he will hear—a beautiful dissonance, the music of the spheres. Then, the dissolution . . .

ESTHER: Dissolution?

LEONARD: In time. We don't know how long—an hour, a day, a year, a decade, a century, an eon—who cares. The tortured ego is gone, the dilapidated personality all disintegrated—erased. Only Life is left and a sense of the universe. And that sense will be back in no time at all, absorbed by a new babe, by other human pores. He will go on and on and on and on—forever Life! Come on Richard, let's bring him out here. (LEONARD *and* RICHARD *exit to bedroom.*)

ESTHER: (*Feeling the drinks.*) Sounds so wonderful.

LOLLY: We'll drink to that. Attila—vodkas—her, me.

ATTILA: (*Holds up two fingers.*) Vodkas! (*Crosses to bar.*)

ESTHER: When Leonard explains it, it sounds so true, so simple, so right. I'm happy for you, Mike.

LOLLY: Yeah, why not? Beats anything else. Good ol' lucky Mike, swimming up there somewhere. Probably laughing at us.

LEONARD: (*Runs out of bedroom.*) I forgive you, Esther! (*Runs back in.* ATTILA *comes back with drinks.* ESTHER *downs hers again.*)

ESTHER: I don't want to be forgiven. I belong to me. Do you hear me, Leonard? I don't want to be forgiven! Get me another drink, Attila—vodka!

ATTILA: (*Jumps up.*) Vodka!

> *Runs to bar. This time while he fixes drink,* ATTILA *drinks one, then another.* LEONARD *and* RICHARD *come from bedroom with* MIKE's *body.* MIKE *has on only purple briefs and a big smile on his face.* ATTILA *shakes head in disbelief, but takes drink to* ESTHER. LEONARD *and* RICHARD *run in and out of bedroom bringing out* MIKE's *clothes.* ATTILA *stares incredulously, goes back to bar and fixes himself another drink, downs it.* RICHARD *and* LEONARD *put* MIKE's *pants on him with some difficulty. The zipper won't zip.* LEONARD *tries and tries, swears under his breath as he tries again.*

LEONARD: The bastard's trying to tell me something.

RICHARD: He's still around.

LEONARD: He's laughing at me! He got Esther. (*Starts to shake* MIKE.)

RICHARD: Take it easy. The poor guy can't defend himself.

LEONARD: Damn it, that's the way I feel. It's a time to be honest, open . . .

RICHARD: His fly sure is. (*Stares at fly meditatively.*) Doesn't really matter, Leonard. It's dead too. Very, very dead. (*Tries zipper. It zips.*) There, I got it.

LEONARD: I'll get the shoes, socks, tie . . . (ATTILA *watches with unbelieving fascination. Remembers* ESTHER. *Crosses to bar to fix her another drink. He drinks one himself, takes another one to* ESTHER. *She drinks it in one gulp. She stares at* MIKE, *blinks eyes.*)

ESTHER: (*Gesticulating.*) From where I stand (*falls back onto couch*) —sit—Mike's ONE GUY. Isn't he, Leonard? (LEONARD *comes running out of the bedroom holding up a pair of yellow socks. Goes to* ESTHER, *shakes them in her face.*)

LEONARD: How could you, Esther! With someone who wore yellow socks! (LEONARD *crosses to* MIKE *and with* RICHARD's *help they roughly put on his socks.*)

ESTHER: (*Stands unsteadily, peers at* MIKE.) He's vanishing. Good-bye, pussy cat. He's going, going, gone—all but the grin.

LOLLY: Look at the way he's smiling. Looks so happy.

LEONARD: Don't rub it in.

RICHARD: (*With bright idea.*) The camera! Over there. We can take a picture of his aura—of ONE GUY, a piece of him anyway.

LEONARD: It's still here? You never took it back?

RICHARD: I couldn't. I had to go to Santa Barbara to protest the oil spill. When Jane Fonda says "go," we go. (*Goes to closet behind plants, rolls out camera toward* MIKE.)

LEONARD: Forget it. We have more important things to do.

RICHARD Just one picture.

LEONARD: I said forget it. Now, go get a drink for Mike. Champagne for everybody. What do you think, Richard? He looks terrible without a tie.

ESTHER: Mike never wore a tie.

LEONARD: Anarchist!

> ATTILA *follows* RICHARD *to bar. They open champagne, fill glasses for everybody.* ESTHER *stands looking around for the Sorcerer's Ear. Sees it on coffee table, picks it up, stares at it.* RICHARD, ATTILA *pass out champagne.* LEONARD *takes a glass, puts it in* MIKE's *hand.* ATTILA *stares at* MIKE, *shakes head, crosses to* LOLLY, *sits next to her. He's quite drunk, starts getting amorous by nibbling her ear.* LEONARD *sees* ESTHER *with plant.*

LEONARD: What's that?

ESTHER: A Sorcerer's Ear. Mike gave it to me. It's very, very rare. Mike was rare. (*Peers at* MIKE, *shakes her head.*) That's not Mike over there. That's just an empty shell. Mike just flowed into this plant. He's inside this Sorcerer's Ear. (*Very konked.*) Hello, Mike.

LEONARD: That's good, Esther. Why not? (*Crosses to* ESTHER *and raises his glass to toast the Sorcerer's Ear.*) Here's to you, Mike. A legacy wide open . . .

RICHARD: (*Crosses over to* MIKE , *inspects zipper.*) I zipped him up, Leonard, don't you remember?

ESTHER: (*Talking to plant.*) We tied up the loose ends, didn't we Mike? You're so beautiful—all those colored veins . . .

RICHARD: Did he suffer from varicose too?

LOLLY: She's talking to the plant, dummy. (*Is bothered by* ATTILA's *nibbling.*) Stop that, honey. Not now.

ESTHER: Oh Mike, would you like me to read something from Omar on this—this joyous occasion? Where's the book?

> *Looks about for book, very unsteady on her feet. She reels, almost falls, but* LEONARD *steadies her.* LOLLY *finds book, hands it to* ESTHER. *She opens it at random, tries to focus eyes on print. She reads a line in great excitement.*

ESTHER: Listen to this! Mike's speaking to us through Omar. "Tomorrow? Why Tomorrow I may be myself with Yesterday's Seven Thousand Years." He's with all time—ONE GUY!

ALL: CALLOOH CALLAY! CALLOOH CALLAY!

RICHARD: Here's mud in your eye!

LOLLY: Here's to purple butts!

ALL: CALLOOH CALLAY! CALLOOH CALLAY!

ATTILA *crosses to* MIKE, *clicks heels, bows, drinks to him.*

ALL: CALLOOH CALLAY! CALLOOH CALLAY!

LEONARD: Share Mike with us, Esther. A strong memory . . .

ESTHER: We have a song, Mike and I. (*She nods at plant in her hands.*) Don't we Mike? (*Begins to sing.*) "Oh, it's a long, long time, from May to December, and the days grow short when you reach September." On Saturday nights we would go dancing at the Crescent Pavilion. (*Tells plant.*) You were the best dancer around and you knew it! Remember the Chinese lanterns around the Pavilion, all lighted up? We would take a walk to the edge of the lake. Around us tree shadows, the rustle of leaves, the smell of the water. Oh, I remember the warm grip of your hand, Mike. I used to think you would never let go. Don't let go, Mike, don't let go . . .

LOLLY: How beautiful. Wasn't that beautiful, Attila?

RICHARD: That was a good memory.

LEONARD: Aren't you the lucky one, Mike. (*Shakes plant.*)

ESTHER: (*Takes plant away from* LEONARD.) Don't be so rough on him! (*To plant.*) Are you alright?

LEONARD: You tell him it's my turn—my turn to have you.

ESTHER: Shhhhhhhhhh.

LEONARD: (*Takes plant from her.*) I promise you, Mike, I'll see to her happiness. So let go, damn you, let go!

ESTHER: Give him back. (*Takes plant from him.*) You'll have to find ONE GUY now, Mike . . .

ALL: CALLOOH CALLAY! CALLOOH CALLAY!

ESTHER: You vanished, but you're still here. You said you would be.

RICHARD: Quiche.

LOLLY: What?

RICHARD: We never finished our lunch. You got anything in the fridge, Esther?

ESTHER: I don't know.

RICHARD: I'll go see. (*Crosses to kitchen.*)

LOLLY: Look at my Attila. (*Kisses him.*) He's been so somber, so understanding, without really understanding.

ESTHER: The room's full of Mike.

LEONARD: To the rafters.

ESTHER: He will mix and melt.

LEONARD: Slowly but surely.

LOLLY: Maybe Attila's not really understanding—maybe he's just smashed.

> RICHARD *comes from kitchen, nibbling on an apple and some celery. Looks out window casually, then does a double take. He makes desperate gestures with the celery in his hand; unintelligible sounds come from his full mouth.*

LOLLY: What's the matter with you?

RICHARD: (*Swallowing.*) Helen—coming up the walk—with people!

ESTHER: What? They're not supposed to come until tomorrow.

LEONARD: Who's not supposed to come?

ESTHER: The Scrimers.

LOLLY: Helen's in-laws. They're Baptists.

ESTHER: What are we going to do? (*Walks every which way, still unsteady on her feet.*) Mike!

LOLLY: Mike!

LEONARD: Don't get hysterical.

> *Doorbell rings. Everybody scatters in all directions; then they stop, come back together again. Start to scatter again.*

LEONARD: Stop! This is a ridiculous way to behave. We're intelligent, rational beings.

LOLLY: What do we do with the body?

LEONARD: Stash it somewhere.

LOLLY: Where?

RICHARD: The bedroom. (*Doorbell rings again. Knocking is heard.* LEONARD *and* RICHARD *pick up* MIKE *and start for the bedroom. Doorknob turns.*)

LOLLY: You left the door open again, Esther.

RICHARD: Doorknob's turning.

LEONARD: Behind the plants. (LEONARD *and* RICHARD *carry* MIKE *to chair behind plants.* LOLLY *follows them.* ATTILA *goes to bar.* ESTHER *falls onto couch.* ATTILA *notices her, fixes drink, crosses to* ESTHER, *stops short, looks at drink, gulps it down himself.*)

ESTHER: Maybe I'll get lucky and pass out.

> *Door opens as* LEONARD *and* RICHARD *prop up* MIKE. HELEN *leads in* DR. SCRIMER *and* AGNES SCRIMER, *who carries a lemon cake.* LEONARD *and* RICHARD *quickly cross to guests, leaving* LOLLY *alone with* MIKE. MIKE *begins to slip from*

chair. LOLLY *props him up pretending to have arms around him.* LOLLY *catches* AGNES SCRIMER *looking at her curiously, so she pretends she's listening to something* MIKE *is saying.* ESTHER *comes to life, jumps from couch a little unsteady on her feet and graciously goes to guests.*

ESTHER: What a lovely surprise!

HELEN: Mother Scrimer insisted on coming over today.

ESTHER: I'm delighted. (*Holds hand out to* DR. SCRIMER.) You must be Bob's father. (*Embraces* AGNES.) And of course, you're Mother Agnes.

AGNES: You do have a pretty mother, Helen. I insisted on today because of this. (*Holds out cake.*)

ESTHER: A cake.

AGNES: My special lemon cake.

SCRIMER: I hope we're not intruding.

ESTHER: Of course not. We're just having a quiet gathering. Dr. Scrimer, Mrs. Scrimer, may I present my friends, Lolly Goldman, Dr. Leonard Ethans, Richard Talisman, and Attila.

AGNES: Attila—just Attila?

LOLLY: Just Attila—like the Hun.

AGNES: Oh, my! How do you do? (*Hands cake to* ESTHER.)

ESTHER: Thank you. Looks absolutely yummy, doesn't it, Lolly.

LOLLY: Yummy.

AGNES: Haven't you forgotten someone?

ESTHER: Who? Where?

AGNES: That gentleman—by the plants. (*Everyone turns head slowly to look at* MIKE, *then quickly turn away.*)

ESTHER: Oh, him . . .

HELEN: That's Mike. My godfather. (*Starts toward* MIKE.) Mike, I haven't seen you for ages. (LEONARD *intervenes, stepping in front of* HELEN.)

LEONARD: Not now, Helen.

HELEN: What do you mean?

LEONARD: He's in the middle of an experiment.

HELEN: A what?

LEONARD: An experiment.

HELEN: What kind of experiment?

LEONARD: A form of autosuggestion—self-hypnosis.

HELEN: Mike?

AGNES: You mean he's in a trance?

LEONARD: In a way.

AGNES: Dear, dear . . .

HELEN: He looks so still.

LEONARD: It's working!

AGNES: What's working?

LEONARD: The hypnosis. It's important that we do not disturb his concentration. He's attempting to reduce his own pulse and heartbeat—he's cleared the mind . . .

AGNES: It's all very strange.

LEONARD: Why don't we all sit down and get acquainted? (*Leads them to couch.*)

HELEN: (*Noticing her mother.*) You've been drinking.

ESTHER: You were supposed to come tomorrow.

HELEN: You're making me nervous, Mother.

ESTHER: Your imagination.

SCRIMER: (*To* LEONARD.) Your friend over there—self-induced, eh?

LEONARD: Yes. Did it all himself.

AGNES: You're not involved in seances, are you?

LEONARD: My dear lady, I don't indulge in parlor games.

AGNES: I'm glad. They're the Devil's work.

LOLLY: That little rascal gets into everything.

AGNES: Rascal? Never thought of the Devil that way.

LOLLY: Oh, but he is—a bloody, red-eyed little rascal. (*Hits* RICHARD's *hand because he's sampling the cake.*) Has his finger in every pie.

AGNES: (*Gives* LOLLY *a long, hard look. Turns to* LEONARD.) What is your field of medicine?

LEONARD: I'm not a medical man.

HELEN: He's a writer, a doctor of philosophy.

AGNES: Oh, one of those. (*Turns to* RICHARD) And you, Mr. Tailman?

RICHARD: Ta-lis-man. (*Picks at cake again.*)

LOLLY: (*Slaps his hand again.*) Like Aladdin's lamp or an astrological amulet with strange powers.

AGNES: Daddy, what does she mean, strange powers?

SCRIMER: Just an example, my dear. What profession are you in, Mr. Talisman?

RICHARD: Protester.

SCRIMER: Beg your pardon . . .

RICHARD: I travel around the country with protest groups—segregation, Vietnam, the nukes, oil spills, nuclear reactors—you name it, I'm there.

AGNES: Is there money in that?

RICHARD: I live for principle and pleasure, Ma'am.

LOLLY: He inherited money—but he doesn't like to talk about *that*.

RICHARD: (*Picking at cake again.*) Your cake is delicious.

LOLLY: Richard's a very good cook. He was a finalist in the Pillsbury bake-off some years back—weren't you, Richard . . .

RICHARD: '68—won with my Angel Divinity.

LOLLY: The little devil. Now he mostly eats—everything in sight. (*Hits his hand again.*)

SCRIMER: Dr. Ethans—Dr. Ethans—seems to ring a bell.

HELEN: He's the author of *The Machiavellian Malaise*. Made the bestseller list. It's done well, hasn't it, Dr. Ethans?

LEONARD: Adequately.

HELEN: He's being modest.

AGNES: Malaise—that's a disease, isn't it?

LOLLY: No less than the clap—oops!—I mean syphilis.

AGNES: Syphi . . . syphi . . . Heavens!

LEONARD: As usual, she's mistaken.

LOLLY: You told me that yourself when you were autographing my copy of your book.

LEONARD: Which you never read.

LOLLY: Which I never read—let me see if I can remember what you said . . . (ATTILA *is nibbling at her neck.*) You said it was about the di . . . di . . .

LEONARD: Dilemma.

LOLLY: Yes, dilemma—the dilemma of modern man, and some rock, and syphilis, and hell.

AGNES: What on earth . . .

LEONARD: A misunderstanding on her part. Let me explain.

LOLLY: But you did say that.

LEONARD: Your scope of comprehension escapes me and depresses me, my dear. (*To* AGNES.) What I gave her was a general overview of my book. Modern man, trapped in a technological, power-structured world, must adopt Machiavellian values to survive, thus little by little giving up his humanity, his natural ability to love. The end result: futility—like Sisyphus straining himself, pushing up that rock in Hades, only to have it roll down again.

LOLLY: I don't remember any Sissy . . . Sissy . . .

LEONARD: I'm sure you don't. There's much that escapes you, my dear.

AGNES: This is the strangest conversation.

SCRIMER: (*Looking toward* MIKE.) You'd think all this talk would disturb him, break his trance.

ESTHER: (*Jumps up.*) Agnes, why don't we go into the kitchen and cut the cake? Helen, come along. Richard, you can make the coffee. (ESTHER *picks up cake.* AGNES, HELEN, *and* RICHARD *follow her to kitchen.* DR. SCRIMER *stands, walks around room, notices camera.*)

SCRIMER: Unusual. What kind of camera is it?

LEONARD: Russian, I believe.

SCRIMER: Russian, eh? Unusual, but awkward. I say, those Russians are still in the backwoods, eh? (DR. SCRIMER *walks about plant area, coming close to* MIKE. LEONARD *quickly steers him away—taking his arm and leading him back to the coffee table.*)

LEONARD: You must see something unusual. (*Picks up Sorcerer's Ear, hands it to him.*) *That* is rare. (LOLLY, *who has been busy extricating herself from* ATTILA's *amorous advances on the couch, pushes him away, jumps up, and crosses to coffee table.*)

LOLLY: You better believe it.

SCRIMER: Interesting. A succulent, isn't it?

LEONARD: Called a Sorcerer's Ear.

SCRIMER: Leaves do look like ears. Mrs. Forbes has quite a collection. (*Eyes fall on* MIKE.) Dangerous . . .

LOLLY: Collecting plants?

SCRIMER: I'm talking about your friend over there. Self-hypnosis can be dangerous. I say, does he have any training? He looks rather pale.

LOLLY: (*Takes* DR. SCRIMER's *arm, leads him to couch, playing up to him as* ATTILA *glares.*) He's done it hundreds of times. You must tell me about Sun City. (*Sits very close to* DR. SCRIMER.)

SCRIMER: (*Clears his throat, somewhat at a loss.*) Well . . .

LOLLY: Esther tells me you're crazy about the place.

SCRIMER: It's—eh—very nice, Mrs. Goldman.

LOLLY: Do call me Lolly.

SCRIMER: I say, like lollypop, eh . . .

LOLLY: Oh, you do have a sense of humor. I love men with a sense of humor.

SCRIMER: Well . . .

LOLLY: Is Sun City a very exclusive place?

SCRIMER: We managed to keep out children, long beards, and foreigners. (*Looks at* ATTILA, *who is glaring at him.*) I say, does he speak any English?

LOLLY: Not a word.

SCRIMER: He's not happy about something.

LOLLY: Oh, never mind him. He gets into moods. Attila, get me a vodka—vodka! Would you like one, Doctor?

SCRIMER: Not for me, thank you. I don't drink. (ATTILA *refuses to budge, crosses his arms, and glares menacingly at them.*)

LOLLY: He pouts too. Just ignore him. Tell me, what do you do for fun in Sun City?

SCRIMER: Fun?

LOLLY: Yes, F-U-N, fun.

SCRIMER: There's bridge . . .

LOLLY: How exciting.

SCRIMER: Sunday's bingo night.

LOLLY: I have a feeling you have a movie theatre that shows nothing but John Wayne movies, am I right?

SCRIMER: We do love the Duke.

LOLLY: And Lawrence Welk, I'm sure.

SCRIMER: Brings his family—ha, ha, that's what he calls his band—down to Sun City two, three times a year.

LOLLY: You should call it Fun City. (AGNES, ESTHER, RICHARD *return from kitchen with cake and coffee.* HELEN *steers* AGNES *away as she stares at her husband making it cozy with* LOLLY.)

HELEN: Would you like to serve the cake, Mother Agnes?

AGNES: (*In a commanding voice.*) Daddy! Come help me . . .

   DR. SCRIMER *jumps up rather guiltily, crosses to* AGNES, *who shoves a plate of cake into his stomach.*

AGNES: Here, you can give this to your friend.

SCRIMER: Yes, dear. (*Hands it to* ATTILA. ESTHER *and* RICHARD *are busy serving the coffee.*)

AGNES: What about your friend over there?

ESTHER: What?

AGNES: Your friend over there, I think he would enjoy a piece of cake.

LOLLY: (*Jumps up from couch, crosses to* AGNES, *takes plate of cake from her.*) I'll take it to him. He's my fiancé.

AGNES: Oh? (*Points to* ATTILA.) Isn't *he* your fiancé?

LOLLY: Him too. It's so hard for me to say no. And men, they simply will not leave me alone.

AGNES: I see.

HELEN: (*To* ESTHER.) What's going on? Lolly's not Mike's girl-friend.

ESTHER: I'll explain later, dear.

HELEN: Don't bother. I'll just wait for the bomb.

ESTHER: Don't be silly. Relax.

HELEN: Mother! (LOLLY *takes the cake to* MIKE, *pretends to talk to him, bends down to listen to something that he's supposed to be saying, laughs merrily, then begins to feed him cake.*)

LOLLY: Oh, Mike, you do say the funniest things! I know, it's delicious cake. (*Eats some cake herself.*) Compliments to the cook? (*Calls out to* AGNES.) Mike says, "compliments to the cook!"

AGNES: (*Quickly, before anyone can stop her, greatly pleased, crosses to* MIKE *and* LOLLY.) I brought you another piece—just for you. (*As* AGNES *tries to hand him the plate she accidentally touches his shoulder.* MIKE *topples to the floor.* AGNES *lets out a scream,* LOLLY *crosses to bar, shrugs shoulders.* DR. SCRIMER *crosses to fallen body.*)

LOLLY: What frigging luck . . . (DR. SCRIMER *bends down and examines the body, doing the usual doctor things; listens to heart, checks pulse, breathing, etc.*)

SCRIMER. This man is dead—has been dead for some time.

ATTILA *has rushed to the scene with everybody else except* ESTHER, *who slumps on the couch as if giving up.* RICHARD *is busily eating cake as he looks over the body. When* AGNES *hears what her husband says, she screams again and falls into a faint right on top of* RICHARD, *who tries to keep her on her feet but instead falls to the floor,* AGNES *on top of him.*

SCRIMER: Agnes, are you alright? Someone bring some water.

HELEN: (*Pacing, talking to no one in particular.*) Why, why does she do these things to me? (ATTILA *observes* AGNES's *situation, rushes to bar.* LOLLY *hands him the vodka bottle, he fills a glass, takes it to* DR. SCRIMER, *who feeds it to* AGNES *thinking it is water. She gulps, begins to sputter and spit.*)

SCRIMER: (*To* ATTILA.) What was in that glass, sir?

ATTILA: (*Clicks heels, bows.*) Vodka!

LOLLY: He's trying to help.

SCRIMER: I think all of you owe us an explanation.

LOLLY: I told you before, he doesn't know a word of English.

SCRIMER: I mean the dead man. He was dead before we got here.

AGNES *is being helped to her feet by* RICHARD; *on hearing her husband's words she falls into another faint, taking* RICHARD *with her.* ATTILA *suddenly burps uncommonly loud,* LOLLY *pats his back.*

SCRIMER: What kind of madness . . .

LEONARD: You're right. Doctor, we owe you an explanation. I do apologize.

SCRIMER: I think the police should be called in on this. The death must be reported.

ESTHER: Police?

HELEN: Why not? Anything goes. The Jabberwock may walk in at any minute . . .

ESTHER: You're not making sense.

HELEN: Do any of you make sense? (AGNES, *still on the floor with* RICHARD, *crawls on all fours toward* DR. SCRIMER. *She holds on to her husband's leg as she speaks, then slowly makes it to her feet, holding on to the doctor.*)

AGNES: Oh, Daddy, that woman was talking to the dead man, hugging him, feeding him *my* cake. "Compliments to the cook," that's what he said, "compliments to the cook." But he couldn't have said it.

ATTILA *burps very loudly, expressively.*

AGNES: And him! That Hun! Always staring like an owl. What kind of language is that? Oh, Daddy, syphilis, hell, seances, lovers right and left—what did our poor Bob marry into?

SCRIMER: Calm down, Mother. I'm sure Dr. Ethans will tell us what it's all about.

LEONARD: It's really very simple.

HELEN: Then, explain! explain! . . . Maybe you shouldn't.

LEONARD: We were attempting to experience death from a unique viewpoint.

SCRIMER: What?

LEONARD: We were celebrating Mike's death.

SCRIMER: Celebrating his death. Wasn't he your friend?

LEONARD: Precisely why we were celebrating.

SCRIMER: I better call the police. (*Crosses to phone.*)

ESTHER: (*Stands in front of phone.*) Must you?

LEONARD: Let him do his duty if he feels he must. (ESTHER *stands away from the phone, then crosses to couch and collapses.* ATTILA *rushes over with vodka. She shakes her head;* ATTILA *drinks it.*)

ESTHER: It's all going to come out.

SCRIMER: (*On phone.*) Give me the police. Thank you, I have the number. (*Dials number.*) Hello, my name is Dr. Scrimer and I would like to report a dead body. (*To* ESTHER.) What's the address?

ESTHER: One, two, three, four, Melody Lane.

SCRIMER: One, two, three, four, Melody Lane. (*Pause.*) We'll be here. (*Puts phone down.*)

HELEN: Mother, I'll never forgive you for this.

LEONARD: Don't you talk to your mother that way.

HELEN: Why does she involve herself in strange, bizarre . . . Why must she live down a rabbit hole?

AGNES: Rabbit hole?

LEONARD: Helen is alluding to Alice in Wonderland. The inhabitants of that land were strange creatures—that's the way Helen thinks of us.

AGNES: How on earth did Helen turn out to be such a wonderful girl?

LEONARD: You think on that, Mrs. Scrimer.

SCRIMER: I'm sure there's nothing wrong with anybody here, if the unusual happenings can be explained.

LEONARD: I take full responsibility for what's happened. Mike died of a heart attack while in our midst. The only indiscretion was not making the usual swift arrangements. That was my doing.

> *Police siren.* DR. SCRIMER *helps his wife to a chair.* RICHARD *is making rounds of the cake plates, eating what's left.* ATTILA *is at the bar, counting empty bottles. The rest are sitting, looking forlorn. Doorbell rings.* LEONARD *crosses to door, opens it to a police sergeant and a rookie.*

SERGEANT: I believe this is one, two, three, four, Melody Lane. We received a report about a dead body. A Dr. Scrimer?

LEONARD: (*Nods toward* DR. SCRIMER.) That's him over there. (SERGEANT *tries to cross to* DR. SCRIMER; HARRY *the rookie cuts in front of him, almost knocking him down.* SERGEANT *closes his eyes as if praying, tries again.*)

SERGEANT: (*To* DR. SCRIMER.) You made the call?

SCRIMER: Yes. The body's over there. (*Points to body.* HARRY *runs in front of* SERGEANT, *gets to body, picks up arm of dead man, lets it fall.* SERGEANT *examines the body while* HARRY *takes out notebook and begins writing with great intensity, walking about, getting in the* SERGEANT's *way.*)

SERGEANT: Harry, stop hovering, O.K.?

HARRY: Yes sir. He looks very dead.

SERGEANT: Smart, Harry, smart.

HARRY: (*Sidles up to* SERGEANT.) The murderer's probably still in this room.

SERGEANT: What murder? We're just answering a call, Harry.

HARRY: Yes, sir. If you say so, sir.

SERGEANT: (*Crosses to* DR. SCRIMER.) Can you tell me what happened?

SCRIMER: (*Points to* LEONARD.) Ask him. I'm just a guest.

SERGEANT: (*Crosses to* LEONARD.) What can you tell me about the death?

LEONARD: He died of a heart attack.

SERGEANT: Just like that, eh? He has a big smile on his face.

LEONARD: Never mind the smile.

SERGEANT: It's unusual. (HARRY *has caught sight of the camera and is examining it.* RICHARD, *still eating cake, rushes over to* HARRY *and pushes the plate of cake on him.*)

RICHARD: Have some.

HARRY: What kind?

RICHARD: Lemon—delicious.

HARRY: (*Samples it.*) Very good.

    RICHARD *starts rolling camera away while* HARRY *is busy eating cake.* HARRY *looks up from cake.*

HARRY: Hey, wait a minute. Stop right there!

SERGEANT: What's the matter?

HARRY: He's trying to hide that thing.

SERGEANT: What is it?

RICHARD: Just a camera.

SERGEANT: Were you trying to hide it?

RICHARD: Absurd. I was just . . . tidying up the place.

SERGEANT: What's your name?

RICHARD: Richard Talisman.

HARRY: (*To* SERGEANT.) You don't believe him, do you? It could be a motive.

SERGEANT: Motive for what?

HARRY: (*Takes notes furiously.*) Murder.

SERGEANT: Will you stop that? We're not looking for motives. You wear me out.

HARRY: I've seen that thing before.

SERGEANT: (*To* RICHARD.) What kind of camera is it?

RICHARD: Russian.

HARRY: The plot thickens. We better call Big Mac.

SERGEANT: Why do you want the FBI on this?

HARRY: Obvious.

SERGEANT: Who let you into the police force?

HARRY: Spies.

SERGEANT: What?

HARRY: Russian secret weapon.

SERGEANT: (*Screaming in his ear.*) It's just a camera!

HARRY: Yes, sir.

SERGEANT: (*To* RICHARD.) Does it belong to you?

RICHARD: Not exactly.

SERGEANT: (*To* DR. SCRIMER.) Know anything about this camera?

SCRIMER: My wife and I are innocent parties.

SERGEANT: Who says you're guilty of anything? Does this camera belong to anyone in this room?

RICHARD: I borrowed it.

SERGEANT Who does it belong to?

RICHARD: You've never seen one like it, have you? Let me tell you something about it. This scientific apparatus is a Kirlian camera invented by one Valentina Kirlian in Russia.

SERGEANT: Scientific, eh?

RICHARD: It photographs the luminescence of human auras, the bioplasmic body . . .

SERGEANT: The bio—what?

RICHARD: Bioplasmic body.

HARRY: Told you it was a secret weapon.

SERGEANT: (*To* HARRY.) Shut up!

RICHARD: It uses a special ray.

HARRY: A death ray!

RICHARD: A gamma ray, to be exact, ultra-fluorescent, revealing the bioplasmic body in photography . . .

HARRY: He's speaking in code—spies, I tell you . . .

SERGEANT: (*To* HARRY.) If you open your mouth with something stupid again . . . (*Shakes his fists in* HARRY's *face.*)

RICHARD *starts to tiptoe away with the camera.*

SERGEANT: You! I still want to know to whom that contraption belongs.

HARRY: (*Remembering.*) It's stolen! It's stolen! I remember where I saw it! The newspaper a few days ago—remember?

SERGEANT: Yeah, for once you're right. I better call Big Mac.

HARRY: That's what I said. (*Follows* SERGEANT *to phone.*) Have Big Mac check up on this guy Talisman. Criminal type. Probably has a record.

SERGEANT: O.K., O.K., I'll check. (*Dials phone.*) Big Mac, have a problem—Sergeant Bacon.

HARRY: (*Looking at notebook.*) Got it all right here, Sarge—possible murder over a secret weapon, disguised as a camera. We're dealing with spies . . .

SERGEANT: (*On phone.*) I've got James Bond with me. Yeah, yeah, it's Harry. You think the department is trying to tell me something? What I'm calling about is that stolen camera from the university. There's a guy here who says he borrowed it by the name of Richard Talisman, T-a-l-i-s-m-a-n, right. Check him out and call me back. Number's 255-5522.

> SERGEANT *puts down phone, crosses over to* ATTILA, *who is leaning against the bar.*

SERGEANT: Your name please.

LOLLY: (*Crosses in front of* ATTILA.) He doesn't speak any English.

SERGEANT: Resident? Visitor?

LOLLY: He's my house guest.

HARRY: Looks Russian to me.

SERGEANT: Does he have any papers on him, lady?

LOLLY: Papers? He's a house guest.

AGNES: That man is her fiancé, so was the dead man. (*Phone rings.* SERGEANT *picks it up.*)

SERGEANT: Yeah. (*Pause.*) Yeah. (*Pause.*) You don't say. I'll take them all down to the station. By the way, there's also a dead man—looks like a heart attack. Send the coroner over, will you? The address is one, two, three, four, Melody Lane—No, I'm not kidding. O.K. (*Hangs up phone.*) Who lives here?

ESTHER: Me.

SERGEANT: And all these people are your guests?

ESTHER: Yes.

SERGEANT: Was the dead man related to you?

ESTHER: No. He was a dear friend.

SERGEANT: I'm afraid I'll have to take you all down to the station.

ESTHER: Why?

SERGEANT: Well, it's getting complicated. Seems Mr. Talisman has a record with the FBI.

RICHARD: I'm proud of it!

SERGEANT: Anyone related to the dead man here?

ESTHER: He has a wife, Dottie.

SERGEANT: We'll see that she's notified. The coroner will be here soon to take the body. The wagon will be here any minute.

AGNES: Wagon?

SERGEANT: Yes ma'am, all of you will be going down to the police station.

AGNES: It's so humiliating.

SCRIMER: I'd like to call my lawyer.

SERGEANT: You can do whatever you want—down at the station. (*The sound of a siren is heard.*) Alright, everybody, let's go.

> As the SERGEANT *herds everybody toward exit,* RICHARD

disappears into kitchen. ATTILA *remains fixed at the bar and* LOLLY *on the couch. Everyone else exits with the* SERGEANT.

SERGEANT: (*As he exits.*) Harry, bring the others.

HARRY: Yes, sir. (*Looks around room and misses* RICHARD.) Where did he go? (*Draws gun.*) Come out, come out wherever you are. ATTILA *starts toward* LOLLY. HARRY *points the gun at him.*

HARRY: Don't move! (LOLLY *crosses to* HARRY *and pounds him with a closed fist over the head.*)

LOLLY: You clown! Don't you point a gun at him!

HARRY: (*Escapes from her blows, turns, then points the gun at her.*) You too, lady! (ATTILA *growls a swear word and tackles* HARRY, *disarms him, then proceeds to sit on him.* HARRY *groans as* RICHARD *comes from kitchen with a package of Oreo cookies.* RICHARD *crosses to* HARRY, *who is lying on the floor with* ATTILA *on top of him.*)

RICHARD: Oreos, anyone? (ATTILA *and* HARRY *take cookies and start munching.* SERGEANT *returns.*)

SERGEANT: Hey, what's holding you up? (*Sees* HARRY *on floor.*) What are you doing?

HARRY: (*Munching away.*) I've been captured.

SERGEANT: How long have you been in the department?

HARRY: Almost six months.

SERGEANT: You'll never make it to a year, Harry. (*Screams at him.*) Get off your ass! (ATTILA *jumps up,* HARRY *scurries to his feet.* RICHARD *offers a cookie to the* SERGEANT, *who simply glares at him. The* SERGEANT *escorts* RICHARD *out;* HARRY *tries to push* ATTILA *without success.*)

HARRY: Come on guy, you got to go. (HARRY *pushes again without success.*)

LOLLY: (*Crosses to* ATTILA.) You just go with him honey—I'll be right behind you. (LOLLY *kisses him and pushes him gently toward the door.* ATTILA *willingly goes out with* HARRY *at his heels.* LOLLY *stands watching them go, then she goes to the phone.* SERGEANT *comes back.*)

SERGEANT: There's only you holding up the show, lady.

LOLLY: I'm going to make a phone call.

SERGEANT: Down at the station.

LOLLY: Right here.

SERGEANT: O.K., make your call.

LOLLY: (*Dials.*) It's me, Lolly. Your mouth hasn't changed, darling. Of course I'm in trouble. Why else would I call? No, your checkbook can't help. Get yourself down to the police station. Really, Jake, don't you know anything else but four letter words? No, the nudist colony is not in trouble. I left the nudist colony last year. They think we're spies. Of course we're not spies. You wouldn't have it any other way, darling. I need your political muscle, Mr. Ex-Mayor. The police chief is in your pocket, isn't he? Alright, I'm exaggerating. But, one word from you and they'll forget about us. Listen, Big Shot, I'll see you in about fifteen minutes—O.K.? (*Makes a kiss.*)

SERGEANT: Mr. Ex-Mayor?

LOLLY: You shouldn't eavesdrop on conversations.

SERGEANT: Political muscle?

LOLLY: You sound like a broken record.

SERGEANT: Police chief in his pocket?

LOLLY: That was an exaggeration. They only play the horses together.

SERGEANT: The ex-mayor, your husband?

LOLLY: Yes, Ex-Mayor Jake Goldman. I'm Mrs. Goldman. Really Sergeant, you're worse than Harry.

SERGEANT: Let me get it straight. The stiff is your fiancé, the deaf-and-dumb one is your house guest, among other things. Then, there's the ex-mayor, your husband. Did I get it straight?

LOLLY: You got it, lover. (*They exit.*)

ACT THREE

wᴗᴗ ᴗᴗᴗ ᴗᴗᴗ

FINAL SCENE

A week later. LOLLY *is leafing through a magazine.* ESTHER *enters.*

LOLLY: You did it?

ESTHER: It's done.

LOLLY: Dottie went along?

ESTHER: Oh, yes. She didn't like the idea at the start, but after a while she realized it's what he would have wanted, the simple, clean way. You know what they gave us at the funeral home?

LOLLY: What?

ESTHER: An urn—to save his ashes.

LOLLY: I can't imagine Mike cramped into an urn—not even his ashes.

ESTHER: We thanked them politely, then we took the ashes in a box out to the lake. It was not the same Crescent Pavilion. Maybe because it was daylight, I don't know. The place looked so ordinary—so old. The lake was beautiful though. I rowed out a way.

LOLLY: Does Dottie know that was a special place for you and Mike?

ESTHER: I don't think so. If she knows, she was very discreet. She sprinkled the ashes into the water, crying so quietly. I cried too—mostly for Dottie and myself, I suppose.

LOLLY: He's free in wind, sun and water.

ESTHER: Why Lolly, you sound like a poet. Yes, he's free. Knowing Mike he would have preferred being used for fertilizer. I thought of it. I thought of sprinkling his ashes into my plants. But I hesitated. Some of the people I know might have thought it too macabre.

LOLLY: I'd still come around.

ESTHER: Have you seen Helen?

LOLLY: She's over at Leonard's.

ESTHER: She hasn't called or anything. I picked up the phone and dialed her number a couple of times—got cold feet.

LOLLY: She's not angry at you. Just worried about you.

ESTHER: She thinks my mind is going.

LOLLY: She thinks you're vulnerable.

ESTHER: Who isn't? What's she doing over at Leonard's?

LOLLY: Trying to convince him that for your good, he should put away all his foolishness.

ESTHER: Throw away what we believe in.

LOLLY: Do you really believe in the Autumn Gold Society after all that's happened?

ESTHER: Nothing happened, except bad timing on the Scrimers' part. I feel so wonderful knowing what I'm all about.

LOLLY: Let's face it—it could be a form of self-delusion.

ESTHER: But everything is, isn't it? We're such little creatures upon this earth, can understand so little, that each of us builds a little web and lives by it, for it. I really believe in Leonard's kind of immortality. I take that back—in my immortality. Never have I been so full of gold.

LOLLY: Well, your daughter has a strong argument, she told me so at the supermarket. I had to catch her first. She was hiding in the aisles, but I cornered her in the frozen food section, her nose buried in the zucchini. That's how I found out she's over at Leonard's now. At this moment she is pleading that he save you from the ridicule and abuse of the world. Poor Leonard. He's going to put aside all he believes in for you.

ESTHER: No, he's not. Why should he?

LOLLY: You knucklehead, he loves you. You're more important to him than any theory.

ESTHER: In his mad, insane way, he does, doesn't he? I have to do something about all this.

LOLLY: Listen, I'm not getting cold feet, but it's kind of breaking up, isn't it? I mean, Richard's in Washington with the women's libbers. And I—I'm off to Buenos Aires in search of Attila.

ESTHER: He'll be waiting for you at the airport. Jake had his hand in it.

LOLLY: Oh, I know it. He had Attila deported. But that's not going to stop me. My ride in the merry-go-round is not quite over.

ESTHER: How long will you be there?

LOLLY: Not long really—just until the merry-go-round slows down, before the music stops. Attila and I have had a good year. But let's face it, love affairs are not meant to go on forever. I want a good exit.

ESTHER: You'll be back then, soon. Richard'll be back in a month or so. I'll hold the fort—the Autumn Gold Society goes on.

LOLLY: Oh, Esther, Esther, Esther! What if Leonard doesn't want to "radiate" anymore?

ESTHER: We'll see about that.

LOLLY: Listen, I gotta go if I'm to catch my plane. (*Crosses to* ESTHER, *they embrace.*) Wait for me—we'll be celebrating before Hallow's Eve. Bye, bye . . . (*Exits.* ESTHER *crosses to couch and sits back. She looks around the room, her eye falling on the Sorcerer's Ear.. She crosses to it, picks it up.*)

ESTHER: I think you need some water. (*Picks up watering pot, puts water in plant.*) You'll always be so special. You're not Mike anymore—just a little plant. But I really think you were once. (*Crosses to window.*) Oh Mike, you're more with the wind and sun now, aren't you? I'm going to go on believing, Mike, just like the Dodo bird said, "the best way to explain it is to do it." I shall celebrate for all things breathing, feel the simple sorrows, the simple joys . . . (*Doorbell rings; it opens while* ESTHER *is still by window.* HELEN *stands there, then she runs to her mother, who holds out her arms.*)

HELEN: Mama.

ESTHER: I feel like saying I'm sorry—but then again, I don't feel like saying I'm sorry.

HELEN: There's nothing to be sorry about. If anyone behaved badly, it was I . . .

ESTHER: No.

HELEN *begins to cry quietly.* ESTHER *embraces her.*

ESTHER: "Consider what a great girl you are. Consider what a long way you've come today. Consider what o'clock it is. Consider anything—but don't cry . . ."

HELEN: That's not Alice. (*She laughs.*) That's the Queen!

ESTHER: That lived backwards, remember?

HELEN: How can I forget all the beautiful things I shared with you as a child?

ESTHER: You've been with Leonard.

HELEN: Yes—how did you know?

ESTHER: Lolly was here. Did you convince him to give it all up?

HELEN: Yes, for your sake. But looking at you, I feel I didn't do the right thing.

ESTHER: You did the wrong thing because you thought it was the right thing.

HELEN: Is that the Queen?

ESTHER: No—Esther Forbes.

HELEN: You're a stubborn Esther Forbes. But I guess I'll just have to learn to accept.

ESTHER: Darling, I've always been off-kilter. You've always been accepting. This is just a little harder.

HELEN: You can say that again! He's coming over, you know. He'll try to convince you that I'm right. Anyway, I thought I was, but I'm not, I guess . . .

ESTHER: This is some conversation! But thank you.

HELEN: I should have understood long ago that people have to be what they believe they are.

ESTHER: I still thank you for "the love gift of a fairy-tale."

HELEN: You and Lewis Carroll!

ESTHER: And the Scrimers? Are they back safe in Sun City?

HELEN: Very much so. They're pretty nice people though. In time the misunderstandings will fade away. Their last words to Bob and me before they left were how bright you were. They'll come around. (LEONARD *appears at kitchen door, crosses to them.*)

LEONARD: Well?

ESTHER: All's well.

LEONARD: Can I take you girls to supper?

HELEN: I'd love it, but I have to pick up Bob. (*Kisses* ESTHER.) See you later, Mama. (*Starts to leave, then stops, comes back, kisses* LEONARD *too.*) I was wrong Leonard, bye. (*Exits.*)

LEONARD: What does she mean by that?

ESTHER: She means she doesn't want you to give up the Autumn Gold Society for my sake.

LEONARD: But . . .

HELEN: I know. She did a lot of convincing. Women do change their minds.

LEONARD: There's a lot of strong points to her argument. It's not going to be easy. You sure you don't want to chuck the whole thing?

ESTHER: Do you?

LEONARD: No. It's just the beginning. I've got great plans!

ESTHER: Insane ones, I hope!

LEONARD: Of course!

ESTHER: Oh, Leonard, I love you.

LEONARD: What did you say?

ESTHER: I love you.

LEONARD: Together—down the rabbit hole, through the looking-glass . . .

ESTHER: CALLOOH CALLAY! CALLOOH CALLAY!

They kiss.

CURTAIN

Blacklight

CHARACTERS

(In order of their appearance)

FOCO	CHROM
AMELIA	TATO
NACHO	VOICE OF ITZAMNA
IXCHEL	CHAC DANCERS
TONIO	SHIRLEY
CUAQUI	CHARLIE
MUNDO	

ACT ONE

SCENE 1

Downstage right. MUNDO's *room, interior exposed. It is set aside from the rest of the house; room extends downstage, parallel to backyard, stage left. Behind backyard area, kitchen entrance. The house, dilapidated, is next to the railroad tracks. Broken-down fence leading left toward tracks, beyond a llano and far away mountains not seen on stage. A border town whose larger population consists of Mexicans who crossed the river into the United States.*

MUNDO's *room: small table, lamp, recorder, tapes on top. Narrow cot angled center of room. Walls covered with drawings of discs, insects, strange faces; on the back wall a pair of huge eyes. Worn cushions strewn on the floor. Room is on a level two steps higher than backyard area.*

Backyard area: upstage—crumbling wall of kitchen, door leading into rest of house. A clothesline, pile of crates, two old cane chairs. To left of yard, runty stalks of corn pitifully breaking through sun-cracked earth. In front of yard, the fence. In front of fence, a pile of discarded tires. Downstage center on side of yard, a post with three finished faces of Mayan gods. Face of ITZAMNA, *god of Night and Day; four faces representing the wind gods right below, then the face of the goddess* IXCHEL. *Post painted in fluorescent paints.*

Time: the present. FOCO *enters, crosses down center. He is a boy about seventeen, head shaved, wearing an old Indian blanket, old pair of Levis. Walks among discards that fill yard of now empty house. Sits on tires, looks around empty yard. Crosses down center, talks to audience.*

FOCO: My name is Foco, a friend of Mundo's. This place's empty now, but it was a special place for all the vatos that came to Mundo's blacklight parties. WOW! Now, everybody's gone. I come around, can't stay away from the place. I'm here to burn that thing! (*Points at post. Since this time is a year after the story, the faces on the post are finished.*) Palo maldito! Nothing but a broken-down stick now. (*Touches it.*) No heartbeat. You think I'm crazy, eh? It had a heartbeat once. Ancient gods came and went, forces that mingled with the sorrows and fears of Mundo's family. No gods now. Just a piece of dead wood. I came to burn it . . . (*Lights a match, looks up at* ITZAMNA.) You were the master here a year ago. You're nothin' now. (*Match burns out. He starts to strike another one, then changes his mind, turns to audience.*) 'Fore I set fire to that thing, I'm going to tell you what happened here a year ago . . .

Fade. A year before. Light on backyard. Post has unfinished faces. It's morning. Sound of train just trailing off. AMELIA *comes from kitchen, crosses to crate, begins to brush hair. She combs it back deftly, twirls it into a bun, then pins it. She stares at the brush, then out into space. She's a sturdy, good-looking woman in spite of the damage of sun and hard work.* NACHO, *her husband, appears at kitchen door. When he sees her, he hesitates to come out into yard. She turns, their eyes meet.* NACHO *goes back into the house.*

AMELIA: Good morning, Amelia. How are you this morning? Angry, angry, angry . . . It's all so senseless. (*Covers face, hardens herself against crying.* MARIA (IXCHEL), *her pregnant daughter, comes from kitchen.*)

IXCHEL: Mamá?

AMELIA: Yes . . .

IXCHEL: Want some coffee? Papá's having some.

AMELIA: Let him have it in peace. All we do is fight these days.

IXCHEL: It's not your fault. It's not his fault either. It's things—the way they are. It's because of Polo . . .

AMELIA: Polo's been dead two years. I stopped mourning a long time ago.

IXCHEL: He was Papá's brother.

AMELIA: We all loved him . . .

IXCHEL: Yes . . .

AMELIA: What time did your papá get home last night? I stopped waiting.

IXCHEL: I don't know. I found him sitting on the ground, there by the door.

AMELIA: When?

IXCHEL: Close to daylight. I got up to get a drink of water, heard him mumbling. I put him to bed.

AMELIA: Mundo's sick. I went to his room this morning. His arm and back, stiff. Claimed he felt fine, but I could tell. His eyes were glassy. The pain showed. He was all bruised. I asked if he'd been in a fight. He started to tell me, but the only word that came out was "Papá . . ." He must have fought with your father. Strange . . . they never go beyond insult . . . I better fix Mundo something to eat. (AMELIA *crosses to kitchen door, disappears. Sound of train is heard.* NACHO *comes from side of house, crosses to edge of fence, watches passing train. As train roars by, he shakes his fists at it.*)

NACHO: Killer!

> IXCHEL *crosses to her father, puts arms around him. He stands, shoulders drooping, head hanging. Turns to* IXCHEL.

NACHO: What can I do?

IXCHEL: The trains are forever.

NACHO: Day after day after day . . .

IXCHEL: They're just trains.

NACHO: Iron killers! Look at the wounds they leave behind. The day begins with their shriek, again and again and again.

IXCHEL: I'm used to them by now.

NACHO: No. They must be stopped!

IXCHEL: That's impossible.

NACHO: Then we must go far away from them.

IXCHEL: Oh, yes! Someday—when there's money.

NACHO: Money . . . there's never any money . . . even when I worked . . .

IXCHEL: This morning I noticed your old lunch pail next to the kitchen window, by the sink. I opened it. It no longer had the smell . . .

NACHO: What smell?

IXCHEL: You know. You would leave it on the kitchen table when you came from work. Sometimes I opened it to see what you had left. It always smelled of banana, bologna, and mayonnaise, all mixed together. I miss that.

NACHO: You're a funny girl. You like the stink of stale smells.

IXCHEL: It is more than that—you and Mamá talking, though you never talked much then . . . You never drank.

NACHO: Catching up with your Tío Polo. He drank for forty years— did nothing much but drink, your great hero.

IXCHEL: Papá, he's dead.

NACHO: He's still here. He never left.

IXCHEL: He's not . . .

NACHO: Shhhhhh . . . hear the moan of the wind? Feel the burning of the sun? They're all here. My little mother, Polo, all the centuries of people who came before me. Mayans circling time.

IXCHEL: Mundo put those ideas in your head with that book of his.

NACHO: I knew them before I saw that book. Mi mamacita, may she rest in Heaven, used to tell me stories about our ancestors, the Mayans. Right here, now, the men of Itza are all around us. I feel the heaviness of their sorrow. They want me to be what I once was.

IXCHEL: What?

NACHO: A warrior.

IXCHEL: You've never been a warrior—in the United States of America?

NACHO: In another time, another place . . .

IXCHEL: See what I mean? You talk in riddles.

NACHO: You'll understand some day. You're right. Here, now, I'm not a warrior, not yet. All I have is desert and the clouds of soot left by the iron devil.

IXCHEL: Mamá worries so about you.

NACHO: Does she . . .

IXCHEL: You don't seem to care. What you're doing is very hard on her. She suffers so!

NACHO: Perhaps she deserves to suffer.

IXCHEL: Papá, you don't mean that!

NACHO: I don't know what I mean. (*A boy of six comes from kitchen, crosses to* IXCHEL, *pulls her skirt. He's the youngest,* TONIO.)

TONIO: I'm hungry.

IXCHEL: Alright, I'll feed you something. But first we find the basin and wash your hands. (IXCHEL *takes* TONIO *by the hand; they go into kitchen as* AMELIA *comes out with a bowl in her hands. Crosses toward* MUNDO's *room, stops.*)

AMELIA: Look at that fence! Can't you do something about it? (NACHO *picks up a broken piece of fence, throws it violently toward railroad tracks.*)

NACHO: Where's the hammer? Nails? Paint?

AMELIA: If you went back to work . . .

NACHO: Don't start. I won't have you nagging . . .

AMELIA: Nagging? I'm desperate. How can I make you see? We all depended on you.

NACHO: I refuse to be a slave!

AMELIA: You were always so eager when a job came along.

NACHO: I had no choice.

AMELIA: You have a choice now?

NACHO: You stop that! You're not going to hound me anymore . . .
I come from the house of Itza, warriors that for centuries resist-
ed slavery. All I was ever paid . . . was just enough to stay alive.
Why? I was one of thousands branded for slavery, a mojado
from across the river. No more!

AMELIA: And what will happen to us? Why all of a sudden, this
terrible pride?

NACHO: I am more than you think I am.

AMELIA: Are you . . . while your family lives off welfare? You think
I like that?

NACHO: We're trapped by circumstance.

AMELIA: How noble that sounds!

NACHO: I am a farmer.

AMELIA: You've never been a farmer. You call that farming—your
sickly corn?

NACHO: I have been a warrior and a farmer for centuries.

AMELIA: Something's very wrong with you, Nacho. Up here, in
the head. I hate this drifting. Nothing to look forward to. I used
to have hope that someday we could move out of this place.
You used to talk about it. You tried to take care of us . . .

NACHO: Were you happy then? I remember tears more than laughter in those days, except when Polo came into our lives . . .

AMELIA: Don't—he's dead. And Mundo's sick. He fought with you,
didn't he? You did something to him.

NACHO: Did he tell you that?

AMELIA: He won't talk about it.

NACHO: Then leave it at that, woman.

AMELIA: What's the use.

NACHO: Gone, gone, gone . . .

    AMELIA *gives him a pitying look, crosses and enters* MUNDO's
room. NACHO *crosses to post with half-carved faces.*

NACHO: Itzamna! Are you deaf and blind? I am Ah Na Itza. (*Begins
to chant from the Chilam Balam.*) "Eat, eat, thou hast bread.
Drink, drink, thou hast water. On that day, a blight is on the
face of the earth. On that day, a cloud rises. On that day, things
fall to ruin. On that day, the tender leaf is destroyed. On that
day, the dying eyes are closed . . . gone, gone, gone." (NACHO
falls to the ground on his knees. IXCHEL, *holding* TONIO *by the
hand, returns with small basin, places it on the crate, lifts* TONIO
to wash his face and hands.)

TONIO: (*Looking toward* NACHO.) What's the matter with Papá?
IXCHEL: He doesn't feel good.
NACHO: (*Stands, shakes fists at* ITZAMNA.) You want my face in the dirt! It wasn't my fault! He killed himself. Maybe he fell, maybe he didn't mean to die. Itzamna, tell me!
TONIO: (*Crosses to father.*) Who you talking to?
NACHO: Itzamna.
TONIO: Oh, Papá, that's a piece of wood.
NACHO: You see with the eyes of a child. Oh, my God! When I look into your eyes I see Polo.
TONIO: Mama says you crazy, Papá.
NACHO: Listen to your mother, boy.
TONIO: Mamá says you crazy . . . (*The sound of another train is heard.* IXCHEL *takes* TONIO *into the house.* NACHO *crosses to edge of fence.*)
NACHO: You iron devil! I'm not afraid of you! I am Ah Na Itza!

SCENE 2

AMELIA *stands by broken fence, tying a bandana over her head.* IXCHEL *crosses to her from kitchen.* AMELIA *turns, watching her pregnant daughter approach.*

AMELIA: I'm leaving.
IXCHEL: Want me to come along?
AMELIA: Look at you! You're no help.
IXCHEL: It's a long walk. I can keep you company.
AMELIA: I can see them, counting out the food stamps, looking at your belly.
IXCHEL: Oh, Mamá, you exaggerate.
AMELIA: Do I . . . No, I've felt the scorn, the humiliation.
IXCHEL: I wish you didn't have to do it.
AMELIA: There's no one else. Look in on your brother.
IXCHEL: Is he better?
AMELIA: He says he is.
IXCHEL: His friends will cheer him up.
AMELIA: His friends!

IXCHEL: They *are.*
AMELIA: Outcasts!
IXCHEL: I like them.
AMELIA: Misfits!
IXCHEL: Don't call them names, Mamá.
AMELIA: What else are they? One out of reform school, one straight out of the crazy house. And the one with the glasses, he's in and out of jail.
IXCHEL: They mean no harm.
AMELIA: My son deserves better. He was a good student.
IXCHEL: It didn't seem to matter when he was kicked out of school.
AMELIA: It wasn't his fault.
IXCHEL: Maybe not, but they still didn't care.
AMELIA: He was sick.
IXCHEL: He was truant.
AMELIA: The school didn't understand—about his illness. He'll go back.
IXCHEL: I don't think he will.
AMELIA: I still have all his report cards, from the first grade on up.
IXCHEL: Much good they'll do him. He doesn't care about school anymore.
AMELIA: No.
IXCHEL: Does it really matter—school, I mean? So many things have changed.
AMELIA: What's going to happen to my boy? Our lives crumbling...
IXCHEL. What we need around here is some kind of faith—in something. I have faith in Joe.
AMELIA: Where is he? He said he'd be here before the baby came. You're due any day now! Promises! (AMELIA *exits.* IXCHEL *crosses to* MUNDO's *room.*)
IXCHEL: Mundo . . . Mundo! (CUAQUI, *the gang's mascot, comes in, loaded down with four six-packs of beer.*)
CUAQUI: Hi.
IXCHEL: Hi.
CUAQUI: Mundo in there?
IXCHEL: Yes.
CUAQUI: Look what I got. Want some?
IXCHEL: No, thank you. Why don't you call him?
CUAQUI: (*In very loud voice.*) Hey, Mundo.
IXCHEL: He heard you. I gotta go in. Lot of things to do.
CUAQUI: Hey, wait . . . when's the baby due?
IXCHEL: Any day now . . .

CUAQUI: You heard from Joe?

IXCHEL: No. But I will. I know I will . . .

CUAQUI: Sure you will . . .

> IXCHEL *crosses to kitchen.* CUAQUI *stands by* MUNDO's *door and whistles, long and shrill.*

CUAQUI: Hey, Mundo! They're coming with your mountain, ése! (MUNDO *comes out of his room. He's a boy about eighteen. Sits on step leading to room.*)

MUNDO: ¡Esa!

CUAQUI: Stole some beer for you guys.

MUNDO: You said something 'bout the mountain?

CUAQUI: Yeah, the guys finished it. Every color in the rainbow.

MUNDO: Suave. That's the best idea I've had for a long time.

CUAQUI: Painting your rock for the blacklight party?

MUNDO: It's not a rock. It's a mountain.

CUAQUI: O.K., O.K., so it's a mountain. Where you find the rock?

MUNDO: In the cemetery. It was growing out of the ground, like some stiff trying to get out.

CUAQUI: You guys spent a lot of time with the stiffs.

MUNDO: Why not? That is a good place, the cemetery—kind of standing still . . .

CUAQUI: Who? You and the guys? Naw . . . you're always up to something.

MUNDO: Where you steal the beer?

CUAQUI: Right off the delivery truck. You know the guys tied up that mountain to three sets of roller skates? Man, it's heavy.

MUNDO: That's cool. It's going to be some party. The rock of Gibraltar, a crater on the moon, Mount Everest, even the Grand Canyon. Wait 'til we turn the blacklight on my mountain. Man, am I going to go places.

CUAQUI: You're always going places, but you never go.

MUNDO: I'm going. Like Tío Polo used to. I mean, he went everywhere . . . New York, Canada, Florida . . .

CUAQUI: Just hopping trains?

MUNDO: Yep . . . He was the king of the hobos. I mean, for real. In the hobo jungle in Chicago, he was elected—just like you elect a president. They cast votes for the best, the very best. That was my Tío Polo.

CUAQUI: You going to be a bum too?

MUNDO: No. No, man, I'm going to go in style. (*Gang enters, rolling in a huge painted rock made of papier-mâché. Los vatos are a strange assortment.* FOCO, *a tall, thin boy, is wrapped in his*

Indian blanket. He's playing on a harmonica. His head is shaven.
CHROM *wears dark glasses and an old gunbelt without guns over worn jeans.* TATO *wears cut-offs, old army boots, a canteen slung over one shoulder.*)
TATO: Esa, Cuaqui, ¿qué traes?
CUAQUI: Four! Four six-packs of beer, guys. (*Boys whistle, pick her up, parade her around. She protests noisily, but enjoys it, giggling. They dump her on the pile of tires.*)
CHROM: Hey, Cuaqui, you kiped it?
CUAQUI: Right off the delivery truck.
CHROM: (*Tries to rub her thigh.*) That's my girl.
        CUAQUI *hits him, almost knocks him down.* FOCO *wraps the Indian blanket around himself with exaggerated ceremony, then sits on edge of broken fence.* TATO *dances around* CUAQUI *and the beer.* CHROM *takes out red rag from pocket, cleans his sunglasses.*
CHROM: Vatos, I shined up the Chevy. Man, it blinds you. It's so beautiful. Hits you right there. (*Pounds his chest.*) Wanna cruise?
TATO: Later, man, later.
        MUNDO *crosses to rock, touches it almost reverently.* TATO *crosses next to him.*
TATO: Just like you wanted . . . (CHROM; *crosses to tires where* CUAQUI *is sitting, gives her a nudge.*)
CHROM: Hey, Cuaqui, get it off. I got a thirst.
TATO: I like mine with salt and lemon. Got any, Mundo?
MUNDO: Don't know . . .
CUAQUI: I'll go see. (*Runs toward kitchen.*)
MUNDO: How long it take you to paint it?
CHROM: Did it real fast. Just closed our eyes and sprayed—like real artists. Came by for you. You wouldn't answer, so we went to the Star Dust. Met a guy from Huntsville, bought us beer. Where were you?
MUNDO: Inside . . .
CHROM: Why didn't you open up?
FOCO: Leave him alone.
CHROM: Let's go cruising by the river . . .
TATO: Later, man, later.
FOCO: We can walk over to our place in the cemetery and drink our beer.
CHROM: Too hot for that. And anyway, all you do is watch them ants. I saw it once and it was enough. You're weird, man.
FOCO: It's not often we see a naked angel with a living halo. I mean,

all those ants streaming over the maguey, jivin' up that tomb-
stone, up between the little fat legs of the angel, all the way up
to its curly head, going round in a circle. That blows my mind,
man.

TATO: Angel ain't naked.

FOCO: Sure it is . . .

TATO: No it ain't. There's no naked angel in a Catholic cemetery.
It's in your mind, man.

CHROM: Know who's buried under the angel? His Honor, the May-
or, back in 1910 . . .

TATO: That cemetery's better than school . . .

CHROM: Or a nothin' job.

FOCO: Or staying home with my father, the bastard.

MUNDO: This is better. The mountain's better.

FOCO: Yeah, our Shangri-la.

CHROM: Our what, loonie? (FOCO *grabs* CHROM *by collar, shakes
him menacingly.*)

FOCO: Don't call me that, chingado.

CHROM: O.K., take it easy . . .

TATO: Why you shave your head, Foco? Tell us.

CHROM: Kojak.

CHROM *takes out his rag, crosses to* FOCO, *looks at* FOCO's
bald head, begins to buff it.

CHROM: I'll shine it up like my Chevy . . .

FOCO: I said leave me alone, cabrón.

CHROM: O.K., O.K., let's go cruising . . .

MUNDO: You got gas?

TATO: His mamá fed him beans. That's the only gas he's got. (CUA-
QUI *returns from kitchen with cut up lemon.* CHROM *picks up
six-pack.*)

CHROM: Shit! It's hot.

MUNDO: Go steal some ice, Cuaqui.

TATO: Or sit on it for a while.

CUAQUI: I'll go to ol' man Charlie's across the street. He's not mind-
ing the store today.

MUNDO: Well, get a move on . . . (CUAQUI *runs off stage toward
Charlie's store.*)

TATO: Man, Mundo, you got you some slave. You could get in her
pants like nothing . . .

CHROM: He ain't interested. He's making it with Charlie's wife.
You're still making it with Charlie's wife? That ol' gringo hates
Mexicans.

MUNDO: Crud . . .

CHROM: If he catches you . . . POW! He keeps a shotgun. You know about the shotgun?

MUNDO: So what?

TATO: Wish I had some tacos to go with the beer.

FOCO: You mamá's not feeding you again?

TATO: On account of my Mosca . . .

Everybody groans.

TATO: Look, over there, behind that tree . . . Mosca's waving at us. Smiling away. Smile back.

CHROM: Go swat your Mosca, O.K.?

TATO: Kill the one I love . . .

FOCO: He's calling you . . .

TATO: I sneaked Mosca inside the house this morning when Mamá was cooking in the kitchen. I put a bib on him so he wouldn't slobber, a fork in one hand, a spoon in the other. Man, he was waiting for that food. That ol' lady of mine—she sees us and starts yelling. Took a broom and beat us out of the house . . .

FOCO: Nobody wants us. I mean nobody! Ain't that grand? (*Drops blanket.*) Got some peyote.

CHROM: Forget it, man. Who wants a cotton mouth.

FOCO: You got joints? Reds? Whites?

TATO: Saw him pick some up at the Star Dust, from the guy we met.

CHROM: Business. Cash, no credit.

MUNDO: Still growing peyote, Foco?

CHROM: Pigs missed his backyard.

FOCO: Chingados, you still owe me for the paint.

TATO: You went wild painting that rock . . .

MUNDO: Mountain . . .

CHROM: I think he was high, sniffing the stuff . . .

FOCO: I'm no fool, cabrón.

CHROM: No, you're Jesus. Oh, I forgot. We don't call you Jesus no more. You shaved off your long hair. Why you shave it, eh?

FOCO: Really want to know?

TATO: Yeah, tell us a little story.

FOCO: 'Cause of Baldy.

MUNDO: That two-by-four assistant principal?

CHROM: The one who personally threw us all out of school?

FOCO: Man, I was rolling around in the lockers, high on peyote, when Baldy caught me. Dragged me to his office and kept screaming in my ear, "Where did you get the stuff?" I told him—my backyard. Called me a liar. Got all red and puffy. (*Jumps on crate.*) So, I jumped up on his desk and his ol' head was shining in my eyes. Big drops of sweat sort of falling—sliding—sliding . . .

CHROM: Talk about stoned.

FOCO: A crystal ball—that's what his head looked like—a crystal ball. I sort of grabbed it—to see my future. He started yelling again, then someone called the cops. They threw me in the psych ward.

CHROM: Why you shave your head?

FOCO: The little guy was sure scared. Why? Maybe bald makes you scared. I wanted to find out. I mean, a guy who wears a suit every day, has money in the bank and a Lincoln. Why was he scared?

TATO: He was scared of you. You went bananas.

FOCO: No. It wasn't me. I know it wasn't me. He was just mad as hell at me, but I didn't scare him. It was the bald head.

CHROM: I don't know what you're talking about, see? You shaved your head for no reason.

FOCO: Maybe. (TATO *pushes* FOCO *off the crate as* CUAQUI *comes in with a bag of ice. Everybody cheers.* CHROM *takes the basin and dumps the ice in it. The boys put beer cans in ice.* TATO *opens a can, gulps.*)

TATO: Ugh!

CHROM: Wait til it gets cold, stupid. You'd drink your own piss. (FOCO *throws his blanket over* CHROM, *follows* MUNDO *to rock.*)

FOCO: That's better than the turning thing on your wall. That is a standing still mountain. It's going to glowwwww. . . . I'm going to feel the sharps and downs, feel it right here (*hits stomach*) in the guts.

CUAQUI: Mundo's freaking out to far places.

FOCO: You're crazy, man. You don't have to go places. It's all there inside of you, the whole mountain. Use your pores. Don't get that stupid mind going.

MUNDO: You go your trip. I go mine. Got new tapes?

FOCO: Acid, man. Vibrations—twang, twang, twang, twang . . .

CHROM: You're sure hung up on your guts.

FOCO: Isn't everyone?

CUAQUI: Can I come?

CHROM: No kids allowed. Anyway—you're a girl.

CUAQUI: How come you let Shirley?

CHROM: Mundo's room—she's his chick. You don't belong to nobody.

FOCO: Cut it out. (*To* CUAQUI) You'll get in trouble with your ol' lady.

TATO: Yeah, stick to stealing.

CUAQUI: I think you're horrible.

FOCO: You made her feel bad. Cut your throat.

MUNDO: Hey, Cuaqui, you're special, you know that. You're our mascot. We don't let any other broad hang out with us.

CUAQUI: Then why can't I come?

MUNDO: You heard Foco. Your ol' lady will skin you.

CUAQUI: I ain't doing nothin' for you guys no more. (*Exits crying.*)

CHROM: She don't mean that. (*Cleans sunglasses again.*) Let's cruise.

FOCO: Eah . . . cruise by yourself.

TATO: I'll go if you stop at the taco place. You got bread?

CHROM: Some. Coming, Mundo?

MUNDO: Thought you had no gas.

CHROM: Got enough to the taco place. We'll figure it from there. Coming?

MUNDO: Naw . . .

CHROM: Foco?

FOCO: I'll stick around.

> CHROM *and* TATO *exit.* MUNDO *and* FOCO *contemplate the rock.*

FOCO: It's going to be some job, getting it into your room. It'll break my back.

MUNDO: It's on roller skates, remember? All we need now is a little leverage . . .

> MUNDO *goes into room, comes back with rope. They roll rock to door.* MUNDO *ties rope around rock, stands in doorway, pulls it into room as* FOCO *pushes from bottom. They manage to get it into room with difficulty.*

MUNDO: Got it.

FOCO: (*Falls to ground.*) I'm dead.

MUNDO: Beer? (FOCO *crosses to basin, squats, stares into basin.*)

FOCO: There's Tato's six-foot fly floating around in the ice. (*Crosses to post.*) Why doesn't your ol' man finish the faces? Started carving them a long time ago.

MUNDO: I'm going to set a match to it.

FOCO: I got one.

MUNDO: Forget it.

FOCO: All those gods real?

MUNDO: What's real?

FOCO: You, me . . .

MUNDO: He thinks they're real.

FOCO: Do you?

MUNDO: You're going to think I'm crazy—but I wonder sometimes. You see, I bring this book about the Mayan civilization some teacher gave me. I read it to the ol' man 'cause he was feeling so bad about Tío Polo. His eyes bugged out. Seems his mamá used to tell him stories about the same gods when he was a kid. So suddenly he's Ah Na Itza—out of the clear blue sky. He sits and stares at the pictures for hours, then comes up with the weirdest things—things he remembers from the past—chants, dreams. . . . Who's putting them there?

FOCO: What you mean?

MUNDO: He never talked that way before.

FOCO: He nver drank before either.

MUNDO: It's like he's many people inside. Man, he's breaking up. They ought to throw him in the drunk tank for good.

FOCO: Won't solve anything.

MUNDO: That's why he doesn't finish the faces. He claims he doesn't have one himself. (FOCO *touches the post, then walks around it.*)

FOCO: This thing feels funny. Something going through me.

MUNDO: You too?

FOCO: Something's happening.

MUNDO: Yeah, my life's messed up . . .

FOCO: You're all different now—your mamá, your ol' man, even your sister, you—ever since Polo died. But your ol' man, he's the worst.

MUNDO: I wish he would explode into nothingness.

FOCO: These gods, maybe he's called them back—from ancient times, I mean.

MUNDO: They ought to come down and knock him around. This goddamned stinking paralysis.

FOCO: You need a shrink. That time you got stoned and told us about your nightmare. I mean, you felt better for days after that. It's all the same thing, you know, your nerves, your dreams. Don't you want to talk about it?

MUNDO: Shut up! Shut up!

FOCO: Hey, listen, I'm your friend. It's getting to me too.

MUNDO: You? Why you?

FOCO: You're my family, man. Sobro en este mundo.

MUNDO: Your ol' man's back.

FOCO: If I stick around that house, I'll kill him.

MUNDO: Been beating up on you?

FOCO: The bastard's afraid of me now—but mi jefa gets it. Minister—ha!

MUNDO: Maybe he just says he's a minister.

FOCO: Who cares what he is? Hates my ol' lady 'cause she's Mexican.

MUNDO: He married her.

FOCO: Came at me with a broken bottle couple of nights ago.

MUNDO: Drunk?

FOCO: Drunk and crazy. Started beating up on la jefita, so I hit him.

MUNDO: Where you been sleeping?

FOCO: Chrom's garage . . . behind the warehouse . . . the cemetery.

MUNDO: You can stay with me.

FOCO: Maybe later. This place, it's special. The way the moon lights up those faces on the stick. There's special feelings in this place.

MUNDO: Yeah . . . sometimes I feel . . .

FOCO: Do you?

MUNDO: Eh—no . . .

FOCO: Listen—I touched that piece of stick. It had a heartbeat.

MUNDO: You're as bad as my ol' man.

FOCO: Your Tío Polo never saw that stick.

MUNDO: No, he didn't need any god to blame things on.

FOCO: He was special. We vatos used to stick around to listen to his stories. He sure got around—like he could do anything, and everything. He felt good about the world.

MUNDO: Do you?

FOCO: I used to ask myself—what's in this life for me, or los vatos? We get drunk, stoned, in trouble. We get thrown in jail or killed. Man, we're down to the ground. But your room—this place— makes me feel special, like the trap ain't for us.

MUNDO: Me—I just want to cut out.

FOCO: Wait 'til you climb your mountain tonight.

MUNDO: Then we'll all feel this place—invisible gods and forces, thick as honey, buzzing and floating . . .

FOCO: And we shall be the chosen ones . . .

MUNDO: Hell, what's the use . . .

FOCO: What's the matter now?

MUNDO: It's crowding me.

FOCO: What?

MUNDO: The nightmares, my sickness, trains, tracks . . .

FOCO: You haven't had a nightmare for a long time.

MUNDO: Came back last night.

FOCO: Do something about it—see that shrink . . .

MUNDO: Oh, yeah . . . I'll go into his ritzy office, put down my cash . . . You don't know what you're talking about.

FOCO: Yeah, I do. Go down where the poor folks do, mental health center by the free clinic, and wait in line.

MUNDO: You've been there?

FOCO: No. Heard about it when they locked me up in the fourth floor.

MUNDO: I don't need no shrink. I know why it came back . . .

FOCO: Why?

MUNDO: Never mind . . .

FOCO: You gotta tell somebody.

MUNDO: Never mind, I said.

FOCO: Why you pick up the pieces?

MUNDO: What are you talking about . . .

FOCO: You didn't have to pick up the pieces of your Tío Polo.

MUNDO: Shut up, chingado, shut up!

FOCO: See what I mean?

MUNDO: I'll tell you, cabrón . . . the fucking placas offered me a fiver, cinco dólares . . .

FOCO: Who you kidding? You didn't do it for that.

MUNDO: I couldn't stand seeing her, sitting and rocking and crying . . .

FOCO: Who?

MUNDO: Mamá.

FOCO: You mean when he got hit?

MUNDO: She saw it all—saw the train hit him, saw the body dragged, mangled. She and me had just said goodbye to him. When it happened, I just stood there. But, she ran to the bloody mess that was left and just sat next to it on the tracks. She was shivering, crying. Someone called the cops. I don't know who. Everybody was asleep—the first train before dawn.

FOCO: Didn't the cops call an ambulance?

MUNDO: Yeah, they called in. The ambulance took a long time to come. There would be another train coming. I remember, they walked around with pad and pencil, taking notes, cracking jokes, like nothing had happened. One of them was chewing gum and talking about the Red Sox . . .

FOCO: Didn't want to bother picking up the body.

MUNDO: Ambulance was supposed to . . . They called again. Still didn't come. One of them tells me, "Hey, kid, want a fiver? Go up there and move 'it' off the tracks." I couldn't take Mamá just sitting there, suffering. I went up to her and tried to pull her away—she wouldn't budge. So I told the cops, "I'll do it if you take her inside." They did.

FOCO: Man, you had some nerve . . .

MUNDO: No . . . it was . . . like it wasn't for real. I pushed the body off the tracks but parts of him were missing—a hand, part of his leg and head. "Hey, kid, pick up the rest of him." I got some grocery bags. I remember the red letters on them, "Safeway." I remember, 'cause when I picked up the pieces, the blood turned them black, 'specially the letters . . . When the ambulance finally came, they took the body and put the grocery bags full of Tío Polo in a big white plastic bag.

FOCO: Shit on the world . . .

MUNDO: It was so quiet. But when we heard the next train coming, I felt this ringing in my ears, I smelled the blood. It hit me then. My mind was flashing pictures—the body sort of rolled up as I pushed it off the tracks, the feel of the hand and leg and part of the brain as I picked them up and threw them in the paper sacks. The ambulance people putting the body on a white stretcher, the whiteness stained in purple brown . . . Funny thing the mind . . .

FOCO: O.K., don't think about it anymore.

MUNDO: Cabrón, you asked for it, remember?

FOCO: Hey, man, I'm feeling with you, all that pain . . .

MUNDO: I was just a kid.

FOCO: You were really close to him.

MUNDO: I liked doing things with him. My ol' man, well, he was different—always sort of uptight, silent. Couldn't talk to him. He thought Tío Polo was a worthless dreamer.

FOCO: Your ol' man didn't like his own brother.

MUNDO: Yeah, he did, just didn't have much use for him, but he'd promised mi 'buelita he'd take care of him. After Tío died, everything bad started happening.

FOCO: I remember . . .

MUNDO: When the nightmares started coming, they'd come two, three in one night—same dream. Still the same last night. I dream I put him together again—the hand, the leg, the head. I try to straighten out the body, but it keeps rolling up, a ball of bloody flesh and dirt. Then it starts rolling away, down the tracks, growing as it goes. I mean, big, like a reddened sun. I run after it. I run so fast, my breath hurts, and I keep calling out, "Wait for me, Tío. I'm going with you this time!"

FOCO: Would you have gone with him—I mean, if he had lived?

MUNDO: I don't know now. The night before he died, I was ready to go with him. But he always made you feel that way. Everything good was going to happen in the world. Jiziz, there was so much gladness in him. Still—I probably would have changed my mind.

FOCO: But you said you were going.

MUNDO: Funny thing. All of a sudden he changes his mind about taking me. Tells me when I'm older. So I just said goodbye to him. After he died, the nightmares were there every night. I'd wake up drowning in my own breath, sweating cold. One night, the shaking and shivering wouldn't stop. Next thing I knew, I couldn't move . . .

FOCO: You're right. You got to leave this place.

MUNDO: I was going to. Now, after last night . . . (NACHO *enters, downstage right, from street. Has a bottle of liquor in his hand. He stops when he sees the boys, glares at them and swears under his breath, takes a drink.*)

NACHO: ¿Qué traen, marijuanos . . .

FOCO: (*To* MUNDO.) See you later . . . (*Starts to run off.*)

NACHO: Hey, oye, you're the crazy one, eh?

FOCO: You know somebody sane? (*Exits.*)

NACHO: Smart mouth! All of you marijuanos have a smart mouth. (*Glares at* MUNDO.) You mad at me?

MUNDO: No. (NACHO *goes to tires, sits on them, beckons* MUNDO.)

NACHO: Get your littl' book and read and read from the Chilam Balam. Conjure up Itzamna so he can give me the power of the jaguar. Read to me, my son . . . You are my son, aren't you?

MUNDO: Give me the bottle.

NACHO: What? Now you give the orders around here, eh?

MUNDO: Give me the bottle. You don't know how to drink, old man.

NACHO: Ah, but your Tío Polo—he drank like an expert, didn't he? He could do anything, couldn't he? He was nothing but a bum.

MUNDO: He was my friend and your brother.

NACHO: A fine brother! He tried to steal you away. That night— the night before he got up on those tracks—he talked you into going with him, didn't he?

MUNDO: Yes.

NACHO: He killed himself. Now, you're stuck here—with your father. And that black demonio wants it that way! But Itzamna will help us. Won't you, Itzamna. We shall pray to you, we shall sing to you from the Chilam Balam . . .

MUNDO *goes back into his room.*

NACHO: Where are you going? Come back! Desgraciado, I order you . . .

Gives up, sits on tires, takes a drink. IXCHEL *comes from kitchen, starts to take down wash. Carefully folds each piece into a basket.* NACHO *watches her with pleasure.*

NACHO: Ixchel!

IXCHEL: You call me, Papá?

NACHO: I love the name "IXCHEL!"

IXCHEL: Mamá baptized me "María."

NACHO: Bah! You are Ixchel—the goddess of making children.

IXCHEL: Was she beautiful?

NACHO: Claws of a tiger, serpent on her head. She fights and clings to life. Can anything be more beautiful?

IXCHEL: You better not let Mamá catch you with a bottle.

NACHO: I will never let your mamá catch me. I may be her prisoner, but she will never catch me. Don't tell her.

IXCHEL: Oh, Papá, you don't make sense.

NACHO: Ah, goddess of the moon. You are the tides of the blood— mother's milk. The claws were a softness then.

IXCHEL: Savages believed in those gods.

NACHO: Ah! Itzamna told me, once in a dream, that savages created all the gods. They're the ones who need gods . . .

IXCHEL: That piece of stick doesn't talk to you. Oh, Papá, what if Joe doesn't come back. Mamá says he's never going to come back and marry me. (*Begins to cry softly.*)

NACHO: He promised, didn't he? Joe's a good boy. He'll keep his word.

IXCHEL: I don't think Mamá wants the baby . . .

NACHO: Of course she wants the baby. She was a good mother to all of you. I want the baby. Joe wants the baby.

IXCHEL *wipes her tears away.*

NACHO: There—you are the beautiful moon goddess—fruitful.

IXCHEL: Papá . . .

NACHO: Yes, my child . . .

IXCHEL: Does Itzamna really talk to you?

NACHO: I hear him—inside me. I look at him and know.

IXCHEL: A dream?

NACHO: Yes and no.

IXCHEL: He's a comfort to you and that's what matters. Oh, Papá.

I can feel your unhappiness. I wish all bad things could be wiped away . . .

NACHO: I want that too, my daughter—all things clean.

IXCHEL: I better finish my chores.

NACHO: No, stay. You and I can talk.

IXCHEL: Because I believe what you say?

NACHO: Because you listen with your heart.

> IXCHEL *kisses him, picks up basket, exits through kitchen door.* NACHO *crosses to* ITZAMNA, *raises arms as if in worship.*

NACHO: Here's the land—pierced by an arrow.

Here's the land—waiting to die.

Here's the land—without seed, without marrow,

Itzamna! heed my cry . . .

> NACHO *crosses despondently to* MUNDO's *door, sits on step, drinks from bottle, dreams . . . Lights become a colored haze. Blacklight on post.* ITZAMNA's *voice comes through the loudspeaker. Music of reed and drums is heard. Four dancers appear—the wind gods, representing the cardinal points: Chac Kib Chac, the red man, East; Sac Kib Chac, the white man, North; Eb Kib Chac, the black man, West; Kan Kib Chac, the yellow man, South. Costumes make this distinction. They perform creation dance of the gods. Dancers chant as they dance; can be backed up by taped chorus.*

DANCERS: Ik, Akbal, Chichen, cimi, Ik, Akbal, Chichen, cimi.

ITZAMNA: Days of evil fortune
        Shall vanish like wind.
        Bring to me Teplictli,
        The mountain of colors . . .
        To please the rain . . .
        Prepare your offering

DANCERS: Manuk, kamat, muluc, ok, Manuk, kamat, muluc, ok.

ITZAMNA: A prince, young
        Who has kept the vigil
        Who has loved Teteo,
        Woman-goddess,
        Make this offering to me

DANCERS: Chuen, Ib, Ben, Ex, Men, Cib, Caban—Chuen, Ib, Ben, Ex, Men, Cib, Caban.

ITZAMNA: The cezantle sings
        of rain
        Of maize fields

Blanketing the earth
The cezantle sings
Of a movable feast
The earth making love
To the rain . . .
Peace.

DANCERS: Exnab, cauac, ahau, imix—Exnab, cauac, ahau, imix

ITZAMNA: Seething life!
Sweet chaos!
Five-petaled flowers!
The Golden Jaguar
Drinks deep
With velvet paws.

ACT TWO

SCENE 1

Midday. The wind is picking up strong. Every so often, the moan of the wind is heard. AMELIA, IXCHEL, *and* MUNDO *are in the back yard.* MUNDO *is sitting on a stool.* AMELIA *gathers his hair in her hands; he pulls away.*

AMELIA: You need a haircut.

MUNDO: Hey, leave it alone.

IXCHEL: There's a sandstorm coming.

AMELIA: (*To* MUNDO.) Take off your shirt. (MUNDO *removes shirt, she inspects his back.*) Oh, my, he really hurt you, didn't he? He's never hit you before.

MUNDO: I fell.

AMELIA: Give me the medicine. (IXCHEL *hands her ointment.*) Where did you fall?

MUNDO: The bushes over there.

AMELIA: By the tracks. Con razón, all that broken glass, rocks. Tracks—oh, my God!

IXCHEL: You fought by the tracks?

AMELIA: No, no, no, no, no, no, no. . . .

IXCHEL: Mamá, what's the matter?

AMELIA: He tried it, didn't he? He tried to kill himself like Polo. That's why you got sick!

MUNDO: It's over, Mamá.

AMELIA: In his state of mind? No, he'll try it again.

MUNDO: We have to get him out of here.

AMELIA: Where? How? Everything takes money. You got sick after the trains passed?

MUNDO: Yes. I managed to drag him off the tracks, then I began to feel the stiffness in my back. He sort of passed out by the door.

AMELIA: What if your paralysis had hit you before . . .

MUNDO: Don't think about it.

IXCHEL: Why would Papá try that, why?

MUNDO: That damned god of his. Something's got him.

AMELIA: It's not that.

MUNDO: Then why did he try it?

IXCHEL: He acts so crazy when he drinks.

AMELIA: It's more than the drink. It has to do with the time when Polo died. He feels guilty about his brother's death.

MUNDO: He wasn't even around. I remember he took off at dawn, with some guys; they were going to Ratón to pick Piñón. He barely made it to the funeral.

AMELIA: What happened the night before . . .

MUNDO: We were all here in the backyard talking, that's all.

AMELIA: You were talking about leaving with Polo. You had never talked that way before.

MUNDO: I wanted to go. I mean, there's nothing for me here. He talked of the ocean. Oh, Tío could make you feel with words. It was like I was smelling the sea. Why not?

AMELIA: After you went to bed, Papá had a fight with Polo.

IXCHEL: I was kind of young, but I remember. You stopped them. I was crying 'cause I had never seen Papá so mad.

AMELIA: Your papá has always been resentful about the way . . . well—the way we took to Polo. When Polo came, the world was suddenly a good place. There are few people with that kind of gift. He was so open, so glad about little things. Found wonder in everything. Your papá is a stern man, a serious man.

MUNDO: I know. I never could talk to him. Oh, but Polo was different.

AMELIA: Your papá felt Polo was destroying his family. As if he wanted us to belong to him.

MUNDO: Polo? He hated possessions. He didn't want to take anything from anybody. He just . . . was.

AMELIA: There was a reason why Papá felt that way. I never told you. But it's time now.

The wind moans sadly, long-drawn, then a whirl of dust hits them. They turn away from the sand that hits their faces. MUNDO *puts his shirt back on.*

AMELIA: It's almost as if the wind knew . . .

MUNDO: Knew what?

AMELIA: Your papá went off to Midland on a construction job seven years ago. You were in the sixth grade, María. The year I made that blue dress. You were reciting in a program at school.

IXCHEL: Oh, yes. Tío Polo came and he thought the dress made me look like a fairy princess. He taught me to waltz, right then and there. And he found the old raft by the river, remember, Mundo?

MUNDO: Took us three days to patch it up. He made a sail for it and went all the way to Fort Hancock with it. It got stuck on a mud bank and we had to sleep in a llano full of salt cedars. I remember how I didn't mind, cause Tío Polo talked about salt cedars late into the night, telling me all sorts of things. How those ugly trees were really beautiful 'cause they could survive anywhere. How they came from Egypt. Then he talked of pharaohs. He knew everything and he never went to school. I remember that summer. That's the summer he took you to a dance at the church hall. You didn't want to go, but he made you, Mamá. Said you needed music in your life.

AMELIA: How can a woman not love a man like that? I knew nothing about tenderness. When we made love, your papá and I, only our bodies were together. Oh, but with Polo, I was he and he was me. He turned me into joy, a living flame . . .

MUNDO: You and Tío Polo?

AMELIA: All that summer . . . Tonio is his son.

MUNDO: Hell!

IXCHEL: Does Papá know?

AMELIA: When I found out that I was pregnant, Polo wanted to take me away. But I couldn't. I confessed to your father. I told him I wanted to stay because I loved him. I do love your papá.

MUNDO: He had a right to kill you both for what you did.

IXCHEL: He forgave you. And Tío Polo came back again and again—and Papá accepted.

AMELIA: I don't think your papá felt anything for Polo or me after that. We just didn't exist. Oh, we did the usual things, life went on, we talked beyond each other . . . He hasn't touched me since . . .

IXCHEL: Oh, Mamá, I'm sorry.

MUNDO: You hate each other now.

AMELIA: No. I'm just desperate. He's been a wild man since he took to drinking. He doesn't work anymore.

MUNDO: You have another Polo now!

AMELIA: Don't.

IXCHEL: How can you, Mundo? Don't hurt her so!

AMELIA: Then Polo died and Papá began to carve out those faces and talk about gods. I don't know what to do anymore.

MUNDO: Can you imagine what's inside that old man?

AMELIA: Yes. And it's my fault.

MUNDO: Yes! We all made a hero of el Tío Polo, right in front of Papá. He tried to take you away, and me . . .

AMELIA: The night they had the fight, Papá told him never to come back. Polo asked for his son. He wanted to take Tonio with him.

MUNDO: I never knew! I never knew!

AMELIA: Your father refused him Tonio and disowned him as a brother. The next morning Polo was dead.

MUNDO: It wasn't Papá's fault.

AMELIA: He thinks it is.

MUNDO: We got to get some help for him. Get him out of this damned place.

AMELIA: There must be places that help—even if there's no money.

MUNDO: I'll find a way. I promise you.

AMELIA: I believe you.

IXCHEL: It'll take some time. What if he tries it again before we find a way?

AMELIA: He will, Mundo, he will . . .

MUNDO: We're all going to watch him, take turns. If he tries it again, we'll just have to hold him down.

IXCHEL: Look at me. I'm so big . . . I can't be much help.

AMELIA: Oh, what if you get sick before all those trains pass? What can I do? (MUNDO *crosses to post, looks at it.*)

MUNDO: Itzamna will help.

AMELIA: What?

MUNDO: I have a rope in my room. We'll tie him to Itzamna.

IXCHEL: Tie him?

MUNDO: Why not? It's possible. We can't take a chance. Where is he?

IXCHEL: I came out earlier and he was sitting on the tires talking about Itzamna and a dream, a promise, then he just took off down the street. (*Another moan of wind, another whirl of sand.*)

MUNDO: Damn winds. I'll be glad when the rain comes.

IXCHEL: You're not going to leave with Shirley?

MUNDO: Who told you?

IXCHEL: She did. You and her were taking off to Califas.

AMELIA: Oh, Mundo, no!

MUNDO: Don't worry. I'm not going anywhere. Not now.

AMELIA: Oh, what would I do without you?

MUNDO: Listen, I'm goin' to lie down for a while. My fingers are stiff from all this talk. (*Exits to his room.*)

IXCHEL: Oh, Mamá, don't worry. Mundo will take care of things.

AMELIA: He should go with Shirley. He always wanted to travel. Polo's fault—filling him with dreams.

IXCHEL: He'll go someday.

AMELIA: I don't know what it is, but something tells me to make him go, leave this place, save himself . . .

IXCHEL: What do you mean?

AMELIA: I don't know. It's just a feeling.

IXCHEL: If only Joe would come. He would help. He said he would come back before the baby came. The baby's due any day now.

AMELIA: If he doesn't, you mustn't . . . (IXCHEL *runs crying into kitchen.* NACHO *enters from the street.*)

NACHO: I saw him sneak into his room. Wants to keep away from me, does he . . .

AMELIA: He's not well. It's so hot and windy out here. Come inside, I'll fix something cool to drink.

NACHO: Keep away from me.

AMELIA: I know about last night.

NACHO: So? Isn't that what you want? To see me dead? muerto? tendido?

AMELIA: No. I want you well and alive.

NACHO: Liar. Just like my brother. Both of you, liars . . . (*Crosses to* ITZAMNA.) Tonight, Itzamna, tonight is the night of Ocna, the full moon in the month of winds. The time to kill the fire. How can I do what you want? A mountain? And who has loved Teteo? Were you telling me there's no hope? You will not give me the power of the golden jaguar to face the iron monster? to avenge my brother?

> AMELIA *goes into the kitchen.* NACHO *crosses to wilting cornstalks. Begins to pull weeds.*

NACHO: You're strangling the life, you and the damned sun. (FOCO *enters, stops to watch* NACHO.)

FOCO: You've got more weeds than corn.

NACHO: What do you want, marijuano.

FOCO: Just watching.

NACHO: Go watch someplace else. (*He pulls weeds in desperation.*) I'll clear the land, burn the brush and purify the house. But the rains must come. How can I bring you the mountain, Teplictli? What are those mountains? (*Points to far away mountains.*)

FOCO: The Franklin mountains. You want a mountain?

NACHO: Yes, I must bring to Itzamna Teplictli, the mountain, to please the rain.

FOCO: Like the one we brought over this morning?

NACHO: What?

FOCO: It's in Mundo's room. Man, if you want to see a mountain, you'll see it tonight when we put the blacklight on that painted rock.

NACHO: Just a rock!

FOCO: Not tonight. Wait 'til you see it . . . Man, look at that sky. It's red with sand. You ought to finish those faces. (FOCO *leaves.* NACHO *goes back to pulling weeds. After a while, he wipes his brow and looks at the corn helplessly. Crosses to tires, sits and stares out into space. Takes a bottle from inside tires, drinks the last of the liquor, throws bottle against fence.*)

SCENE 2

Sunset. MUNDO's *room.* SHIRLEY *enters from street. Goes into* MUNDO's *room. He hears her, turns to watch her, up on an elbow, head resting on hand. She leans over, kisses him.* MUNDO *traces outline of her body during kiss, then pulls her down to bed. Kiss again and again.* SHIRLEY *breaks free, walks around bed to table, looks through tapes, chooses one, puts it in recorder. Soft, romantic music fills the room. She hums tune as she dances seductively, standing before* MUNDO. *He reaches out for her. She falls on bed. Quiet for a minute, then she reaches for a cigarette, lights one for him, one for herself. She puts her head on his stomach, they smoke in silence. He touches her hair, cheek, then rests his hand on her breast. She drops her shoes, puts out cigarettes. He undresses her slowly, kissing neck, shoulders, etc. Fall into bed to make love. Slow fade.*

Lights up on backyard. AMELIA *and* IXCHEL *are sitting in back-yard area. They listen to poignant music from* MUNDO's *room. A full yellow moon rises, Ocna.*

IXCHEL: Why, Mamá, why doesn't he come? I want him so.

AMELIA: The ways of men are not our ways.

IXCHEL: Shirley and Mundo are making love in there. I wish it were Joe and me.

AMELIA: As big as you are . . .

IXCHEL: Doesn't that music make you yearn?

AMELIA: Yes.

IXCHEL: For Polo?

AMELIA: No. For Papá . . .

IXCHEL: You should tell him. He needs you as much as you need him.

AMELIA: Polo was like that music. Someone in a dream, too good to be true. Things like that don't last. I was so foolish to dream.

IXCHEL: You think it's like that with Mundo and Shirley?

AMELIA: Maybe. I hope it is . . . Why are we talking like this?

IXCHEL: It's the moon and the wind and the smell of rain. Makes me a little mad. Don't you feel it?

AMELIA: I did, a while ago.

IXCHEL: When?

AMELIA: A little while ago. Papá fell asleep. His face was clean of hurt, guilt. He looked so young, so strong. I felt this fire surge through me. My breasts rose like a young girl's. But I dared not kiss his lips.

IXCHEL: You should have.

AMELIA: No, I know too well the consequence of rashness, of taking what you want. You pay for it.

IXCHEL: Mamá, I want you to understand—it wasn't like that with Joe and me. I knew nothing about love. Neither did he.

AMELIA: Both of you are still children! I know. Children love in innocence. Discover each other in a special magic, and for a while love is eternal for both—because they are children.

IXCHEL: I'm a woman now . . .

AMELIA: Are you . . .

IXCHEL: It's strange, isn't it, the many kinds of love there are? Was it like that with you and Polo?

AMELIA: In a way. The miracle was there, the discovery of something beyond the physical pleasure. My body was nourished, my spirit. A return to innocence, you could say, in spite of all the scars and fears . . . (*Far-away thunder.*)

IXCHEL: It's going to rain.

AMELIA: Not in this desert. The thunder and the lightning dance overhead and take the rain with them to some green land.

IXCHEL: He'll come.

AMELIA: Joe . . .

IXCHEL: Yes. (*Places hands on back hips.*) Oh, I'm getting pains.

AMELIA: (*Laughs.*) The consequence of love! Come, I'll help you to bed. Let's see how often the contractions come. It is time. (AMELIA *and* IXCHEL *exit through kitchen door. Fade on back-*

yard. Lights up in MUNDO's *room.* MUNDO *is still in bed.* SHIRLEY
is sitting up. She begins to dress.)

SHIRLEY: Mundo, baby, it's going to be a blast. We'll be free.

MUNDO: I know—free, honey, when you are in my arms.

SHIRLEY: Oh, I love you, I love you, I love you . . .

MUNDO: Take it easy. The guys'll be here any minute.

SHIRLEY: I saved eight hundred dollars. I bet you never saw that
much money in your life.

MUNDO: Nope.

SHIRLEY: The car's in my name.

MUNDO: What do I take?

SHIRLEY: Yourself, baby, you're worth a million.

MUNDO: We'd just be running away. Free is something else.

SHIRLEY: Getting as far away as I can from ol' stinking Charlie,
that's freedom to me.

MUNDO: You married him.

SHIRLEY: You think I wanted to? My ol' lady bitched and bitched
until I did. She said there was only the street or Charlie for me.
Sometimes I think picking up johns would have been better. I
didn't mean that, lover. It'll always be you, you, you, just you.

MUNDO: Charlie's due back.

SHIRLEY: After midnight. That's why we gotta take off early, before
the sun comes out. What's the matter?

MUNDO: Why?

SHIRLEY: You're not excited like before.

MUNDO: I'll tell you later.

SHIRLEY: Tell me what? (MUNDO *gets out of bed, goes to window.*)

MUNDO: It's getting dark. Man, I gotta unwind, fly, fly out of myself
into something, something vast . . .

SHIRLEY: Vas . . . what you say? You think too much.

MUNDO: Like dying, you sort of become a part of all the bigness.

SHIRLEY: Stop that dumb talk. Come kiss me . . . (*They kiss.*) You
flying?

MUNDO: Oh, honey, I love the way you feel. Your hair smells so
good. You're so warm, alive . . .

SHIRLEY: Then quit talking all that jazz . . .

MUNDO: Look at that moon rising behind those black clouds.

SHIRLEY: It's orange, so big . . .

MUNDO: Ocna.

SHIRLEY: What?

MUNDO: The full moon of Ocna. The winds will die down.

SHIRLEY: There you go again, with your dumb stuff. You sound like a Dracula movie.

MUNDO: The Mayans have a festival when the wind is still and the rains are about to come.

SHIRLEY: You making it up?

MUNDO: No. It's in the Maya's sacred book. Ocna means "enter the house." The wind gods, the Chacs, come into the house to cleanse it of evil, to kill the fire. Then it is offered to the rain. The house is restored.

SHIRLEY: Cut it out, will ya?

MUNDO: (*Making an offering.*) Wind gods! Come. Purify this house. Kill the fire. Give us hope.

SHIRLEY: You sound like your ol' man . . .

MUNDO: He and I are one—bound to the centuries of our people.

SHIRLEY: I'm not going to listen to you anymore. (*Crosses to rock.*) That's some rock. Purple running into blue, blue into red. Gives me goose pimples.

MUNDO: Wait 'til it's lighted . . . See all those grooves? The electricity of the soul. (CHROM *appears at the door. Crosses to* SHIRLEY *and* MUNDO, *contemplates rock.*)

CHROM: Yeah—that thing's beautiful. Man, we're all fused. I've got the grass.

MUNDO: Enough?

CHROM: Sure.

MUNDO: Where you get it?

CHROM: Across the river. (TATO *walks in.*)

TATO: Esos. What you say about the river? (*Crosses to* SHIRLEY.) Esa, gringuita.

SHIRLEY: Hi, Tato.

TATO: Hey, you guys, I crossed the river the other day. You know what happened? Made myself a raft and the federales blew it up. I was drowning, man. Then—DADA! The biggest fishie that you ever saw, bigger than my fat Mosca, came along and carried me across.

CHROM: You should have brought it with you and we could have had ourselves a fish fry.

TATO: Don't eat my friends, man.

CHROM: You know what I wish?

SHIRLEY: What?

CHROM: I wish I could cross the river with two bags of hash under my armpits. Where's Foco, el loco?

TATO: This strange creature was trailing me—he's right behind me.

(MUNDO *stands. Makes a ceremonial gesture with his hands, looking solemn and serious.*)

MUNDO: Enter the house.

CHROM: What's with him?

SHIRLEY: (*Giggles.*) He's inviting some gods to come and join the party.

TATO: Hey, that's cool. What kind of gods?

SHIRLEY: His papá's gods. (FOCO *appears at the door. Sits on floor at edge of semicircle.*)

CHROM: Let's light up. (*Lights a toke.*)

FOCO: Did you all see that post outside?

CHROM: Don't tell us. The gods are gone. They're coming to the party.

FOCO: They're still there. But you should see how the moon is shining on those half-faces. Better than blacklight. Man, they look so alive. I thought they were going to jump down and follow me.

TATO. They did—they did Now, don't sit on them. They're next to you. Give 'em the toke. (*Everybody laughs except* MUNDO, *who seems to be in a trance.*)

MUNDO: Gods, kill the fire. We have an offering—this mountain.

CHROM: You can't fool 'em. They know it's a rock, man . . .

MUNDO *turns on the blacklight, turns music on. All the pictures on the wall come to life. The rock is one huge splendor.*

CHROM: Man, you're right. It's a mountain! (*A pair of huge purple eyes on the back wall are nebulous and hazy during the beginning of the scene. At the end of the scene, they are a bright, living purple, yellow and black. Boys light up another toke.* MUNDO *goes to window, stares at moon. Indian music begins to intermingle with acid rock. Imperceptible at first, then becomes dominant over the rock.*)

TATO: Know what I saw today?

FOCO: What?

TATO: A floating Goodyear tire up in the air.

CHROM: You mean the zeppelin, pendejo.

TATO: Bigger than my Mosca.

MUNDO: Consecration . . .

SHIRLEY: What's he talking about?

MUNDO: Shhhhhhhhh! Ocna!

SHIRLEY: Cut it out, Mundo.

MUNDO: A mass—the offering of the blood and the body—to purify, to purge the evil.

CHROM: He's not even stoned. Hey, Mundo, ain't you going to join us?

MUNDO: What?

SHIRLEY: What's the matter with you? You give me the creeps.

CHROM: Here . . . (*Offers* MUNDO *the toke.* MUNDO *takes it, joins them in the semicircle. A clap of thunder is heard. The group listens to the music and smokes. The wind is blowing hard and wet. A figure appears from the darkened area of backyard. It is* NACHO. *He peers into* MUNDO's *room. Sees the rock. Crosses to post.*)

NACHO: (*Shouting against wind.*) Itzamna! Teplictli, the mountain of color! For you, Itzamna. Now, send to me the woman-goddess. I burn with your passions. Send her to me! I shall make love to her! Fulfill her like the rain fulfills the earth. . . .

> *Another figure appears from darkened backyard area. It is* AMELIA, *her hair loosened, dressed in a thin, revealing nightgown. The wind blows the gown against her body.*

NACHO: Teteo!

AMELIA: Are you alright?

NACHO: Teteo! I want you . . .

AMELIA: Oh, my love . . . (NACHO *takes her in his arms, kisses her passionately, picks her up in his arms, takes her through kitchen door. The* CHAC GODS *appear.* KILLING OF THE FIRE DANCE. *They run in carrying fire in their hands to purify the house.* [*Long nylon scarves, sprayed with fluorescent paint, make very impressive fire as they dance.*] *The dance is wild and passionate. The music is now totally Indian, reed and drums* [*Villalobos*]. *Group is still in the semicircle, oblivious to what happened.* MUNDO, *however, senses something, stands. Runs out of his room toward post. Dancers intermingle with his presence, nearly touching him. He cannot see them, but feels them.*)

SHIRLEY: Hey, where you going?

FOCO: Leave him alone.

CHROM: He's by the post with the faces.

TATO: Talking to the gods.

FOCO: It ain't funny, guys. There's something in this room and out there.

CHROM: Told you you were loonie.

SHIRLEY: What gods? I don't see no gods.

FOCO: You unbelievers!

CHROM: Shut up!

MUNDO: Itzamna, are you real? Papá's right. You're reaching out from the centuries. You're in our blood.

CHROM: (*Standing in doorway.*) Hey, Mundo, you freaked out? (*Thunder is heard.*)

SHIRLEY: It's going to rain soon. I don't want him out there getting wet. we're leaving for Califas at dawn.

CHROM: You and Mundo?

SHIRLEY: Yes.

FOCO: You sure?

SHIRLEY: We've been planning it for weeks.

TATO: WOW!

CHROM: Wait til your ol' man finds out.

SHIRLEY: We'll be gone by the time he finds out.

CHROM: Hey, Mundo, come on, let's celebrate.

FOCO: I'll get him.

> CHROM, SHIRLEY, *and* TATO *sit in their semicircle, pass the toke, and contemplate the rock.* FOCO *crosses to* MUNDO *by post.*

FOCO: I'm glad you're leaving.

MUNDO: What?

FOCO: With Shirley. I have a feeling this place is not for you.

MUNDO: I'm not going.

FOCO: Shirley know?

MUNDO: I'm going to tell her.

FOCO: You're crazy, man, you gotta go.

MUNDO: My ol' man got up on those tracks last night and tried to kill himself.

FOCO: Shit.

MUNDO: I'm not going to let him.

FOCO: (*Pointing to post.*) Look, look, at that thing. Something terrible is going to happen.

MUNDO: You think I'm going to let it happen? I'm keeping him off those tracks.

FOCO: Damn you! It's you that thing is after. (*Nods toward* ITZAM-NA.)

MUNDO: You're crazy . . .

FOCO: Don't you feel it?

MUNDO: Sort of . . .

FOCO: See what I mean! They're crowding in on you. Take off. You better! I'll stay here and keep your ol' man off the tracks even if I have to punch him out.

MUNDO: It has to be me, don't you see?

FOCO: I can handle him.

MUNDO: Papá must see that I care—that I'm here to take care of him, that I love him. So much has happened to the poor old man.

FOCO: All this scares me. (*Sits on doorstep.*)

MUNDO: It's up to me to save this family . . . (*Inside,* CHROM, TATO, *and* SHIRLEY *are still contemplating rock.*)

TATO: (*Calling out.*) Hey, Mundo, look at your rock.

CHROM: It's a rainbow blob, like a beating heart—ping pang, ping pang, ping pang. (FOCO *and* MUNDO *go back into the room and join the circle. They all sit in silence listening to the music, smoking, staring at the rock. Outside, the dancers reappear, bearing the fire. Voice of* ITZAMNA *mixes with drum beat, gathering intensity. Thunder is heard.*)

ITZAMNA: Sacrificio
                Son for Father
                Fire killing fire . . .

    Dancers disappear. Inside:

CHROM: Hear something?

TATO: Music turned weird.

SHIRLEY: It's the rainbow rock. It's growing.

FOCO: Save yourself, Mundo!

MUNDO: I can't! (*Clash of cymbals.*) LOOK! (*The purple glowing eyes are staring at him.*)

ACT THREE

FINAL SCENE

Almost dawn. However, there is little light, for the sky is dark with heavy thunderclouds. The storm hasn't broken. MUNDO'S *room.* SHIRLEY *is startled into wakefulness by the sound of* CHARLIE'S *truck at the store across the street. She jumps out of bed, dresses quickly.* MUNDO *awakens as she looks about for her things.*

MUNDO: What time is it?

SHIRLEY: It's so dark. I can't tell. Close to dawn, I guess. (*Crosses to window.*) Charlie just drove up. We have to get out of here.

MUNDO: Did you leave him a note saying you were splitting?

SHIRLEY: No. He'll think I'm at my mother's, but he'll check right away. Unless . . .

MUNDO: He knows about us.

SHIRLEY: Oh, Mundo, I'm scared. Hurry up.

MUNDO: Calm down, will ya?

SHIRLEY: He has a shotgun. Sometimes he just stands there, pointing that thing at me. Says if he ever catches me with another man . . . please, Mundo, let's go.

MUNDO: Where's your car?

SHIRLEY: At my girlfriend's.

MUNDO: Then, take off.

SHIRLEY: What do you mean? You're coming with me.

MUNDO: I can't go, baby. Not right now.

SHIRLEY: Then I'm not going either.

MUNDO: Drive on to Yuma, like we planned.

SHIRLEY: Without you?

MUNDO: Yes. I promise you, I'll get there. Just wait for me.

SHIRLEY: Mundo, why? Why aren't you going with me?

MUNDO: My ol' man's sick. I gotta stay.

SHIRLEY: What difference will a few days make?

MUNDO: I gotta make arrangements, find somebody that will help me with him. It'll take a few days, that's all.

SHIRLEY: Why can't your mother do it, or María?

MUNDO: No one can handle him but me, O.K.?

SHIRLEY: Oh Mundo, you promised. You said you loved me. You don't owe your family anything.

MUNDO: He's my father. I want to stay.

SHIRLEY: I hate you! You promised!

MUNDO: (*Holds her.*) Honey, honey, listen, I love you. I'll get to Yuma. All I need is a little time.

SHIRLEY: Oh Mundo, come with me. In a few days we'll be there. Imagine, seeing the ocean together for the first time. Everything new, waiting for us. Now, Mundo, now.

MUNDO: We're going to see it. Do as I say. You better go. Charlie will be out looking for you soon.

SHIRLEY: You know what'll happen if he knows about us?

MUNDO: We don't know that he does. I can handle him.

SHIRLEY: Oh, Mundo. Hold me. (*They embrace, kiss.*) I'll wait. I love you.

MUNDO: I love you. Now go. (MUNDO *leads her to the door. She is still hesitant, but leaves reluctantly. She walks away, stops, looks, looks back, then breaks into a run.* MUNDO *watches her until she's out of sight. The whistle of the first morning train is heard. In the backyard area, there is a stool next to the post, a knife on the stool. The faces are now completely carved out.* AMELIA *comes out of kitchen door, sees* MUNDO *in his doorway, crosses to him.*)

AMELIA: Look at that sky. I wish the storm would break. I'm glad you're up. I was coming over to wake you. It's Ixchel's time.

MUNDO: Baby's coming . . .

AMELIA: The pains are one on top of the other. I have to be with her.

MUNDO: She alright?

AMELIA: Fine. I'll have to deliver the baby. But it's not my first time.

MUNDO: Want me along?

AMELIA: No. That's just it. I'm worried. Have you seen your father?

MUNDO: He's asleep, isn't he?

AMELIA: When I woke up he was gone. It's strange. But what worries me is that. (*Points to carved-out faces.*)

MUNDO: He finished them! When?

AMELIA: During the night, I guess. You have to look for him. The liquor bottle is empty. I didn't think he would do that, not after . . .

MUNDO: After what?

AMELIA: Last night, your papá and I—we were together.

MUNDO: You and papá?

AMELIA: I haven't got time to tell you now. I don't want that baby to come without me there. But—find him. If he drank all that liquor, his mind may still be on those trains. (*The sound of the train is now close. It roars as it passes.*)

MUNDO: To think we've been waking up to that every morning for years. There's still two more trains to go. I'll be on the lookout. Don't worry.

AMELIA: Thank you, son. I think things are going to be alright.

MUNDO: I'll make sure of that.

AMELIA: (*Touching his face.*) My son! (AMELIA *exits into kitchen.* MUNDO *sits on step of his doorway, looks up at sky. There's a roll of thunder and, very far away, the whistle of the second train.* NACHO *comes from the side of the house, ignores* MUNDO, *goes up to post.*)

NACHO: Itzamna. You can see now. Wind gods, Ixchel, you can see now. You are finished. I have kept my promise. Now, Itzamna, you keep yours.

MUNDO: Papá . . .

NACHO: What do you want?

MUNDO: What did he promise you?

NACHO: You wouldn't believe me if I told you.

MUNDO: Try me . . .

NACHO: I don't trust you. Why all this interest in Itzamna? You don't believe.

MUNDO: You finished the faces.

NACHO: When the winds died down and all of you had gone to sleep, I came out here. Itzamna was waiting for me. You should have seen him, bathed in moonlight. I knew he wanted me to finish his face. Took me the rest of the night, but I finished. His eyes tell me he will give me the power.

MUNDO: What power?

NACHO: The power of the golden jaguar.

MUNDO: All those stories are nothing but fairy tales. Don't be a fool.

NACHO: I shall never die.

MUNDO: All that liquor has made you crazy in the head. You're planning something. I can tell. (*Train whistle is heard, much nearer.*)

NACHO: When Itzamna dies in battle, he is born again. He will face the iron devil by my side. Iron men with iron faces and iron

ways. Metal screaming, "no hope, no hope, no hope, no hope..."
No. There is no more fear. For I am Ah Na Itza and I will face
the Iron Devil.

MUNDO: You idiot! You'll be torn to pieces. You think I want to see
that again? Oh, you—what do you care about us?

NACHO: It is because I care. I must send the black smoke, the red
fire, down to the bowels of the earth. Hear it? It grinds and
twists and squeezes the life out of me. The god of Night and
Day has made me his warrior.

   MUNDO *goes quickly into his room.*

NACHO: Where are you? Soot all over the world. Black cancer
clouds eating up our lives. I will face that iron devil, Itzamna.
Yes, yes, I know you're pleased. And when I'm done, will I
ride a winged horse across the sky by your side? Ah, we'll scatter
milky stars into the darkness. I dreamt of that, Itzamna . . .

   MUNDO *returns with rope, crosses behind* NACHO.

NACHO: You! Don't try to stop me.

MUNDO: Of course not. You are Ah Na Itza. You will face the Iron
Devil and die to be reborn. Itzamna has said so.

NACHO: Yes, yes . . .

MUNDO: Why don't you face the truth like a man.

NACHO: Truth?

MUNDO: You want to get up on those tracks because you want
to die!

NACHO: No, no . . .

MUNDO: You're so full of guilt, it leaves no room for anything else
in your life. Why? You weren't to blame for Polo's death.

NACHO: Leave me alone, chingado.

MUNDO: No. You're going to listen. You're a coward.

NACHO: Maldito! (NACHO *sees the knife on stool, crosses to it,
picks it up, throws it at* MUNDO, *misses.*)

MUNDO: I don't care if you want to kill me—but you'll face the
truth.

NACHO: I killed my brother, that's the truth!

MUNDO: No, you didn't.

NACHO: I told him never to come back. I refused him his son. I
negated him as a brother. That's why he killed himself. Oh,
Mamá, forgive me!

MUNDO: Polo did not kill himself. He was no coward. He loved
life too much to give it up. Don't you see? He was a force in the
world. He celebrated life! He would never kill himself, no

matter what you said or did to him. The world doesn't destroy men like Tío Polo, only accidents, old age . . .

NACHO: Desgraciado, I know he was your hero.

MUNDO: Tío Polo was going to hop the morning freight and slipped. It was that simple. An accident.

NACHO: Liar! Your hero.

MUNDO: You're my hero, Papá. That's why I can't bear to see you this way. (*The roar of the train is near.*)

NACHO: (*Screams to* ITZAMNA.) Did you hear that? He called me a coward! Ah, but Polo, he says, is a force in the world! Tell him, Itzamna. I have the power of the golden jaguar! I'll show him . . . (*The train is almost upon them.* NACHO *runs toward train.* MUNDO *follows him. The train thunders by. As the sound of the train subsides, a struggle is heard.* NACHO *runs into yard,* MUNDO *following.* MUNDO *picks up rope as the distant sound of the last coming train is heard.*)

MUNDO: (*Out of breath, straining; it is apparent that his illness is upon him. Holds out rope before him, standing between* NACHO *and tracks.*) You're not going to do that again . . .

NACHO: Try and stop me, desgraciado!

NACHO *attempts to make a run toward tracks;* MUNDO *lunges at him, brings him down, hits him, dazing* NACHO *for a moment. Enough time for* MUNDO *to tie his hands, then he drags* NACHO *to the post.*

NACHO: Chingado! Let me gooooooooo . . . . . .

MUNDO *holds him up roughly while* NACHO *struggles.* MUNDO *manages with some difficulty to tie him to the post.*

NACHO: Itzamna, free me!

MUNDO: Yes, you tell Itzamna to free you. He will do as you say. (*Begins to cry.*) You old bastard, I love you so!

NACHO: Mundo . . .

MUNDO: Papá . . . (*Embraces his father.*)

NACHO: Let me go. I won't try it again. I don't know what came over me. I thought Polo had taken you away from me . . . let me go.

MUNDO: No. Not until the last train passes. You see, I can hardly stand on my feet. I'm about to pass out, you understand? You stay there, you stay there until the train passes . . . (*Walks unsteadily to room, can barely make it up the steps.*)

NACHO: Please, Mundo, son, I just want to help you. Please. You're sick.

MUNDO *goes into his room, falls before making it to his bed. He falls close to the painted rock. Tries to use it to raise himself. Doesn't make it. Passes out holding on to rock.*

NACHO: Itzamna! The power of the golden jaguar! I have felt you, sensed you, believed in you! Itzamna! I made you offerings. The mountain of color, Teplictli. You sent me Teteo, woman-goddess, soft, giving, full of fire. . . . No, No! It was Amelia, my Amelia . . . Amelia! Where are you? I need you!

The roar of the coming train drowns out his cries. CHARLIE *appears carrying shotgun.* NACHO *realizes what he is about to do.*

NACHO: (*Frenzied whisper.*) Charlie . . . Charlie.

CHARLIE *stops, turns to look at him but does not speak, then continues to* MUNDO's *room.*

NACHO: (*Struggling desperately.*) My fault—my fault. Charlie, wait! It's me you want. Tell him Itzamna! You are my strength. I felt your compassion. I am Ah Na Itza. You want a sacrifice, Itzamna? You want nothing less than the living flesh? Oh . . . no. It's always been the same! Why must gods demand the living flesh? Charlie, listen to me. Don't be a coward. He can't defend himself. Do you hear me, coward? Please . . .

CHARLIE *points the gun at* MUNDO's *head.* MUNDO *is unconscious, hugging the rock.* CHARLIE *pulls the trigger.* NACHO *slumps on the post. The train thunders by. Then the storm breaks; heavy, warm drops of rain fall steadily. From the house, there is the first, lusty cry of a newborn baby.*

CURTAIN

Sor Juana

CHARACTERS

(In order of their appearance)

SOR JUANA INES DE LA CRUZ
  (at forty-two)
SOR FELICIANA
SOR CATARINA
JUANA ASBAJE (at eight)
SLAVE JUANA (at nine)
ANDRES (at eleven)
LADY LEONOR MARIA DE
  CARRETO (LAURA)
LADY BEATRIZ
LADY MARGARITA
BERNARDO
FATHER ANTONIO NUÑEZ
  DE MIRANDA
MARQUIS DE MANCERA

SCHOLAR
ALTAR BOY
CANON
SLAVE JUANA (as adult)
DR. IGNACIO PAVON
COUNT DE PAREDES
COUNTESS DE PAREDES (LISI)
BISHOP MIGUEL FERNANDO
  DE SANTA CRUZ
FATHER JUAN IGNACIO
ANDRES (as adult)
PRIEST
SOR BARBARA
SOR CELESTINA

NOTE: To give validity to the historical sequences, a large cast is necessary. However, the play lends itself well to double casting. In my production I combined the roles of Canon, Father Juan Ignacio, and the Priest to be played by one actor. The noble ladies in Act One became the sisters in the final scene. Other double castings are possible.

ACT ONE

𑁋𑁋𑁋𑁋𑁋

SCENE 1

The Convent of St. Jerome, Mexico City, 1693: The near empty cell of SOR JUANA INES DE LA CRUZ. *It contains a cot, a chair, and some boxes containing the last few possessions of* SOR JUANA. *On top of one of the boxes are lighted votive candles, on another, a yucca whip.* SOR JUANA, *a slight, thin figure, forty-two years old, is dressed in a single white chemise. She kneels down center, holding a huge crucifix over her head.*

SOR JUANA: (*In prayer.*) Sweet Jesus, Jesús del alma mía, me entrego a tu compañía. Perdóname mis pecados. Forgive my arrogance, my pride, my selfishness. Oh, Sweet Jesus, I have forsaken my vows. You, Who are all merciful, do not desert me in this, the hour of my need. Let your angels surround me. My strength has left me. My mind has left me. I am empty. Oh, Divine Spirit, fill this sorrowful vessel with your compassion. Dear Christ, my body shall feel your pain, your wounds. (*She beats her breast, lowers head to floor, begins to unbutton top of her garment, rising. Kisses crucifix, crosses to box, lays crucifix on top, drops top of her garment down to her waist; back to audience, picks up whip.*)
  The red haze, symbolic of the Misery, the penitence ritual of SOR JUANA, *begins to fade gradually.* SOR JUANA *blows out candles. Total darkness. There is the sound of a whip descending upon bare flesh, a suppressed groan. Another whip lash, the sound of suffering sobs.*
SOR JUANA: Oh, my God! Here's my soul! Take it from me! See? My blood runs free. I feel your presence. Touch my wounds. They are your wounds. I shall not sleep—el dormir es el ensayo del morir. (*Sound of the whip, a long, deep moan.*) My life! My life! All ashes.
  Red haze gradually returns. SOR JUANA *rises, lights candles. She covers exposed body, then takes candles down center,*

places them on both sides of her as she kneels and prays feverishly.

SOR JUANA: *Domine, non sum dignus.* Oh, Lamb of God! Cleanse my spirit. Soul of Christ, sanctify me. Body of Christ, save me. Blood of Christ, inebriate me. Water from the side of Christ, wash me clean. Passion of Christ, strengthen me. Oh, Good Jesus, hear me. Within thy wounds, hide me. In the hour of my death, call me and bid me come to thee, that with thy saints I may praise thee and be thine, forever and ever . . .

BLACKOUT

SCENE 2

Sunrise. Two days later. SOR JUANA *is asleep on the cot.* SOR FELICIANA, *her young niece, is sitting by her side.* SOR CATARINA *comes in quietly with a bowl of soup, crosses to bed, looks over* SOR JUANA.

SOR CATARINA: She's so pale. She slept around the clock, though.
SOR FELICIANA: Fitfully, I'm afraid. She cries out in her sleep and tosses so.
SOR CATARINA: This soup will do her good. (*Places soup on top of one of the boxes.*) She hasn't eaten for days.
SOR FELICIANA: All those weeks of scourging herself. I'm glad you broke the lock.
SOR CATARINA: She was half dead when we found her. All that blood! And that whip has got to go. Enough is enough. We should have interfered before. It's not natural, to whip yourself. Not for a Hieronymite. She's sinking into some terrible darkness. We simply will not allow it anymore. I'll burn that infernal whip.
SOR FELICIANA: It's all because he's gone.
SOR CATARINA: Father Antonio?
SOR FELICIANA: Yes.
SOR CATARINA: It's much more than that. She's warring with herself. And with her capacity for passion . . . No. We shall put a stop to it.

SOR FELICIANA: When she wakes up she will force herself to go to San Hipólito. You know how far she walks each day? Seven miles—in her condition.

SOR CATARINA: That seems to be her life now—worrying about those starving people in the barrios, taking whatever she can. Feed her the soup when she wakes up. Tell her Sister Sofía and Sister Magdalena will go to San Hipólito in her place. There is grain to give. I have written to Father Antonio. If he gets my letter he will come.

SOR FELICIANA: The Holy Company forbids it.

SOR CATARINA: After what's happened to Mexico City, to Sor Juana, *that* is of little importance. What we need now is a miracle. Father Antonio is our miracle. To have him back would raise her from the dead.

SOR FELICIANA: She loves him so!

SOR CATARINA: (*Crosses to door.*) I leave her in your care. Stay with her. I think she needs that soup more than sleep now. Wake her gently and make her understand God wants her well and strong.

SOR FELICIANA: Yes, Sister.

> SOR CATARINA *exits.* SOR FELICIANA *goes to the bed, smooths* SOR JUANA's *hair, takes her aunt's hand in hers.*

SOR FELICIANA: Juana . . .

SOR JUANA: Shhh . . . Listen—Do you hear the cowbell?

SOR FELICIANA: How are you feeling?

SOR JUANA: I heard the cowbell. Was it in my dreams?

SOR FELICIANA: Most likely. There is no cowbell.

SOR JUANA: The cowbell means Andrés will come along with his flute.

SOR FELICIANA: It was a dream. Andrés is d . . .

SOR JUANA: Is what?

SOR FELICIANA: Dead . . .

SOR JUANA: It must have been a dream. We were children again. We were climbing the cowpath, Juana, Andrés and I. To the rocks where Andrés found a cliff rose once, so long ago. Where's Juana?

SOR FELICIANA: You gave her her freedom. Don't you remember? She's living somewhere in the zambo barrio—with an aunt, I think.

SOR JUANA: Freedom? Juana is my sister. Andrés, my brother.

SOR FELICIANA: They were your mother's slaves, and when you came into the Order, your mother gave you Juana to attend you.

SOR JUANA: No. I'm not thinking clear . . .

SOR FELICIANA: You lost much blood . . .

SOR JUANA: Listen, I hear the cowbell . . . (*Blackout on stage area. Sound of cowbell as light comes up on flashback area. Time: 1659.* JUANA ASBAJE *is eight.* JUANA, *the zambo slave, is nine, her brother* ANDRES, *eleven.* ANDRES *is leading, playing his pito (flute). Suddenly he stops, takes a corn cake out of his pocket. Divides it in three parts, gives each little girl a piece.*)

SLAVE JUANA: You took it when Mamá Seya wasn't looking. I saw you.

ANDRES: (*Stuffing mouth.*) Mamá Seya doesn't mind. (*Turns to* JUANA.) Eat it, coya.

SLAVE JUANA: Tastes best when you're on a cowpath and the sky is blue.

ANDRES: (*Looks at sky.*) All blue—nothing but blue . . .

JUANA: All the way to Mexico City?

ANDRES: Sure. You see when you go there. Same sky.

JUANA: I wish you could go with me. That's what I wish.

ANDRES: Who would take the cows to pasture?

SLAVE JUANA: Who would feed the chickens and help Mamá Seya in the kitchen?

JUANA: I must go. I must show people how well I read and write. I will read my poems and sing my music.

SLAVE JUANA: People will go to see you like in the circus.

ANDRES: Like a dancing bear. People will come from all around.

JUANA: I'm not a dancing bear. (ANDRES *takes out his pito and begins to play a tune.* SLAVE JUANA *pretends she is a dancing bear.* JUANA, *eating her cake, dances too. Still playing his pito,* ANDRES *starts walking up the cowpath.*)

SLAVE JUANA: Wait for us! (*Starts after* ANDRES.)

JUANA: (*Following.*) You know that in Mexico City there are more books than in my grandfather's library? I've read all of those, you know.

ANDRES: I cannot read.

SLAVE JUANA: All the books, could they make a mountain?

JUANA: Lots of mountains.

SLAVE JUANA: Will you forget about the sun?

ANDRES: And the river?

SLAVE JUANA: The bird songs?

ANDRES: The stars behind the mountain?

JUANA: Don't walk so fast.

ANDRES: (*Stops, takes cup from inside shirt, shows it to girls.*)
Look!

JUANA: You're going to milk . . .

SLAVE JUANA: Let's catch a cow . . . (*All three run off as light fades, light comes up on cell area.*)

SOR FELICIANA: You're lightheaded. You've fasted too long. Sister Catarina brought some soup for you. (*Crosses to box, brings soup to* SOR JUANA. *Tries to feed her, but she is too absorbed in thought.*) Please drink it, Tía. You need the strength. (SOR JUANA *takes some spoonfuls.*)

SOR JUANA: (*Pushing spoon away.*) Not too much. (*Looks at bruises and open gashes now cleaned.*) You washed it off, all the blood. How long did I sleep?

SOR FELICIANA: Around the clock. You needed it.

SOR JUANA: San Hipólito . . .

SOR FELICIANA: Don't worry. Sister Sofía and Sister Magdalena will give out grain today.

SOR JUANA: (*Tries to get up.*) I should go with them.

SOR FELICIANA: (*Stops her.*) No. You are to rest. We're not going to let you have your way anymore, dear Tía.

SOR JUANA: And what is my way?

SOR FELICIANA: No more scourging, no more fasting, and the barrios in San Hipólito can do without you for a few days. Sister Catarina took the whip to burn it.

SOR JUANA: (*Pushes* SOR FELICIANA *away.*) No! (*She gets out of bed.*) I must suffer the wounds of Jesus for what I made of my life . . . In a windstorm, I stripped a yucca of its leaves, braided them, soaked them in salt water—to make the whip flexible, to feel the sting of salt upon my open wounds.

SOR FELICIANA: No more, Sor Juana. It is insane what you have done to yourself. It is not you. Not a Hieronymite.

SOR JUANA: You forget—I was a Carmelite. Their faith is pure—pure—that is its strength, isn't it? That clean faith without doubt, without words—I didn't have it then. I want it so now. I want it so. Faith—Faith—Faith—Oh, Feliciana, what am I?

SOR FELICIANA: The most faithful, but you should be in bed.

SOR JUANA: I am not an invalid. I feel strong. This isn't the first time I've spilled my blood or fasted. But with the coming of a new day, God has always given me strength.

SOR FELICIANA: Please—you are forcing yourself. I can tell. I don't understand this delirium that has taken hold of you for so long.

SOR JUANA: (*Weak, shaking, with great effort crosses to chair, holds it for support.*) There's nothing wrong with me. I'm—I'm fine.

SOR FELICIANA: You're so stubborn! (*Crosses to her aunt.*) Here, let me help you back to bed. (*Touches her aunt's forehead.*) Why, you're burning up with fever. You must go back to bed.

SOR JUANA: There's so much to do. So much I've left undone. Let me be. Go away.

SOR FELICIANA: Sister Catarina said I must stay with you.

SOR JUANA: Don't be foolish, my child. How can I make you understand that all this pain, this confusion, this emptiness inside me, has to be purged? It is between me and God. No one else. Go!

SOR FELICIANA: I wish I could help you . . .

SOR JUANA: You can help me by respecting my solitude.

SOR FELICIANA: Will you stay and rest—sleep some more? You're so frail. You're body cannot take much more . . . Will you promise not to leave your cell?

SOR JUANA: There are so many things to be done that I've left undone . . .

SOR FELICIANA: I will not let you walk off into the desert to follow the moan of the wind as you did before. We couldn't find you! By the time we did, you were half-frozen. You might take it in your head to go to San Hipólito after all. Your body cannot stand it! This energy you have is not energy. It's some obsessive agony . . . Please, Sor Juana, I understand your need to be alone, and I will go if you promise to stay.

SOR JUANA: The people in San Hipólito need coal. They need fires to feed the children, to keep them warm.

SOR FELICIANA: (*Crosses to bed, picks up* SOR JUANA's *only black habit at the foot of the bed.*) Not today, Sor Juana.

SOR JUANA: What are you doing?

SOR FELICIANA: I'm taking your clothes with me.

SOR JUANA: No . . .

SOR FELICIANA: (*Crying softly.*) It's the only way. (*Goes to door with* JUANA's *only habit.*) I'm sorry. (*Exits.*)

SOR JUANA: (*Goes to door. Leans against it, turns, collapses to floor.*) No . . . (*Tries to sit up with great effort; folds arms, rubbing.*) I'm shivering . . . cold, cold, cold. Oh, God, do not forsake me! I'm so cold. (*Rises unsteadily, goes to cot, takes blanket from bed, wraps herself in it; touches forehead.*) I'm burning up. Why am I so cold? I think it's April. The sun . . . (*Crosses to window.*) Ah, yes . . . warm, warm, warm. (*Stares out into convent garden.*) Cornstalks! The flowers—where are they? Where are my people? Laura? You died so long ago! Lisi? What's happened to Lisi? They loved me well . . . Oh, Father Antonio, I need you so. Jesus, help me understand. Was I a willing bride? I remember my own happiness so long ago—when I told myself, "I shall discover God through knowledge, and the Church will let me learn. . ." Was that good enough reason to become your bride? (*Crosses down center.*) Sweet Jesus—love? Pure, clear, the flower of faith? That was not my offering to you, Jesus. But I was so young, so hurt . . .

> *Lights fade out on cell area, come up on flashback area. It's 1667, the Viceroy's palace, Mexico City. The garden. One chair on a raised platform, appears throne-like. The Marchioness, Lady Leonor María de Carreto, known as* LAURA *to close friends, enters followed by* LADY BEATRIZ *and* LADY MARGARITA. LAURA *crosses downstage, and with a sweep of the hand that holds an open fan, she gestures to an area at a distance.*

LAURA: Over there—see them? Bronze, blue, green—aren't they superb? Peacocks from my husband! How dear of him. Just what my garden needs.

LADY MARGARITA: Such a garden! It's a woodland.

LAURA: One of the splendors of our new land.

LADY MARGARITA: We saw your peacocks on the ship. Now, they're free.

LAURA: A safe arrival. Now you two are in my care for a little while. I heard the ship was chased by English pirates. Infamous English! The waters in the Gulf are infested with them.

LADY BEATRIZ: Fearful experience. Our ship fled against southerly winds.

LADY MARGARITA: With the help of God we arrived safely in Vera Cruz.

LADY BEATRIZ: And the help of Count Camborio. He kept our spirits up all during the chase.

LADY MARGARITA: We stayed at his villa when we arrived in Vera Cruz.

LADY BEATRIZ: Marvelous place. He has twenty-four slaves— humble, curious people. He told us slaves were abundant and your criollos were good at civil work and the like. We are not so fortunate in Spain. But tell me, Laura, why didn't Bernardo go to Vera Cruz to meet me?

LAURA: I don't know, really. I'm sure it was some pressing business.

LADY BEATRIZ: I shall be very angry with him. When we were first betrothed, he was so eager for an early marriage. Now that I've set a date, you'd think he'd be anxious.

LAURA: Tell me, will you be married in Toledo?

LADY BEATRIZ: Yes. At the great *catedral*. I shall take Bernardo back with me. Oh, Laura, you must go back to Spain with us— you must attend the wedding.

LAURA: Oh, I do long to see the Spanish sun again, but I cannot. The building of the great *catedral*, here in Mexico City—it has been my husband's dream. It is almost finished and we are preparing for a celebration. A sonnet will be written by Sor Juana Asbaje for the occasion in honor of Diego de Ribera.

LADY MARGARITA: Isn't she the one who wrote that poem on the death of our late King Phillip? I remember someone reciting it some years back. They mentioned it was written by some child in your court, some criolla. Is she still with you?

LAURA: Oh yes. In fact, it was that poem that brought her to my court. I insisted on meeting her. She was thirteen at the time. She came from a village called Amecameca, demanding that she be allowed to study at the university. Amazing, precocious girl. Of course she was not allowed to enter the university. I took her under my wing.

LADY BEATRIZ: So you let her run loose in your garden.

LAURA: Come to think of it, she did go off this morning with your Bernardo at her heels. They are good friends.

LADY MARGARITA: Ah, Lady Beatriz, you came just in time.

LADY BEATRIZ: Don't be absurd, Margarita. (*To* LAURA.) I suppose you keep her for the court's amusement.

LAURA: Oh, no. I love her dearly. I wish I could arrange a good marriage for her, but unfortunately she is the illegitimate offspring of some Spanish captain and a farm girl. She has no dowry. A great beauty, though, and a brilliant mind.

LADY BEATRIZ: Not advantageous to a lady, I would say.

LADY MARGARITA: I agree with you. A woman with a mind is no more than a curiosity to men.

LADY BEATRIZ: I am sure that is all she is to Bernardo.

LAURA: Tell me, will your uncle, the Bishop, perform the wedding?

LADY BEATRIZ: Yes. The whole Spanish court will attend.

LAURA: How exciting. (*Starts to leave, continuing conversation.*) I suppose Princess Mariana will attend.

LADY BEATRIZ: So will the young king.

LADY MARGARITA: He goes wherever she goes.

LAURA: So what I've heard is true . . .

LADY BEATRIZ: And what is that, M'Lady?

LAURA: It is really Princess Mariana who rules Spain. You must know all the intrigues. Do tell me . . . (*They exit.* JUANA ASBAJE *enters, a slender, tall girl of sixteen with wide-set eyes and chestnut hair, broad brow, quick smile, straight nose, determined chin.* BERNARDO *catches up with her.*)

BERNARDO: Wait. You must understand.

JUANA: I do. She's come to fetch you back.

BERNARDO: It was arranged years ago—by our parents.

JUANA: You never told me. Why?

BERNARDO: I don't know—except that all I could see in the world was you and I.

JUANA: You are mocking me.

BERNARDO: Please, Juana . . .

JUANA: Maybe you were just indulging yourself. A favorite pastime at court—with you nobles.

BERNARDO: I love you, Juana Asbaje.

JUANA: You pretend to know about love?

BERNARDO: I know how I feel and how you feel.

JUANA: Don't presume, Sir! How inconsequent and variable is your reason.

BERNARDO: You have a right to be angry.

JUANA: I have no rights, Bernardo. In your game, only gentlemen with titles and ladies with property have rights.

BERNARDO: I'd give anything in the world if I could change the consequence of who I am, what I am committed to. What you and I feel is beyond all measure . . .

JUANA: Your words burn in the sun. They will disappear with the wind, ashes without voice. I am numb, Sir. I have no feeling. When you go, what I shall feel for you, I do not know, but I've learned much from this episode.

BERNARDO: Episode?

JUANA: What would you call it?

BERNARDO: Much, much more. It's not that simple.

JUANA: For both our sakes, it had better be.

BERNARDO: I wish . . .

JUANA: Your wishing could well cause harm.

BERNARDO: You're right. What I want and truly wish—they're not part of the scheme that's planned for me. My obligations, loyalties . . . I'm not free. Oh, I wish I were . . .

JUANA: How strange—the ways of enslavement. Please go . . .

BERNARDO: I feel like some kind of coward.

JUANA: No—don't feel that way. It's something much bigger than you. Marry your noble lady. Go, please go! (BERNARDO, *struggling with his feelings, hesitates a moment, then leaves. When* JUANA *senses him gone, she falls into* LAURA's *chair, crying.* SLAVE JUANA *enters, goes to her, kneels by chair.*)

SLAVE JUANA: No llore, coya, el thielo sonlei.

JUANA: Oh, I'm glad you're here—even if it's for a little while. I'm so alone.

SLAVE JUANA: Dry your tears. Your mamá in San Miguel will not want to hear about your tears when I go back. You are so happy here! So many fine gentlemen and fine ladies! You say that all the time—how happy you are!

JUANA: Right now, I wish I were back home with all of you. Such happy years—reading my grandfather's books at Poanyán, listening to Mamá Seya's stories by the kitchen fire. Does your mamá still tell stories to the little ones?

SLAVE JUANA: All the little ones still come to her and sit in a circle at her feet like we used to do.

JUANA: And market day . . .

SLAVE JUANA: We would watch the tocotines dance and sing.

JUANA: Oh, how I long to hear the sweetness of the Náhuatl tongue . . .

SLAVE JUANA: And the songs we used to sing. Remember? (*She stands.*) Come, come . . . (*Begins to clap hands, snaps fingers, beats out a rhythm with her feet, begins to sing.*) Tumba, la, la, la—La tumba la, la, la . . .

SLAVE JUANA *takes* JUANA's *hands, pulls her to her feet, turns her around, continues singing and dancing.* JUANA *hesitates, then joins* SLAVE JUANA *in the song and dance.*

SLAVE JUANA and JUANA: La otra noche, con mi conga, tuvi sin durni. Pensaba—que no quele gente pliete—como aye so gente branca—Tumba la, la, la—Tumba la, le, le. Y en este sueño facho . . . (SLAVE JUANA *notices the entrance of* FATHER ANTONIO, *stops, puts hand on mouth, runs off.* JUANA *sees him, runs to him, attempts to kiss his hand. He gently withdraws it.* FATHER ANTONIO NUÑEZ DE MIRANDA *is a Jesuit, forty-eight years old. Behind his glasses are eyes that are intelligent, piercing, full of humor. There is an extraordinary aliveness about him. He is famous for practicing religious severities as a member of the Inquisition Council. Yet, he is a simple man of peasant*

stock, a man of the earth. Everything about him—his manner,
his voice, his attitude, his walk—suggests balance. He is known
to be a man who measures realities with great exactness.)

FATHER ANTONIO: (*After withdrawing his hands.*) No need, my
child. Who was the girl you were dancing with?

JUANA: One of the slaves from my mother's farm. She is like my
sister. She will go back soon and I shall miss her so! At times like
this I miss my valley. The slaves had songs for everything—joy,
sadness, love . . . songs about the blueness of the sky, counting
stars behind the mountain of Anahuac . . .

FATHER: And what times are those?

JUANA: What?

FATHER: You said—at times like this . . .

JUANA: Sad times, I suppose . . .

FATHER: You've been crying.

JUANA: Doesn't matter anymore.

FATHER: Forgotten what you were crying about?

JUANA: I'm not a child anymore. It's not that easy.

FATHER: Would you like to talk about it?

JUANA: Oh, Father Antonio, tell me—what's to become of me? I
don't belong here.

FATHER: You have always loved this life. Three years I've been your
confessor—you have never said otherwise. And what's this
about, "What's to become of me?" It should be—what do *you*
want to become?

JUANA: It's not what I want to become, but what I want, Father . . .
(*Crosses to Laura's chair and sits.*)

FATHER: Is that what you want?

JUANA: What do you mean?

FATHER: To be a viceroy's lady, perhaps?

JUANA: I, who am the lowest of the low . . .

FATHER: Now, what caused that? Have you had a fight with your
young man?

JUANA: He is not my young man. Never was.

FATHER: So that's it.

JUANA: His future bride, Lady Beatriz, daughter of the Duke of
Airon and Marquis of Valero, has crossed the ocean to claim
him. They will be married in a great *catedral* . . . Oh, Father,
I'm so miserable . . . (*Goes into his arms.*)

FATHER: Just cry it out . . .

JUANA: I've already done that—and tears are silly, aren't they?

FATHER: They are not silly when you have something to cry about.

JUANA: Well, I won't cry anymore. What's inevitable is inevitable...

FATHER: And what is inevitable?

JUANA: The closed doors. First, they refused to accept me at the university. Women, they informed me, should not attempt to seek the clearer eye, logic, wisdom. And today I discovered I don't belong here. My future has no certainty. I cannot hope for a good marriage like the noble ladies of this court. I have no dowry, no title . . . how dare I hope! I am no more than a curiosity at this court!

FATHER: Lady Laura loves you dearly. Everyone in this palace is fond of you, proud of you . . .

JUANA: Oh, Father, how can that give meaning to my life? Fond of me, proud of me . . . those are just vagaries. Am I to be at the mercy of such vagaries all my life? I must be something! Belong somewhere!

FATHER: The reputation of your brilliance grows . . .

JUANA: Another vagary!

FATHER: Go back home, then. Marry an honest man . . .

JUANA: No, I know now marriage is not for me. My greatest hunger is the need to know, to learn, to understand everything in the miracle of Creation. I want to read all the histories, all the poetry, learn all the sciences of the world. I need freedom for that, and freedom is hard to come by for a woman.

FATHER: Turn to God . . .

JUANA: I do not even know Him.

FATHER: You are pious.

JUANA: That is the way of women. God becomes a comfort early in our lives. Where men fail us, God doesn't. An expedient? No, I cannot believe in God through faith, or fear, or need. I must know Him through the intellect. Then I can say that I know God . . .

FATHER: The best way to serve God and men and thus find salvation is through humility and faith, the way to self-perfection.

JUANA: The principle of St. Ignatius of Loyola! You are humble! Your faith shines. That is your meaning. Oh, Father, I must get away from the frivolous passions in this court, from the superficial promises. You've warned me, again and again, and I never listened. Some time ago you told me my future would not be found at court. I didn't hear you. I was dreaming of a young man who promised me his love. Again you cautioned: April is no more than one month . . . The good face of a poor woman is a white wall where fools throw mud . . . Trampled flowers are wasted. Beauty, a man's love, all disappear on land, in smoke, in dust, with shadows . . . You told me all this, and I could not hear, for I was remembering the hot, demanding mouth of a lover . . .

FATHER: The answer is God . . . (*Light fades on flashback area, comes up on cell.* JUANA, *covering face with hands, is kneeling down center.*)

JUANA: (*Stands.*) No! I say no to You, God! They are right. No more whip! No more pain! No more vague, undefined guilt. I shall stand and reason with You, God, for it is through reason that I found You, gave myself to You and loved You. Oh, God, reason and You shall give clarity to my guilt. (*Goes to window.*) I became Your bride without really knowing You, Sweet Jesus. What took me to the Convent of San José was some stubborn pride, a blind self-pity. Oh, I remember the Mother Superior with her cadaverous, hollow-eyed face. Oh, the light of her spirit and her face is still with me. She told me the convent was a refuge for the frightened and the lost, and I was both. Becoming a nun is another thing, she said. A struggle more fearful than the struggle of Jacob and the Angel. I took the vows though the struggle was dark and seething inside of me. I became a Carmelite. I could not find You through faith. I wanted faith. I was jealous of the other sisters' faith. You are so big to them. Prostrate before You, God, they are glorious forgotten queens, so sure of knowing You, loving You, living for You . . . Faith burst forth fully developed like Athena out of Zeus' head, for them! for them! not me! I took to fevers and delusions. I left the Order in delirium. What was my life? What is my life? (*Crosses to box, begins to take out books.*) Back to the Viceroy's palace, to dear sweet Laura, so full of sympathy. I went to the Marquis and begged him to intercede once more with the university, to influence them. Knowledge, I was certain, was going to be my salvation . . .

Fade out on cell area, light goes up on flashback area. The audience room in the Viceroy's palace. The MARQUIS DE MANCERA, DON ANTONIO SEBASTIAN DE TOLEDO, *is sitting by his wife,* LAURA, *upstage right.* JUANA, *seventeen, stands by a podium, down left. In the audience are forty of the most learned men from the university, classical men, theologians, philosophers, mathematicians, humanists. One of the* SCHOLARS *rises.*

SCHOLAR: Very well done, Juana Asbaje. You have proved your genius. One last question: What is your definition of wisdom?

JUANA: Wisdom is a delicate fabric within "being." For no other reason is the angel more than man, and by the same token, the lack of wisdom makes man brutish.

SCHOLAR: Bravo! I am amazed. Not once have you faltered in your answers. I am sure that all the gentlemen with me are as impressed as I am. All of us, the mathematicians, the philosophers, the scientists, are full of admiration for the scope of your great knowledge. (*Applause.*)

JUANA: I thank you, but I must be honest. I feel no gratitude for your praise, for it is only praise. All of you have refused me entrance into the university. The forty of you were asked to come here by my mentor and friend, the Marquis of Mancera, for the sole purpose of disproving the belief that mine is only a smattering of knowledge. You have witnessed that it is not; yet, if I were to beg you here and now to voice approval for my entering the university, I know there would only be silence. (*Pause.*) I am only a girl, you say . . . And all of you believe that women should know only enough, for more than enough is harmful. It is not meant as an accusation against you. It is a sad, hopeless fact. But I, a woman, know better. A whole lifetime of striving to learn and know is not enough for man or woman, and in my struggle with self, with my own femininity, I know there is no difference between the mind of a man and the mind of a woman. Why the barriers? Why the fears?

MARQUIS: Now, Juana Asbaje, you have won the battle. Hasn't she, gentlemen? You stood before these prudent gentlemen like a royal galleon beating off the attack of a few enemy sloops, taking on all questions without task, replying to all arguments, to each in his own specialty. You stand vindicated. My dear, I am proud of you. All of Mexico is proud of you . . . (*Applause.*) And now, gentlemen, if you will follow me, I will show you another marvel. This way. My herbarium is beyond. Come, come, gentlemen, you shall see no less than one hundred and fifty species, the largest collection of Indian herbs in the New World. This way . . . (MARQUIS *exits.* JUANA *stands at podium, covers her face. She is crying in anger and defeat.*)

JUANA: (*Pounds on podium.*) It happens again, and again, and again!

LAURA: My dear, what on earth is the matter? You astounded them all. You've proven what you are.

JUANA: What I am? What am I? That's what's wrong. M'Lord says, "Another marvel . . ." You say I astound . . . Am I no more than a circus? I thought I had found where I belonged at the convent, but I failed there too . . .

LAURA: You're so frail. Their way of life was repugnant to your nature—such rigid denials!

JUANA: Where do I belong then?

LAURA: You are making a name for yourself in the literary world.

JUANA: A name? One doesn't belong to a name! Father Antonio convinced me I belonged to Jesus. But did I? I was too rash, too eager to get away from here. This palace—the garden—even in the corridors I would sense that Bernardo was behind me, at the turn, about to open a door. He was everywhere and my yearning for him was so painful. The jasmine outside my window, the soft wanting dark of spring, awakened every memory of what we were to each other. I wanted to forget. To put all those memories away forever. The only time I forget the bittersweet hurt, the only time I do not feel the longing is when Father Antonio comes. I want so much to be like him.

LAURA: Oh, I know how faithless love can be. What woman doesn't? Many women have taken orders for similar reasons. There is no reason to reprimand yourself.

JUANA: How defeating for our kind! Oh Laura, I don't want to run away from anything in my life now. You and Father Antonio were by my side all during my illness. I remember the strength of his hands, the sweetness of your voice. I did not die, and somehow during my fever, when I was burning up, my mind was clear as crystal. I was one with God. Then when I could again fill my lungs with pure air, when I heard the calling of the Angelus, God became very real to me. I felt as if I were a tiny flame struggling in the fire of His Love. It was something beyond faith, beyond intellect. I can't explain it.

LAURA: You want to be a nun.

JUANA: Yes, oh yes—but I have failed that.

LAURA: Father Antonio told me you had found your calling after the crisis. How strange that he should know! He sat by your bed after a whole night's vigil when they thought you would not live. He prayed so for you, held on to you as if refusing death the gift of you. The next morning when the doctors said the danger was over, Father Antonio kissed your hand and turned to me and claimed, "She belongs to God."

JUANA: He was right. He's some kind of miracle in my life. I think I lived because I could not bear to leave him.

LAURA: Juana, he has arranged it all. Father Antonio and I were going to tell you later, but you need to know it now . . .

JUANA: Arrange what? Know what?

LAURA: Last week he came for me and we drove out to the border of the city, south. To the Convent of St. Jerome.

JUANA: The Convent of St. Jerome! Most of the Hieronymites are daughters of the very rich . . . I could never hope . . .

LAURA: It's all arranged! You have more friends than you think. Don Pedro Velásquez did not allow my husband to pay your dowry. He insisted on being your mentor since he is your relative. And two knights of the Order of Santiago, Don Antonio Mejía and Don Gaspar, have purchased the property of your cell, gifting it to you.

JUANA: I don't understand . . .

LAURA: Father Antonio convinced all of us that it was the perfect order for you. He told us St. Jerome wanted women to learn. It should be wise women who teach young girls instead of men. The Hieronymites are teachers. Their *locutorio* is a meeting place for learned people. Now, with you there, it shall become the meeting place for the nobility. The Marquis and I and my court shall attend vespers at St. Jerome.

JUANA: Oh, Jesus be praised! St. Jerome, a lover of knowledge! A defender of women! Oh, it *is* the place.

LAURA: Another surprise! My husband has convinced the Bishop to give you certain privileges. You can have books and whatever you may need to study and learn . . .

JUANA: I shall read Virgil, St. Augustine, St. Jerome, in the tongue of the Church. I shall journey the whole world through my books . . .

Fade on flashback area, light comes up on cell area. JUANA *sits on one of the boxes holding a book.*

JUANA: Oh, I know what You think of me, God! A hypocrite—is that what You think I was? No, no, You simply loved me. And I? I forgot about You! Do You hear? Not even in the silence of the church, kneeling before You, feeling my love for Jesus, did I doubt myself. How funny it seems now—when I understand it all. St. Jerome was never a haven from the world. I simply brought the world to St. Jerome. That was another world, a world now lost. Father Antonio knew—from the very first he warned me. During my novitiate, he was troubled by all the gifts, the plans, the privileges given to me. The bookshelves that were built for me right here in this cell, the fine furniture, the rugs, all this bothered him so! But I was so full of joy because of the freedom I now had to learn, to study, to write. I remember the afternoon, the very eve before the taking of my vows. I remember . . . Oh, God! a hypocrite and more. There was the joy, the excitement and then what I felt that eve, that confused passion for that serious, earnest man. I tell you now, if he had not been of the Faith—if I had not planned to take the veil, I would have gone to the ends of the world with him. I loved him fiercely and silently for so long. A love more than spiritual, total, full of desire . . . I can still remember that eve . . .

Lights fade on cell area, come up on flashback area. The foyer where the Register of St. Jerome is kept. It lies on a small table. JUANA, *dressed as a novitiate (simple grey gown, white cloth covering hair) enters, leading* FATHER ANTONIO *by the hand.*

JUANA: It's dark in here. So silent. (*Notices candle on table.*) We can light that. I will need light to sign the register.

FATHER ANTONIO: (*Goes to table, lights candle.*) I still think you should do this the proper way.

JUANA: No. The Mother Superior gave me permission.

FATHER: After the Marquis persuaded her. You are spoiled!

JUANA: Why should it be a festive affair, the signing of the register? Why should there be others here? I only want you.

FATHER: You told me there was another reason.

JUANA: (*Goes to register, opens it, points to several places in the book.*) Look—all of them, entries made by novitiates—I, so and so, legitimate daughter of . . . I, so and so, legitimate daughter of . . . See—all of them. I cannot claim the father who sired me. He never claimed me, did not marry my mother . . . What shall I do?

FATHER: How you sign it is of little importance.

JUANA: Legitimate daughter of . . . a lie.

FATHER: Only the keeping of your vows matters. You shall vow to live in poverty, to own nothing, to live in obedience . . . What I have seen—gifts, privileges . . .

JUANA: Don't scold! I shall bring honor to St. Jerome.

FATHER: I do not doubt that. What about your own salvation?

JUANA: Knowledge will be my path to salvation. I do not have your humility. Your whole life—feeding the hungry, healing the sick. You love the poor so!

FATHER: And you love the rich Spaniards so!

JUANA: They are my friends and I am grateful for what they've done for me. Let's not quarrel. It is you I love the most. Look at you! (*Touches his forehead to erase the frown on his face.*) There! That's better.

FATHER: I always give in to you, don't I? You are a beautiful bird, singing as it flies. You do not touch the earth . . .

JUANA: Oh, Father, what's important is that you will never leave me. You will help me be what you want me to be . . .

FATHER: What God wants you to be . . .

JUANA: At this moment—what you want me to be . . .

FATHER: Daughter . . .

JUANA: And you? More than father—brother, lover . . .

FATHER: Juana . . .

JUANA: I'm not saying sinful things. My heart says this and I merely speak it. It says you are my other self—the one still unborn . . . (*She embraces him, then goes to register, picks up pen, and writes as she speaks.*) I, Sor Juana Inés de la Cruz, legitimate daughter of Don Pedro de Asbaje y Vargas Machuca and Isabel Ramírez, for the love of Our Father, the Virgin Mary, and our glorious Pastor, St. Jerome, and Our Mother, St. Paula, choose and promise God, Our Father, and His Grace, Don Antonio de Cárdenas y Salazar, canon of this *catedral*, provisional judge of the archbishopric in whose hands I profess in the name of the Honorable Francisco Payo de Ribera, Bishop of Guatemala, Archbishop of Mexico, and all his successors, living and dying in my time, in the space of my life, to live in obedience, in poverty, owning nothing, promising chastity and accepting perpetual confinement, as is the rule of Our Father, St. Augustine and the rule of our Order. I sign my name in Faith the 24th of February, 1669. (*Puts pen down, turns to* FATHER ANTONIO.) Father . . .

FATHER: Yes, my daughter . . .

JUANA: One candle to light the darkness. So many shadows!

FATHER: Don't be afraid. Tomorrow, all will be light.

JUANA: How many days did you spend in the cellar making all those luminaires?

FATHER: They line all the gardens and the path to the church and surround the church. They will light up the whole of Mexico City. This very eve, they will be lighted. In all God's brightness, Satan cannot come to tempt you!

JUANA: May God make me saintly . . . (*Blows out candle. Lights fade out on flashback area. Total darkness. Singing begins.*

[*Baroque Spanish Mass.*] *Lights come up on flashback area again. A kneeling pew covered by white cloth is at center. Music—the benediction. An* ALTAR BOY *appears with cushion holding crown and ring. He is followed by the* CANON. ALTAR BOY *crosses up center,* CANON *to right of kneeling pew.* CANON *prays over crown and ring, blesses them.* JUANA, *dressed as a bride, enters, crosses to kneeling pew, kneels before* CANON. [*For simple staging: procession could be included with convent nuns.*] *After* JUANA *kneels, the* CANON *holds the gold crown over her head.*)

CANON: Come, bride of Christ, and receive the crown that God prepared for you all through eternity.

JUANA: All my days I shall follow the angel of Our Father who is the Tabernacle of my body. I renounce the kingdom of the world and its vanities for the love of Jesus Christ whom I saw, whom I love, whom I believe, and whom I made the object of my predilection. I am His servant and I shall serve Him humbly. (*The crown is removed. The* CANON *places the ring of Fidelity on* JUANA's *finger.*)

CANON: On your finger I place the distinct pledge of the Holy Spirit. Thus you are named the wife of God. (*Choir voices rise in final benediction as lights dim at the end of Act I.*)

ACT TWO

⟨decorative glyphs⟩

SCENE 1

The next evening. Rosary bell is heard. JUANA, *sitting cross-legged in bed, wearing a sackcloth wrapper, is playing a flute very softly, awkwardly, stopping every so often to touch it. She stops to listen to church bell, then covers face with hands. A tray of untouched food sits on one of the boxes.* SOR FELICIANA *enters, crosses to tray, inspects it.* JUANA *puts flute under pillow.*

SOR FELICIANA: You didn't touch your food.

SOR JUANA: I drank my tea. Stopped the shivering . . .

SOR FELICIANA: (*Crosses to bed, touches* SOR JUANA's *forehead.*) You're still feverish. Did you sleep?

SOR JUANA: I don't want to sleep—I don't want to dream.

SOR FELICIANA: (*Sits on bed next to* SOR JUANA.) I wanted to spend the day with you. We went out for wood and had such problems!

SOR JUANA: There's no more coal?

SOR FELICIANA: Supply wagons cannot get into the city. They're ambushed by the people up on the mountain. No fruits or meat . . .

SOR JUANA: They're starving, those people up on the mountain. They need the food more than we do. It's all so different, so terrifying. (*Crosses to window.*) Look, out there, the *locutorio*, silent, dark. Over a year now. Is the whole world like that now?

SOR FELICIANA: They're all dark now, all the *locutorios* of Mexico. Don't you remember? The Commissary of the Inquisition decided on that long before the burning of the city. I hear they are dark all over Spain too.

SOR JUANA: Sinful. Isn't that what the *locutorios* are supposed to be? And my plays? And all the festivals for the saints? I believe it now. My whole life was sinful . . .

SOR FELICIANA: That's not the truth, Sor Juana. The *locutorio* of St. Jerome, thanks to you, was the spiritual center for the devout. Great people, great minds, gathered out there. They all found a path to your door. You have always been faithful to the precepts of St. Jerome, to knowledge.

SOR JUANA: Faithful to knowledge, but not to my vows . . .

SOR FELICIANA: You're never going to get well with all that guilt inside of you. You never did anything wrong. You, of all people, the most gentle, the most wise.

SOR JUANA: I miss the garden so. Where there were flowers, there are turnips now. But we cannot eat flowers, can we . . .

SOR FELICIANA: After rosary services, I'm coming back with hot soup, and you're going to eat it. I'm going to make you. Food, rest will get you well . . .

SOR JUANA: You think so? I wonder where he is right now . . .

SOR FELICIANA: Who?

SOR JUANA: My confessor, my tormentor . . .

SOR FELICIANA: The last I heard, Father Antonio was leading a wagon train with food and medicine for the starving of Zacatecas. No harvest there.

SOR JUANA: Always with the poor, the sick, the hungry. But he knows how to gain Heaven, on earth as well. I didn't understand before, but now I wish I had spent my life the way he has. But he's so old. He shouldn't travel long distances any more. If only I could see him, talk to him one more time . . .

SOR FELICIANA: Oh, dear Aunt, you will see him. Sor Catarina has sent for him.

SOR JUANA: But he was forbidden to ever see me again.

SOR FELICIANA: That won't stop him if he knows you have been ill.

SOR JUANA: Oh, dear God, thank you for the hope! Days will be good again just waiting for him! (*Rosary bell rings again.*)

SOR FELICIANA: (*Kisses* SOR JUANA, *crosses to door.*) I must go now, but I'll be back after services. (*Exits.*)

SOR JUANA: (*Crosses to window.*) I miss the flowers so!

Light fades on cell, comes up on flashback area. A table down right; a chair with a flower basket full of bouquets next to it. SOR JUANA *enters with a handful of cut ribbons;* SOR FELICIANA *follows. St. Jerome has been the home of* SOR JUANA *for seventeen years. She wears a tunic of white wool, blue-edged, double-sleeved. Outside sleeve is bell-shaped, giving a certain elegance to the habit. Over the tunic is a long black scapulary (two small slips of cloth almost the length of the tunic underneath). The scapulary is six inches shorter than the tunic. On the front piece of the scapulary is an image over the chest area. Emblem of the Annunciation, the Virgin*

Mary standing to the right of a recliner where a book lies open. The left hand of the Virgin lies on the book. Opposite the Virgin, on the other side of the recliner, is the imprint of the Archangel Gabriel with folded white wings. On her head, SOR JUANA *wears a white toque and over that a long black veil. On her waist is a wide leather belt with a brass buckle. On her feet, plain black closed shoes and cotton stockings. Around her neck and falling parallel to the scapulary is a black rosary (fifteen mysteries). The large gold cross of the rosary is adjusted high on the left sleeve of her tunic. The habit of the Order of St. Jerome.* SOR JUANA *and* SOR FELICIANA *put a ribbon around each of the bouquets. A children's choir begins to sing as they go about their labor.*

> Aquella zagala
> Del mirar sereno
> Hechizo del soto
> Y envidia del cielo
>
> La que el mayoral
> De la cumbre excelso
> Hirió con sus ojos
> Hirió con sus ojos . . .

Harmony without lyrics is heard.

SOR FELICIANA: The legend of the nymph. How beautiful, your words, your music.

SOR JUANA: My farewell gift for Lisi. The nymph that disappears in light. Oh, why must the people we love leave us . . .

> La ninfa del valle
> Donde nací
> Vuela, bailando
> La escala de luz
>
> En alta peñasca
> Donde tiembla el sol
> Canta la ninfa
> Canta, canta
> Con voz celestial.

SOR FELICIANA: There. All done. After they sing, each child will offer a bouquet to the Count and the Countess.

SOR JUANA: Overwhelmed by flowers. My last festivity for them. They love this garden so, dear Count, dearest Lisi . . .

SOR FELICIANA: Dr. Pavón is due any minute now . . .

SOR JUANA: Oh dear, I forgot all about the interview. I suppose I must find the time since I said I would, but I do have so many preparations yet for the festivities tomorrow.

SOR FELICIANA: Would you like to see him here in the garden?

SOR JUANA: Yes, send him out here.

SOR FELICIANA exits. SOR JUANA notices her slave.

SOR JUANA: There you are. Go tell Timoteo I would like the chairs set up this afternoon. A canopy over the Count and Countess' chair . . .

SLAVE JUANA: Mistress . . .

SOR JUANA: Let's see. I've taken care of the pastries, the chocolate came in from Chiapas. The Count's favorite wine must be chilled. And more flowers—of course, I must see to the flowers. (*Notices her slave.*) Go, girl, do as I say.

SLAVE JUANA: You said I could go and see Andrés.

SOR JUANA: What?

SLAVE JUANA: You forgot about Andrés . . .

SOR JUANA: Oh, I'm sorry. It did slip my mind. How is he? You saw him yesterday?

SLAVE JUANA: He beat bad. He and Camila hide. I go take them food.

SOR JUANA: You must be careful not to implicate yourself . . .

SLAVE JUANA: He my brother.

SOR JUANA: What he did is considered a most serious crime. He has run away from Don Martín many times before, but this time he turned on his master. That is a serious crime. Have you heard? Is Don Martín dead?

SLAVE JUANA: Don Martín evil man. Good if he die.

SOR JUANA: May God forgive Andrés . . .

SLAVE JUANA: And you . . .

SOR JUANA: Juana!

SLAVE JUANA: I beg you buy Andrés away from Don Martín . . .

SOR JUANA: You know I spoke to him about it, again and again. A stubborn man—a slave is a slave to him.

SLAVE JUANA: The Count, the Countess, your friends—they could make him. They are important people. They could force Don Martín . . .

SOR JUANA: You don't know what you're talking about. It's a delicate subject. There are certain unspoken rules about a master and his slaves. I cannot take sides.

SLAVE JUANA: You forgot Andrés was like your brother long ago.

SOR JUANA: I have not forgotten. But that was long ago. It's a different world.

SLAVE JUANA: You not love Andrés. You not care. Andrés and Camila go to mountain where people hide. Soon they will fight!

SOR JUANA: Fight? That is only fearful talk. It will not come to that.

SLAVE JUANA: You do not see because your nose in book all the time.

SOR JUANA: Enough. If only all men were equal. Perhaps some day this will be, through the help of God, knowledge . . .

SLAVE JUANA: Your head stuffed with words, Sister. Pretty, silly words, Sister.

SOR JUANA: How dare you . . .

SLAVE JUANA: You say I is like your sister.

SOR JUANA: You are also my slave.

SLAVE JUANA: Then why you say we is equal?

SOR JUANA: Go to Andrés. Help him as best you can. Tell him I will pray for him.

SLAVE JUANA: Many starve on mountain.

SOR JUANA: I will pray for them too.

SLAVE JUANA: That will not fill their bellies.

SOR JUANA: Prayer moves mountains . . .

SLAVE JUANA: Don't move mountain. Just give more food.

SOR JUANA: I said enough! Now go.

SLAVE JUANA: (*Turns to go, then stops.*) Andrés and Camila will not come back this time. They will not be caught. They have wagon and gun.

SOR JUANA: May God keep them safe. (*Watches* SLAVE JUANA *go, puts hand to forehead as if head hurts.*) Why must the world change so? I remember slaves singing at the plow. But I was a child then. I cannot bridge the years anymore. Oh my, I must see to those flowers . . . (SOR FELICIANA *enters with* DR. IGNACIO PAVON, *a Peruvian poet who has come from Lima to interview* SOR JUANA.)

SOR FELICIANA: Sor Juana, this is Dr. Ignacio Pavón. He has come all the way from Lima, Peru, just to interview you.

DR. PAVON: Sor Juana Inés de la Cruz, a great honor. (*Kisses her hand.*)

SOR JUANA: Dr. Pavón.

SOR FELICIANA: You'll forgive me. I have duties to attend to.

DR. PAVON: Thank you for leading me to this garden and to this great lady.

SOR FELICIANA: Goodbye, Dr. Pavón. (*Exits.*)

SOR JUANA: You have caught me in the midst of preparations—a farewell party for the Count of Paredes and his wife, Lisi.

DR. PAVON: I am intruding . . .

SOR JUANA: Oh, no, please! This is the perfect time. I need someone to cheer me up. A poet, you are!

DR. PAVON: A humble one in the light of your great fame. Beautiful place, St. Jerome.

SOR JUANA: My home for seventeen years.

DR. PAVON: Fruitful years.

SOR JUANA: They have not been idle. May I offer you some refreshment?

DR. PAVON: Not at the moment, thank you. I have come across an ocean to set eyes on the Tenth Muse.

SOR JUANA: So, I am pursued into pagan temples! My church is Christ's church.

DR. PAVON: In your writings, you have given that Christian humanity to the pagans. You cannot deny you love the Greeks.

SOR JUANA: The Greeks are the open door to our humanity. Tell me of your work, your country.

DR. PAVON: What does a poet do? I'm a man coiled in his own passions, unwinding, discovering, and sometimes, and mind you only sometimes, attempting to re-create with words some kind of energy lost in my people. A sad attempt to remold our poor misguided civilization.

SOR JUANA: Unwinding passions—how beautifully you put it. We are creatures of passion, are we not? Writers! What a lot we are!

DR. PAVON: All I've read by you, of you, is full of passion.

SOR JUANA: My greatest passion has been to learn and learn and learn. My way to God.

DR. PAVON: There is, of course, your strong faith.

SOR JUANA: I shall share a secret with you.

DR. PAVON: A secret?

SOR JUANA: You journalists are always looking for something new. For a long time now, I have come to believe that my love for knowledge is much more than a passion. It's madness.

DR. PAVON: Madness? I don't understand . . .

SOR JUANA: Some time ago, a holy and candid abbess who was my superior forbad me to study. I was ordered not to read a single book. She believed that knowledge was a form of inquisition. I did as I was told. I did not study. I did not even take a book into my hands. A very difficult thing for me to do.

DR. PAVON: She had no right . . .

SOR JUANA: Oh yes, she did! She was a most holy abbess. She was true to her vows. She lived by faith alone. Her path to God was different from my own. Well, when I could no longer read, I found myself overwhelmed by a curiosity. I studied the things that God created, all around me—little things. One morning walking through the doorway ot my bedroom, I observed that though the lines of the two sides of the hall were parallel and its ceiling was level, the eye pretended that its lines leaned toward each other and that its ceiling was lower in the distant part. I inferred that visual lines run straight, but not parallel, forming a pyramid figure. I told myself that was the reason the ancients doubted that the earth was spherical. But then I told myself it could be a trick of the eyesight. Thoughts came like this one, one after another, day after day. It was like a fever consuming me. More than a passion.

DR. PAVON: But such journeys of the mind are exciting.

SOR JUANA: My mind would not rest. I remember watching the little girls we teach here at St. Jerome playing with a top one day. I noticed the easy movement of the spherical form and how long the impulse lasted once it was independent of its cause. I ran to the kitchen and took a handful of flour. I sifted it on a table, then took the top and spun it on the table. I spun it thus to see if the circles made by its movements were perfectly circular or not. I discovered that only some spiral lines lost their circularity as soon as they transmitted their impulse. Then to my mind came the thought that in the study of music, harmony is circular. A spiral! Such thoughts invaded my mind, invade my mind still these days, though I now spend long hours reading, experimenting. God wants me to understand my universe. Did you know I had been accused of heresy for doing what I do? The Bishop of Puebla does not approve of me. They would like me to study more of the sacred theology. Little do they know that both can be reconciled . . .

DR. PAVON: You have found a way . . .

SOR JUANA: Of course! Without Rhetoric, how could I understand the figures, the tropes, the locution of the Holy Scripture? Or, without Physics, how could I understand the many natural problems of the nature of sacrificial animals? Without Arithmetic, could I understand the computations of days, months, hours, weeks as mysteries, as were those of Daniel? How without Geometry could I measure the Holy Chest of the Testament and even the Holy City of Jerusalem, whose mysteries thus measured form a cube? All those dimensions! And the marvelous distribution of all its parts! Without Architecture, how could I understand the Great Temple of Solomon? God Himself was the Architect who gave the disposition and plan. The Wise King was only the foreman who executed it. They accuse me of loving knowledge more than God.

Light fades out on flashback area, comes up on cell area. SOR JUANA is still by the window, looking out. She suddenly turns, crosses to bed, takes out flute from under the pillow. Plays a few notes softly, then touches it tenderly.

SOR JUANA: You gave this to me, Andrés. Your one possession. You and Juana said goodbye forever. Yes, it was forever! We were children, free . . . (*She plays a few more notes, then hugs flute, crosses to window again.*) Oh, God, are You out there in the hovels where children cry of hunger? Are You out there in the ashes that were the marketplace, where the hanging tree sways with the wind? Are You here, with me and my pain? No! I want to remember happy times. The garden full of people and laughter . . . the last party we ever had in the garden. The very last one. Even then the sounds of a wounded world, heavy with pain, hung in the air . . .

Light fades on cell area, comes up on flashback area. There are three chairs, very ornate under a canopy. The center chair is raised slightly above the others. A single ordinary chair is outside the canopy. SOR JUANA is seated on the raised chair. The COUNT DE PAREDES sits to her right. LISI, his wife, sits to her left. DR. PAVON sits on the single chair outside the canopy.

LISI: I shall remember this day. The children were lovely, all our friends so kind! I hate to say goodbye to Mexico.

COUNT: I too shall miss Mexico, though I confess the Mexico outside these walls is not to my liking. The Indian, the sambo, has forgotten the good we have brought to this new world. We civilized a primitive people. Now they turn against us.

DR. PAVON: I equate civilization with violence, M'Lord. The white man has been less than a humanizing force.

COUNT: Did you hear about Don Rafael Martín? Attacked by one of his slaves. Found unconscious in the granary.

SOR JUANA: Will he die?

COUNT: He'll recover, but two slaves are gone, his wagon, his horse, and stores from his warehouse. Who is safe these days!

SOR JUANA: Humane masters, perhaps. Don Martín treats his slaves like animals.

COUNT: Do you condone the crime?

SOR JUANA: I don't condone crime, but all circumstances must be understood before the word "crime" is given to a single desperate act.

COUNT: Those runaway slaves have a good head start into mountain country. Don Martín's soldiers gave up the chase. I suppose you're glad the two slaves escaped. I'm afraid the mountains have their own merciless bondage. They may starve, freeze to death, become the prey of wild animals.

SOR JUANA: May God protect them and keep them safe.

COUNT: Would you say the same prayer for Don Martín?

SOR JUANA: There is no need. He is surrounded by comfort and care.

LISI: M'Lord, let's enjoy our last visit to St. Jerome. Oh, the memories I take with me—music, laughter, brilliant conversation. Sor Juana drawing, quoting her poetry, or passionate over a new scientific finding. Sor Juana, the center of our lives . . . I shall miss you so, dear friend.

COUNT: We should not be at odds, Sor Juana. I know you love us well. Ah, the peace of this place. Such flowers!

SOR JUANA: I shall miss you both. Six years. I've known you and loved you both for six years. And you have done so much good, M'Lord.

COUNT: I hope that during my reign I made the right decisions. I tried to. I pride myself in being a man in touch with the times. But dreams erode. The world is full of wolf packs and each great nation in time falls victim.

SOR JUANA: Ah, Dr. Pavón. There is much to say about His Excellency. He has been a compassionate ruler, just and right as if he were born to be nothing less.

DR. PAVON: I have heard the like said of him. But you are right, dear Count, the wolf packs are growing. When I arrived in Vera Cruz, a French pirate ship had gone into Acapulco and carried off forty women.

COUNT: The Gulf is infested. Another problem for the new viceroy.

DR. PAVON: Ah yes! Count Monclova is a favorite of the Peruvian court. Has an arm made of silver. Lost it in a naval battle. For many years he was the companion of Her Excellency, the Vicereine of Peru. He carries a gold casket aboard his ship. It's said to be full of gold and diamonds and a bone belonging to St.

Rose of Lima. It is his protection against pirates. He will rule with a silver arm . . . preferable to ruling with an iron hand, eh? (*Laughs.*)

LISI: Alas, he has no wife. No one to lead him to this wonderful place. I daresay he will come to meet you, Sor Juana, and will attend one of your gatherings in the *locutorio.*

SOR JUANA: I fear it will not be so. There is the weight of too much criticism—of me, of St. Jerome, of *locutorios* in general. It can only get worse.

LISI: You have our protection even from across the sea.

SOR JUANA: I know it and I thank you.

LISI: Whatever happens, your work will be published. I'm taking all you have ever written to a publisher in Madrid.

SOR JUANA: They are the only children I have conceived. Imperfect, but they are yours . . .

LISI: They shall belong to the world . . . (*Light fades on flashback area, comes up on cell.* SOR JUANA *sits on bed and begins to play flute. Stage slowly darkens.*)

SCENE 2

The next afternoon. SOR JUANA *and* SOR FELICIANA *are standing over the boxes.*

SOR JUANA: I want all articles and letters in this small box. Books in the large one.

SOR FELICIANA: Are you up to doing this?

SOR JUANA: Of course I am. Look at me. You fed me last night. I ate everything this morning. My fever's gone—and Father Antonio might come today. It's Wednesday, isn't it? He always came for tea on Wednesdays when he was in the city, remember?

SOR FELICIANA: Don't set your hopes too high . . .

SOR JUANA: It's a beautiful day, isn't it? Anyway, let's put all these things away. Once everything is put away I shall feel that I have turned another page in my life, and the page is clean, waiting for new experiences. We shall bury these things deep in the dungeon of this convent . . .

SOR FELICIANA: There's no dungeon . . .

SOR JUANA: Very well. We shall store them somewhere dark where spiders can build their webs. I do not want my past.

SOR FELICIANA: I see your guilt did not disappear with the fever.

SOR JUANA: He will never recognize this place. I don't even have a table to serve tea! I must have a table . . .

SOR FELICIANA: We'll find one if he comes . . .

SOR JUANA: Of course he's going to come. Let's start with this box. (*She kneels on floor and starts taking books and papers from a box to sort them. Comes across a copy of her love sonnets. She turns the pages.*)

SOR FELICIANA: What's that?

SOR JUANA: Poems . . .

SOR FELICIANA: May I? (SOR JUANA *hands book to her.*) Your sonnets! How beautiful.

SOR JUANA: Not now . . .

SOR FELICIANA: Wait! (*She begins to read.*) "Love begins, a faint restlessness, a burning wakeful anxiety, growing in slopes, transsections, feeding on tears, entreaty . . ."

SOR JUANA: Ancient, ancient feelings.

SOR FELICIANA: Your feelings?

SOR JUANA: All mine. The pain of youth . . .

SOR FELICIANA: (*Continues reading.*) "Love, shadow of my scornful good, bewitched image, fair illusion for which I'd gladly die, sweet confection, for which I live in torment . . ."

SOR JUANA: They sound so awkward—such rash feelings.

SOR FELICIANA: Someone hurt you very much.

SOR JUANA: We suffer so when we are young. The howls of my pain.

SOR FELICIANA: Is that why you took the veil?

SOR JUANA: Who knows one's reasons for doing those things that change one's life? What comes to mind is a childhood memory. There was a mulatto on my grandfather's farm, a misshapen man, an idiot, they used to say. Even as a child I could read the hurting loneliness in his eyes by the way he walked and held his head. Poor creature! One morning when the dark was dissolving, I followed him out into the desert wondering what he did out there so early in the morning. He ran to the middle of a sand hill. The wind moaned and the dust curled under his feet. He held up his arms as if pleading with the morning sky, then fell to his knees. Suddenly he raised his head and howled. Just howled— a long, sad, empty sound that ran into the stillness of the sun. That was his loneliness, his pain. He freed himself of the heavy cutting burden, to face the day.

SOR FELICIANA: How sad. What happened to him?

SOR JUANA: He disappeared. I always imagined he had walked off into the desert and found a place where he was like everyone else. Those words are just the way I howl . . .

SOR FELICIANA: Your sensitive, beautiful words?

SOR JUANA: Why not? The writing of those sonnets washed me clean. The anger, doubt. bitterness. all washed away.

SOR FELICIANA: Who was he?

SOR JUANA: A young nobleman, foolish and unwise, no different from myself.

SOR FELICIANA: It must have been so painful . . .

SOR JUANA: The grave agony that begins with desire, then that sudden rushing melancholy, evaporating contradictions. Those are the contradictions.

SOR FELICIANA: (*Reading through the pages.*) You speak of deception, again and again. (*Reads.*) "Triumph, my love, you who kills me with disdain. And he who loves me, I myself, kill, for he loves in vain. I do not know if love is hate, or hate is love, for both are fires that prick the skin and move the heart and sweeten all the air . . ."

SOR JUANA: He will come today. I know he will . . .

SOR FELICIANA: It's not a certainty.

SOR JUANA: I am not at my best . . . my wool tunic, the blue-edged one—the embroidered scapulary, the one from Spain . . . Look at me—so disheveled . . .

SOR FELICIANA: All you have is what you're wearing.

SOR JUANA: How stupid of me! I forgot. Is there some tea left in the kitchen? Just a little . . . (*Looks around room.*) He will be shocked, the way I look, the room—so empty, bare . . .

SOR FELICIANA: You sold everything. Do you regret it? All your beautiful things, your books, your instruments.

SOR JUANA: No! There's no regret. My empty cell will please Father Antonio. It vexed him so, my having all those luxuries. May God forgive me! Is it three o'clock? He always came at three . . . so punctual!

SOR FELICIANA: It's closer to five.

SOR JUANA: Five . . . No! Sister Catarina sent for him. It's been two weeks now.

SOR FELICIANA: We have not received word as to his whereabouts. The fact that it's Wednesday doesn't mean . . .

SOR JUANA: I wanted him to come today. I need him to help me creep out of this darkness. Never mind the books. We'll see to them later. I'll watch for him at the window

SOR FELICIANA: Do you want me to watch with you?

SOR JUANA: No. Go about your business. Thank you. I'd rather sit here by myself.

SOR FELICIANA: I'll check on the tea—just in case . . .

SOR JUANA: Yes, yes—do that.

SOR FELICIANA: (*Crosses to exit, turns.*) I'll stop by after supper. (SOR JUANA, *staring out into the garden, doesn't answer.* SOR FELICIANA *leaves.*)

SOR JUANA: I have cast off pride, possessions, so my flight to Heaven will not be cumbersome. Oh, Father, you were right! Knowledge more easily breeds arrogance than it does humility. Oh, Father Antonio, I know myself now! I've opened the door to the prison I created. It's not a blind creature you will see before you . . . No more . . .

Light fades on cell, comes up on flashback area. There is a statue of the Virgin Mary backing a font of holy water. To the left is a confessional. SOR JUANA *comes out of the confessional, crosses herself, goes to font, dips fingers in holy water, crosses herself again.* FATHER ANTONIO *comes out of the confessional.* SOR JUANA *turns, hands reaching out to welcome her confessor.*

SOR JUANA: My prayers of penitence can wait!

FATHER ANTONIO: You are forgiven, my child.

SOR JUANA: Trees are blooming, and the last time I saw you I was worried about the frostbite on your nose. (*Touches his face after looking at it intently.*) There are tired lines around your mouth. You are too old for long trips over mountains! Where were you?

FATHER: Manzana. I found a miracle there. (*Takes out folded printed sheet from pocket, hands it to* SOR JUANA.) See . . .

SOR JUANA: (*Unfolding sheet.*) My mysteries! I wrote them a long time ago. Where did you find them? Manzana—an Indian village, isn't it?

FATHER: Isolated, and now its people are dying of the plague like flies. I exhausted all my energies, not fighting for peoples' lives, but preparing them for Heaven. The last rites become swollen ritual words in my mouth. So many! One night, they forced me to rest and gave me a fish for supper. I sat down at a table, too weary to protest, and unwrapped my fish. There it was—your mysteries.

SOR JUANA: Someone wrapped a fish with it?

FATHER: There it was, your name, your words, at a time like that! I forgot my hunger and fatigue. I read your prayer by a wavering flame in the cold room—your fourth mystery to the Virgin Mary. It made me new. I read it again and again and held it in my hand while I slept. A miracle.

SOR JUANA: These were distributed in the *catedral*, thousands of them, two years ago. This one fell into your hands . . . and all those months I longed for you so, imagined you falling off a horse, or getting sick. There was no more waiting at the gate for you, and somehow days became blurred and empty.

FATHER: When there is time to breathe or rest, you are in my thoughts too.

SOR JUANA: But my prayers have been answered. I hear you were recalled by the bishop. I heard the Tribunal had reprimanded you for neglecting your duties as an officer of the Inquisition. You have been ordered to remain in Mexico City and I'm glad, glad, glad!

FATHER: I doubt that you are glad about my misfortune.

SOR JUANA: It isn't that to me! Someone younger, with more energies, can take your place with those people.

FATHER: How little you understand. North of Coahuila—immolation—anger against the God we gave them. Their most insane pagan god is better to them than the God given to them by the Conquistadores.

SOR JUANA: They have lost the Way . . .

FATHER: I'm not so sure. I have been one of them for too long not to understand their anger and their fear.

SOR JUANA: All that I care about is that you're safe and that you're here and that I shall see you often.

FATHER: How blind you are, my daughter. The palace, the convent, that is not the world—nor those books that consume your life.

SOR JUANA: I know that these are rebellious times.

FATHER: How well you mouth the words of your masters.

SOR JUANA: My masters!

FATHER: For almost two decades you have spent your life writing, singing the praises of the masters. *Villancicos* for a long parade of viceroys, vicereines—loas and sonnets about the Spanish great. Your praises have been bountiful for those who have conquered your people, exploited them.

SOR JUANA: They are my friends. They are the only world I know . . .

FATHER: Have you forgotten your beginnings? You are mejicana!

SOR JUANA: I will not take sides! I dream, I hope for, I work for the brotherhood of all men . . .

FATHER: What substance is there in the words you write, the ideas you express, when in this very city you hear the sad songs of the zambo slaves living in the hovels behind the rich man's house? The cry of women whose children are in pain because of hunger? Look upon the earth to find your Heaven, child. It is not in pretty words.

SOR JUANA: Why do I wait for you with such eagerness? There is no peace between us.

FATHER: Have you made peace with yourself?

SOR JUANA: I do not know what you mean. I just confessed my sins to you. You have absolved me . . .

FATHER: Oh, the triviality of your sins! You're not even aware of your sins!

SOR JUANA: You don't love me! You take such pleasure in trying to destroy what I believe . . .

FATHER: What you believe! It's what you *are* that's important. Look to your own people.

SOR JUANA: What would you have me be?

FATHER: In Fresnillo, where I was born, there is a dry, brittle shrub that clings ferociously to life. Its roots dig into the sand, the hostile sun violates. The tempestuous wind twists the shrub, strips it, wounds it, until it structures itself against its own nature, pulling away, pushing away, just to stay alive, just to survive. Its thorns, empty of the milk of hope, prick your finger. The shrub shrivels up against the violence around. That is the Mexican today—the Indian—the zambo slave. My spirit is like that shrub, my soul, my passions. I am a Mexican, so I fight! I beg money off the rich, I hide the fugitive, I scramble around for food and medicine, because their hunger, their pain, their enslavement, their deaths wound me, consume me . . .

SOR JUANA: I feel with you, but you must understand—I fight the same struggle. My voice carries all over, my words of love, compassion, brotherhood, peace . . .

FATHER: I'm speaking of human beings—not words!

SOR JUANA: You refuse to understand!

FATHER: And you refuse to see! (*Light fades on flashback area, comes up on cell area.* SOR JUANA *is still by window.*)

SOR JUANA: He's not coming. He may never come. (*She crosses to a box on the floor and rummages through it desperately until she finds a packet of letters. She looks through them until she finds the one she is looking for. It is a letter written to her by one Sor Filotea de la Cruz. She stares at it, then crumbles it in her hand.*) They deceived me with this! Conspiracy! The Holy Company against one lone woman. Cowards! (*She begins to sob.*) They took him away from me . . . they took him away from me . . . (*Light fades on cell area, comes up on flashback area. May 1691. The Bishopric in the diocese of* BISHOP DON MIGUEL FERNANDO DE SANTA CRUZ, *in Puebla.* BISHOP *is sitting behind desk, looking at three documents. A published postulate written by a renowned Jesuit, Father Antonio Vieira, an intellectual giant, entitled* The Greater Good of Jesus. *The second document is a letter written by* SOR JUANA *as an answer to the third document, supposedly a letter written by one Filotea de la Cruz, Convent of the Holy Trinity.* FATHER JUAN IGNACIO, *the* BISHOP's *secretary, enters.*)

BISHOP: We have a problem.

JUAN IGNACIO: You speak of Sor Juana Inés de la Cruz.

BISHOP: Precisely. Hostile forces within the Church and outside the Church are shifting and changing to create dissension. As the Bishop of Puebla, it is my duty to maintain some kind of balance.

JUAN IGNACIO: I understand, Your Holiness.

BISHOP: Don Francisco Aguiar y Seijas has changed the face of Mexico.

JUAN IGNACIO: Our esteemed Archbishop has seen to it that all comedies in print be burned and has successfully replaced his most holy book among the faithful, Consolations for the Poor . . .

BISHOP: You can imagine what he thinks of Sor Juana's pagan plays! Mexico shall be well rid of impure customs, sinfulness. Sor Juana may find herself in the Index one of these days. When our Archbishop first came to Mexico six years ago, he found a country beset by vices, devoid of virtues . . . The time has come for great piety among the faithful. Festivities in the Church have been abolished, convent *locutorios* are now closed. You would think Sor Juana would see the light, but her pen has not stopped. And her latest—her criticism of Vieira—that is too much for the Holy Company to endure. A hornet's nest . . .

JUAN IGNACIO: Of course! Her Athenagoric letter. It has caused a sensation. She claims it was not meant to be published.

BISHOP: I had it published. I also called it, appropriately, the Athenagoric Letter. Rather well titled, wouldn't you say?

JUAN IGNACIO: A clever insinuation on your part. She does love the Greeks. It's there, in all she writes. She is an Athena . . .

BISHOP: I assumed that if I had it published, she would be proved a fool! She is a fool! How dare she criticize the postulate of the most brilliant of Jesuits!

JUAN IGNACIO: There is no greater Catholic Predicator than Father Antonio Vieira.

BISHOP: The audacity of that woman! A man of the world! One who has mingled with great minds! To find himself opposed by this upstart—a nun with a parochial mind! He must be highly amused.

JUAN IGNACIO: A great part of the public is siding with Sor Juana.

BISHOP: I simply cannot believe—refuse to believe—that the ravings of a simple-minded maid should be preferred over the subtle discernment of the Holy Scripture in Vieira's argument. But then, Vieira's views are beyond common intelligence.

JUAN IGNACIO: A great man.

BISHOP: A man of action too! A long service as advisor to the king of Portugal, and later, standing before his Christian pulpit in Brazil, he gave voice to the abuses of the rich. He fears not! The powerful Brazilians used their influence at the Vatican to have him censored. But he went to Rome himself and pleaded a brilliant case before the Pope. Even the Pope gave in . . . Vieira went back to Brazil with a papal order in his pocket exempting him from the jurisdiction of the Grand Inquisitor. Vieira's postulate questions the old dogmas. So, no one agrees with him. They dare not! And many just simply cannot grasp the brilliance of his concepts. Then came Sor Juana with a rehash of old stale beliefs—the kind that people cling to. That woman is a parrot. Oh, she praises with rhetorical passion. She loves, she discusses, she reasons, she exalts . . . then, there's that curious humility in her words—so female. How dare she! A mere—mere . . .

JUAN IGNACIO: Woman. Your plan didn't work, then. When both arguments were published side by side, she was not discredited.

BISHOP: The public applauds her! This cannot be forgiven. That *gongorina* feeds the reading public the fare they prefer. I should have foreseen it. Vieira's postulate on the "greater good of Jesus" makes people uncomfortable. The greater good, he forwards, is God's deliberate absence from Mankind. That is a shocking idea to the ordinary layman or the ordinary churchman. Why didn't I foresee . . .

JUAN IGNACIO: Everywhere one goes, everything one hears—well, a battle on church doctrine is well on the way.

BISHOP: She must be forced to put down her pen.

JUAN IGNACIO: I doubt that it is possible . . .

BISHOP: My dear Father, you give up too easily. I have found a way. I sent for Father Antonio Núñez de Miranda. She loves him well—too well, I'm afraid.

JUAN IGNACIO: I doubt that Father Antonio can persuade her.

BISHOP: His absence from her life might persuade her! I hear she is eager for his visits. She relies and depends on him. Off and on, they have been companions for almost a lifetime. He will come to see me this very day. In fact, I expect him now. (*Pause.*) Before he arrives, I would like to take you into my confidence regarding a delicate matter.

JUAN IGNACIO: How can I be of service . . .

BISHOP: Remember the letter I dictated to you a month or so ago? (*Goes to table, picks up letter from Sor Filotea and hands it to* JUAN IGNACIO.)

JUAN IGNACIO: I remember it well. At the time I thought it strange that you did not sign your own name to it, but used the name Sor Filotea, Convent of the Holy Trinity, Puebla de los Angeles. I know you had your reasons.

BISHOP: Very good reasons.

JUAN IGNACIO: It was a kind letter—praising Sor Juana's considerable talents, stating great affection for her.

BISHOP: I thought that if Sor Juana read the letter as from a fellow sister, a woman, she would heed the soft current of advice I offered. In the letter I urged she give up her worldly writings and return to her vows.

JUAN IGNACIO: Did she answer you?

BISHOP: Oh, yes. She sent the letter to the Convent of the Holy Trinity addressed to Sor Filotea. It was turned over to me.

JUAN IGNACIO: How did she reply?

BISHOP: See for yourself.

Crosses to table, picks up the answer to Sor Filotea written by Sor Juana, hands it to JUAN IGNACIO. *As* JUAN IGNACIO *reads the letter,* BISHOP *paces floor around his secretary.*

BISHOP: It's no use. She refused my advice. Look, pages and pages explaining her obsession—yes, I said obsession! Things of the mind control her. Oh, she is humble and apologetic. See? All a trick, I assure you. A letter of merit, I agree, but one that reveals the stubbornness of her nature. So this scheme failed. (*Pause.*)

I shall ask a favor of you. Do not mention this letter to anyone. It could prove an embarrassment . . .

There is a knock at the door. JUAN IGNACIO *opens it to* FATHER ANTONIO. JUAN IGNACIO *leaves as* FATHER ANTONIO *enters.*

BISHOP: Ah! Father Antonio—it has been a long time.

FATHER ANTONIO: Your Holiness.

BISHOP: I hope you have had a taste of our hospitality here in Puebla.

FATHER: Yes. Thank you.

BISHOP: Come, sit down. I have brought you here all the way from the capital for good reason.

FATHER: Your message said the "utmost urgency."

BISHOP: It is—and you are the only solution.

FATHER: I—am a solution?

BISHOP: The problem is Sor Juana Inés de la Cruz.

FATHER: That furor over her criticism of Viera? It's gotten out of hand. Her criticism was not meant for publication. It was her own private exercise . . .

BISHOP: She has said that of all her writing, yet it seems to get published in Madrid. Her words exercise a modesty that she does not truly have.

FATHER: I know her—and I do know her very well—to be a modest person. She has never considered what she calls her "scribblings" worthy of print.

BISHOP: You, who know her so well, believe her?

FATHER: It is not a matter of belief. Sometimes our own words belie us. What motivates her to write, to some extent, is an audience. It's a worn ritual in her life. She claims she is pressed by others to write. But her writing is her own search for God.

BISHOP: Absurd! When has this woman been true to her vows? That is the way to God!

FATHER: Hers is not an ordinary case. The world makes demands of her, the court . . . she has a genius, a talent.

BISHOP: Indeed! If this is foremost in her life, why even pretend piety? She serves not God, but the world! What happened to her vow of poverty? Where is her humility?

FATHER: The *locutorio* of St. Jerome has never made it possible. She has been a light, drawing to her the writers and intellectuals of her time. You cannot blame her for the circumstance of her fame. The church was very pleased by this not so long ago.

BISHOP: You, my dear Father Antonio, know that times have changed. The *locutorio* of St. Jerome is now closed as are all *locutorios* all over Mexico. Our Archbishop considers the frivolities that *locutorios* are famous for a mark of shame in church history.

FATHER: I doubt that history will see it thus.

BISHOP: You are a member of the Inquisition Council. You know very well the severe austerity that cloaks the Church these days. Sor Juana's horizons differ greatly from those of our Archbishop. Now—this thing with Vieira.

FATHER: It was not of her own doing. She was urged to write it.

BISHOP: Who does she blame?

FATHER: She blames no one in particular. According to her—many people. Sor Juana does not run from any labor that gives her the exercise of reason. She admires Vieira greatly. She stands in awe of his intellect.

BISHOP: I know! I know! Nevertheless, what did she do? You must admit her postulate cannot compare with Vieira's. She says nothing that has not been said before.

FATHER: I will not judge either argument. Each has its merits.

BISHOP: There is the matter of her worldly possessions. Her cell is a luxury in itself—expensive gifts, fine furniture, thousands of books! The gardens of St. Jerome are a showplace . . .

FATHER: How am I a solution to all this?

BISHOP: She is very well aware of the Church's displeasure. She is aware of her enemies, yet even after the Vieira episode, she wrote a silva for the Viceroy, Count Galve. And those new *villancicos* in honor of St. Catherine . . . She's very, very clever.

FATHER: You still have not answered my question . . .

BISHOP: In time. First, I must make you see why you are the last resort. You have read her *villancicos* on St. Catherine?

FATHER: They are pure music and her most intimate convictions.

BISHOP: They are a weapon against her censors!

FATHER: I can't believe that you . . .

BISHOP: Wait! Hear me out first. Sor Juana has many persecutors, so she claims. Did not St. Catherine suffer the great persecutions of Maximino? Sor Juana is accused of confusing the scholars of our day. Was it not the same with St. Catherine? St. Catherine, as Sor Juana puts it, was a martyr to Wisdom. Do you not agree that Sor Juana believes herself to be the same? St. Catherine was condemned to a horrible death, placed on a wheel of knives, then beheaded. But her wisdom triumphed even over her death. The angels carried her up to Moses' mountain to be buried. So our Sor Juana stands before us, the martyr, the triumphant one. Do you think she would like her own Mt. Sinai?

FATHER: It's not fair! Your whole argument is a distortion . . .

BISHOP: Very well! You do not see it my way, but on one thing you have to agree: Everything she writes has the stamp of arrogance!

FATHER: I cannot help you if you think that way . . .

BISHOP: This is an order from the Inquisition Tribunal, Father Antonio. I'm afraid it's not a matter of choice.

FATHER: What order?

BISHOP: You are forbidden to see her again. (*Lights fade on flashback area, come up on cell area.* SOR JUANA *puts down the letter, crosses to window again, looks out into the night.*)

SOR JUANA: They took you away from me. I did not believe that you would do as they ordered. Ah, but you, the true Jesuit, must obey. Why did they torture me by taking you away? That last time you warned me that my words were my own prison. Words, I told you, are all I have. Words caress me, fulfill me, warm me . . . not any more, not any more, not any more! I must not write, you said. I cannot help it, I said, I succumb, my fingers nervous, careless, to please others—imperfect scribblings. I'm only a woman incapable of changing worlds. You warned me about what was happening outside the walls of this convent: missions abandoned in the province of Coahuila—Indian uprising—multitudes hiding and starving in the mountains. I didn't want to hear about the world falling apart! I had my compass, books, pen, harp. I had conceived a world of my own in my mind. The mind knows passions, feelings, beauty, order, I said. I listen only to the reasoning dimensions of scientific laws, human poetry, philosophy, the words of God . . . a city had to burn, a brother had to die, and you left me—before I could understand. My journey is at an end, my purpose chills, but I wait. Oh, I wait for you, Father, and a tenderness grows inside of me—the resurgent language of the heart. I dare not open this window to breathe in the spring, for I would die of longing—for God? For you? It's grown so dark, I must have some light in here. (*Goes to box where candle stands, lights it.*) Your single flame is like my heart, impervious, waiting, like stars lost in the immense darkness of the sky. (*Crosses window, opens it; sounds of night birds are heard, she looks at sky.*) How silent you are! How sweet is the night! Oh, but I remember the bells! The bells that pierced the sanctuary of my world . . .

Light fades on cell, comes up on flashback area. The church bells of the whole city are ringing. On the walk leading from the garden to the chapel of the convent, SOR JUANA *waits for* SOR FELICIANA *to catch up. From a great distance the muffled sounds of shouting and screaming and the sounds of gunfire are heard. The red glow of a burning city inflames the skies. The* VICEROY's *palace, the marketplace in the Plaza Mayor, municipal buildings are on fire.*

SOR FELICIANA: Where have you been?

SOR JUANA: I was down by the gate. The sacristan from San Angel came with the latest news.

SOR FELICIANA: Has the fire been contained?

SOR JUANA: Yes, but the marketplace was burned to the ground, and the Viceroy's palace suffered from the fire too.

SOR FELICIANA: Thousands came down from the mountains, from the starving pueblos. They headed for the palace, ragged Indians, women, children . . . they came down only to beg for food.

SOR JUANA: Is it true all the houses closed their windows so as not to hear them?

SOR FELICIANA: Even at the palace. The crowd screamed for the Viceroy, then someone picked up a stone and threw it at a window when no one answered. Soon, everyone was throwing stones. Some of the starving made their way to the warehouses behind the palace, broke down the doors and took the grain. Then someone threw a torch . . .

SOR JUANA: And the Viceroy? His family?

SOR FELICIANA: They fled to the monastery of San Francisco, where they were given refuge.

SOR JUANA: The sacristan told me the Archbishop headed a procession out of the *catedral* to appeal to the crowds, calling among the faithful. They threw stones at the Archbishop, so he went back to the *catedral.*

SOR FELICIANA: The palace guard and the soldiers from the garrison opened fire on the people.

SOR JUANA: Fired among women and children? Those starving people have no weapons!

SOR FELICIANA: All the faithful in the city are being called to prayer.

SOR JUANA: Volumes and volumes and volumes of prayers.

SOR FELICIANA: Come, we must hurry . . .

SOR JUANA: The sky is red with anguish . . .

SOR FELICIANA: Come, we must not be late. (SLAVE JUANA *runs in greatly frightened, face stained with tears, falls to knees before* SOR JUANA.)

SLAVE JUANA: Sister . . .

SOR JUANA: What's wrong?

SLAVE JUANA: Andrés . . .

SOR JUANA: What about Andrés?

SLAVE JUANA: He is here, in the garden, hurt.

SOR JUANA: Blessed Mother! (*Motions for* SLAVE JUANA *to lead her to him.*)

SOR FELICIANA: Sor Juana . . .

SOR JUANA: Go on, go to prayer. I'll take care of this.

SOR FELICIANA: But, Sister . . .

SOR JUANA: Go on, I said.

> SOR JUANA *follows* SLAVE JUANA *to garden;* SOR FELICIANA *goes toward chapel.* ANDRES *lies prone on the ground.* SOR JUANA *kneels beside him, strokes his face.*

SOR JUANA: Andrés, can you hear me?

ANDRES: Yes . . .

SOR JUANA: Where is your wound? Were you shot?

ANDRES: Yes . . . my leg.

SLAVE JUANA: He tired, Sister. Soldiers chase him. He got away. We got to hide him. (SOR JUANA *looks at wound, rips worn leg of cotton pants.*)

SOR JUANA: He's bleeding still. We need something to staunch the wound.

SLAVE JUANA: My poor brother! My poor brother!

SOR JUANA: Go get some clean cloth and some wine from the cupboard. (SLAVE JUANA *is still crying.*) Did you hear me?

SLAVE JUANA: I get them—I get them. Will my brother die?

SOR JUANA: Of course not. Stop crying and hurry. (SLAVE JUANA *exits.*) Juana says soldiers were chasing you. Did they see you come here?

ANDRES: I run fast—is dark . . .

SOR JUANA: Why were they chasing you?

ANDRES: I kill soldier . . .

SOR JUANA: Why?

ANDRES: He shot Camila—she with child. He shot her in the stomach.

SOR JUANA: Oh, my God, no! (*She kisses* ANDRES' *face and holds him close.*) I'm so sorry. They went straight to Heaven, Andrés, straight to Heaven. Oh my brother, your pain is my pain . . .

ANDRES: I killed him with his own gun.

SOR JUANA: May God forgive you.

ANDRES: You not know Camila . . .

SOR JUANA: I'm sorry. But she must have been beautiful. I wish . . .

ANDRES: What you wish?

SOR JUANA: Why didn't I go to you, to your family? I feel so badly about not . . .

ANDRES: No time to cry now. That was long ago. I remember like dream. You are the little girl?

SOR JUANA: Yes, my brother. I have your flute. I still play the song you taught me . . . Forgive me, Andrés!

ANDRES: Don't cry, coya, the sky is smiling.

> SOR JUANA *holds him close, crying.* SLAVE JUANA *returns with cloth and wine.* SOR JUANA *puts bottle to* ANDRES' *lips. He drinks. She tears piece of white cloth into shreds, uses one to staunch blood, then binds the wound. She uses another piece to cleanse his face very tenderly.*

ANDRES: (*Tries to raise himself.*) I hide . . .

SLAVE JUANA: You hide him here, Sister.

SOR JUANA: Yes, yes . . . but where? I know! The main altar in the chapel. There's room there. After the service this evening we'll take you there. Now, you must stay in my room. Can you walk?

ANDRES: Yes. (*He holds on to* SLAVE JUANA *and* SOR JUANA.)

SOR JUANA: This way . . . (*There is pounding at the convent gate. The sound of a soldier's voice: "Open this gate, in the name of the Viceroy!" Someone else calls out, "Break it down. He's in there. Break it down!" Sound of hacking on wood as the two women lead* ANDRES *away.*)

> *Lights fade on flashback area. Slowly a red haze comes up on cell. The sound of a flute is heard.* SOR JUANA, *sitting on the center of cot, crosslegged, is playing the flute. She stops.*

SOR JUANA: I am without illusion now—distrusting even stars. (*Leaves bed and goes to window.*) And dreams? Persuasions of the blood. (*She plays flute as she crosses down center.*) But dreams have freed me as faith has not. That dream, that first dream, where I was one with God. I still remember the terror of my smallness. A sleeping world—my spirit leaving the vegetative state of my body. I flew to the pyramidal shadow of the earth until it came to touch the lunar sky. Ah . . . through me poured a great silence. All things were purified. I became a whirlwind. Yes! a whirlwind penetrating the immensity of Heaven. My eyes saw thousands and thousands of things, variations that confused my understanding. And I hungered so to

understand! Secrets beyond me . . . I felt the breath of God. I
knew my smallness then. Suddenly, the terror! I felt Him, my
God! (*She begins to play the flute again.*) Remember, Andrés?
My brother . . . you taught me that song when I was but a child.
They dragged you away from here and put a rope around your
neck. Your eyes were dark with fear. I saw you dangling from
the hanging tree. My eyes cannot erase it. My mind cannot
erase it. A sovereign fact, this death of yours which was . . . a
death of me. Oh, the raw concreteness of the world! The mind
is not enough, is it? Oh, I have wept loudly in the dark and felt
a copious guilt . . . And that dark, mysterious flow where no
words exist—I found it, didn't I? Faith . . .

ACT THREE

㸚㸚㸚㸚㸚

SCENE 1

1693: JUANA's *cell. There is a small table with two chairs. On the table are cups, spoons and saucers. The boxes have been cleared away.* SOR FELICIANA *is straightening out the cot as* SOR JUANA *arranges cups and saucers on table.* SOR CATARINA *comes in with teapot containing steaming tea.*

SOR CATARINA: Here you are. Mint tea. I wish it were some other kind . . .

SOR JUANA: Oh, it's fine. Thank you.

SOR CATARINA: I found a little sugar . . .

SOR JUANA: How wonderful of you!

SOR FELICIANA: (*Looks out the window.*) He's coming through the garden.

SOR JUANA: He's here? (*Goes to window.*) How old he looks!

SOR CATARINA: We'll leave you now so you can enjoy your visit. It's Wednesday and exactly three o'clock.

SOR FELICIANA: I'll be by for rosary . . .

SOR CATARINA: We must see to Sister Magdalena now. I'm afraid it's the plague. We were hoping the convent would be spared. May God help us.

SOR JUANA: I should be helping you.

SOR CATARINA: There will be plenty for you to do—but not today. Enjoy your afternoon.

SOR FELICIANA: He's here. He's finally here. (*Kisses her aunt on cheek.* SOR CATARINA *and* SOR FELICIANA *exit.* SOR JUANA *takes a small missal out of her skirt pocket and places it on the table. There is a knock at the door.* SOR JUANA *hurries to the door, then stops for a moment, her hand upon her heart. She takes a deep breath of joy, then opens the door to* FATHER ANTONIO. *They embrace without a word, then* SOR JUANA *takes his hand and leads him in.*)

SOR JUANA: This is a day I've waited for. Oh, my spirit's voice, angels have brought you to me in brighter dreams. I saw your face so clearly.

FATHER ANTONIO: Juana . . .

SOR JUANA: You cannot imagine my life without you!

FATHER ANTONIO: You're thin. You've been so gravely ill.

SOR JUANA: My soul, my spirit. But I've made peace with myself.

FATHER ANTONIO: (*Looks around cell.*) Everything's gone.

SOR JUANA: The money I received was put to good use.

FATHER ANTONIO: You gave it to the poor.

SOR JUANA: It was not enough. There never is enough, is there? You've helped such people all your life—did you ever feel it to be a hopeless cause?

FATHER ANTONIO: My hope has been tried many times.

SOR JUANA: Hope! Come, Father, sit down. There's tea. (SOR JUANA *and* FATHER ANTONIO *sit at the table.* SOR JUANA *pours tea.*)

FATHER ANTONIO: It's wonderful—the tea, sitting across the table from you. You were always in my thoughts.

SOR JUANA: To hear the sound of your voice again!

FATHER ANTONIO: I'm here to stay. I'm back at my old church.

SOR JUANA: I shall go help you sweep your church on Saturday mornings. You used to do that, remember?

FATHER ANTONIO: And wash my supper dishes on Tuesday nights . . .

SOR JUANA: As an offering to the Virgin Mary. Oh, Father, I bow my head each day at dusk in special prayer for the people who are part of me now . . . the people from the barrio in the gulch in San Hipólito.

FATHER ANTONIO: I know it well. I worked with the inmates of the asylum at the edge of the barrio.

SOR JUANA: I went to the asylum . . . remembering you. I stood by the door where you stood so many times, putting coins into wavering hands. All those people, lost forever—it's heartbreaking! I can do so little. These are times of desperation . . .

FATHER ANTONIO: But you never give up . . .

SOR JUANA: Never! My world has contracted to Tomasita, Carmela, the children . . .

FATHER ANTONIO: Who are they?

SOR JUANA: People who need me. Tomasita is old and blind, and she lives in one cold room. I keep a fire going for her and she holds my hand for hours. I take bread to Carmela, who has six children. She's so brave, so beautiful . . . the fierceness—to feed her children, to love them, keep them safe. Once a week I sit on a tree stump, with a comb in my hand and a can of kerosene.

Mamas send their children for miles around to be deloused! But what the Sisters of St. Jerome do for the barrio is not enough. We need many more to help . . .

FATHER ANTONIO: I shall go with you.

SOR JUANA: Father, to have you by my side . . .

FATHER ANTONIO: It shall be so for the rest of my days.

SOR JUANA: I am content . . .

FATHER ANTONIO: And your quest—to find God through the intellect?

SOR JUANA: He is all the life around me . . .

FATHER ANTONIO: Amen.

SOR JUANA: The art of love—the art of finding God—lies not in words, does it? Having learned this so late in my life, I am now afraid . . .

FATHER ANTONIO: Because your name is in the world . . .

SOR JUANA: Yes. What I have written to be truth is not the truth I see before my eyes each day . . . except for love and dignity. I see that in the barrios every day. It embarrasses me to sound full of self-importance. They will say that all good things evaporated in Mexico with the coming of rebellion, that I was forced to give up my possessions, my writing. They will make of me a martyr. I am not. I simply faced myself and found myself wanting. My knowledge could not dissolve the terror of death and violence. My books could not suspend the suffering of so many! Words became only words; for that reason I saw them as a form of deceit. It would be a prideful thing to say such things with words.

FATHER ANTONIO: You do not write anymore?

SOR JUANA: During my time of trial, my penitence, some inner force made me take up my pen. Once, when I was mad with guilt, I spilled my blood and wrote out a legal petition for forgiveness. (*She goes to missal, takes out one of the papers, hands it to* FATHER ANTONIO.) My confession in blood, to wash away my sins . . .

FATHER ANTONIO: This is not you! Destroy it!

SOR JUANA: No. It shall be sent to the Divine Tribunal.

FATHER ANTONIO: There's no need.

SOR JUANA: Oh, I know the Holy Company! This legal petition is exactly what they want. If my enemies want it, they can have it. The guilt belonged to another Sor Juana. In spite of all their accusations, perhaps all they fear is my being so singular. Strange—that very singularity denied me myself!

FATHER ANTONIO: You have learned humility.

SOR JUANA: I do not mind being the lowest of the low . . . but that is silly, isn't it? There's no such thing. Last Friday, before vespers, the air was heavy with spring. Again, I picked up my pen. (*Goes to missal, takes out another piece of paper, hands it to* FATHER ANTONIO.) I wrote this . . .

FATHER ANTONIO: (*Reads it aloud.*) "Oh mad Hope, green loveliness that gives meaning to our lives, intricate delicate dream of wakefulness, vain treasure, heart of the world—imagined decrepit Spring, the 'now' desired by the joyless, and for the joyful, the tomorrow . . . A mystery! Let it follow your shadow when you search for the day, a day with magic windows, windows where you paint what you desire to see. For I, I have the measure of my fortune in my hand, my eyes, and see only what I touch . . ."

SOR JUANA: (*Crosses to window.*) I must get up at sunrise and pick my turnips tomorrow. Sister Catarina says I'm well enough to take the wagon to San Hipólito.

FATHER ANTONIO: Will you stop by the church for me?

SOR JUANA: Yes.

SCENE 2

Lights come up on flashback area. February 17, 1695. A room in the parish house of San Angel. SOR JUANA *kneels in the shadows, upstage right. She is praying the Fifteen Mysteries on her rosary. Once she coughs, a harsh, deep, rasping cough, then returns to the prayers. In the center of area, on his deathbed, lies* FATHER ANTONIO. *A* PRIEST *is administering Extreme Unction. He holds a small vessel with olive oil. He dips his thumb into the oil, then makes the sign of the cross over* FATHER ANTONIO's *eyes, ears, nose, mouth, hands, and feet. As he anoints:*

PRIEST: Through this holy anointing, and His most tender mercy, may the Lord forgive you whatever sins of sight, hearing, smell, taste, speech, touch, and steps . . . Amen. (*Continues praying in silence. Then he makes a sign of the cross, goes to* SOR JUANA, *touches her shoulder to console, and exits.* SOR JUANA *crosses to bed, kneels, takes* FATHER ANTONIO's *hand, kisses it, puts her head down on his chest, wanting to feel his last warmth. She raises her head, lovingly traces the outlines of his thin face.*)

SOR JUANA: Oh, how the world has tired you! But you love it so, don't you? You will take that love with you to Heaven. But loving has always been so easy for you, my shepherd, my love . . . Can you hear me? Of course! You have always heard me, you will always hear me. You bent and twisted with the wind, my dear old shrub, and your roots are alive and well in me and the many you have loved. I shall be so alone, so alone. No, you have filled my emptiness too well, for my days, all my days . . . they won't be many, I think, for all that is me will reach out for you . . . Oh, Sweet Jesus, Sweet Mother, hold him unto You. He is so precious . . . (*She strokes his head, then opens his shirt, listens to his heart; then she kisses his chest and lays her head on it.*) You smell as sweet in death as you did in life! Do you think I can be upon this earth without you?

Lights come down on flashback area. A REQUIEM CHANT *is heard as the lights begin to dim. It continues in the darkness. Suddenly the Chant is broken by the sound of a flute. The lights go up on cell area.* SOR JUANA *is sitting crosslegged on her cot, playing the flute of her childhood. Around her, sitting, standing, are* SOR FELICIANA, SOR CATARINA, SOR BARBARA *and* SOR CELESTINA. *The last two are very young. They have been nursing their ill sisters, for the plague has hit hard. All four wear work clothes and simple kerchiefs to cover their heads. Almost as if they have left all the cures of the world behind them, they seem like young girls, free of care as* SOR JUANA *plays her tune. She blows a wrong note. They all laugh. The laughter is broken by the knelling of the church bell, funeral bells.*

SOR BARBARA: I can't stand them. All day long. Half of the sisters at St. Jerome gone. Death, death, all around us . . .

SOR JUANA: Shhh! Don't think about death. Think about being alive.

SOR BARBARA: That's hard these days.

SOR FELICIANA: Think of the nice dinner we had.

SOR CELESTINA: Chicken soup!

SOR CATARINA: Miracle of miracles. Where on earth did you get a chicken, Sor Juana?

SOR JUANA: I was hoeing at sunrise, by the garden gate. Suddenly I had this feeling that I must open the gate. I did, and what did

I see? A chicken stumbling over a mudhole, coming toward me.

SOR CELESTINA: An angel must have sent it.

SOR JUANA: (*To* SOR BARBARA.) There, you're smiling. Isn't it wonderful, to see the sunrise, to walk with the winds, to look up to the Heavens and know that God is watching over us?

SOR BARBARA: You're so brave.

SOR JUANA: And you, so young. How old are you?

SOR BARBARA: Nineteen.

SOR JUANA: And already you embrace God without misgivings. That's why you must think of being alive. I'm glad to be me. Aren't you glad to be you?

SOR BARBARA: Yes . . .

SOR FELICIANA: (*To* SOR JUANA.) All the guilts have melted away.

SOR CELESTINA: What guilts?

SOR JUANA: My guilts. You and Sor Barbara have been in the order, let's see, how long now . . .

SOR CELESTINA: Two years. To be part of St. Jerome, of Sor Juana!

SOR CATARINA: You are one of our shrines, Sor Juana. Long after the Order is gone, you'll still live!

SOR JUANA: Don't . . . don't kindle the old pride, It still lurks like a monster, waiting to take possession. Have pity on me!

SOR FELICIANA: I'm proud of all you have been all your life.

SOR JUANA: Like my guilts, my regrets of the last year are dispersing in the heat of our desert sun. Sometimes I feel . . . I feel almost weightless. (*She coughs.*)

SOR FELICIANA: You alright?

SOR JUANA: Of course. I'm feeling so whole these days. (*Begins to sing softly.*) "Coya, coya, coya, ja no llore ma', el thielo sonlei, el día lindo va . . ."

SOR BARBARA: I heard you sing that song, walking home from Father Antonio's burial. I thought it was kind of strange . . .

SOR JUANA: I *am* strange. Andrés, my brother, sang that song when we climbed the hill behind my grandfather's farm. Oh, memories are good (*crosses to window, traces thread of sunlight*) . . . like this thread of sunlight that holds all the mysteries of Creation. What's more wonderful, my mind does not question anymore.

SOR FELICIANA: But all the wonderful things you've written were written because your mind questioned.

SOR JUANA: I'm not sorry for the old me. Even that I accept. It just took me longer to know my God. (*To* SOR BARBARA *and* SOR CELESTINA.) For you, there was the straight path of Faith.

SOR CATARINA: The old passions, they're still part of you.

SOR JUANA: Only this morning, before going out to hoe, I found this old letter I never mailed . . . (*Hands it to* SOR CATARINA.) To Father Kino.

SOR CATARINA: It's dated 1686, almost nine years ago.

SOR JUANA: Speaking of passions. He stood very much alone, defending his concepts of comets against the censorship of our conservative Holy Fathers.

SOR CATARINA: (*Reads.*) "Dear Holy Father, I agree with you, comets are not omens from an angry God. They are just like any other heavenly body. My findings are most inferior compared to yours, Father Kino, but I thoroughly agree, and cite from my own notes the position of the comet in relation to other celestial bodies, its magnitude, its distance from the earth, its velocity—all verify your concept of harmony in our Heavens . . ."

SOR JUANA: Stop! See, little sisters (*to* SOR BARBARA *and* SOR CELESTINA), I was even stranger in earlier years.

SOR BARBARA: But it's wonderful, all your knowledge.

SOR JUANA: No, what is wonderful is the Faith that soars in my blood today. My memories of loving people, in my poor clumsy way. What is wonderful are the shadows in this room in the quiet of the afternoon. What is joyous is being with you, playing this flute badly and remembering . . .

SOR FELICIANA: Oh, dear Aunt, you are growing wings, or becoming wind . . .

SOR JUANA: To the hill, to the hill! Run! Fly, my shepherd, quick! For Our Blessed Virgin melts into the air . . .

SOR FELICIANA: Oh, I remember when you wrote those words . . . "Run! Fly! Quick! Quick! For She takes our heart and soul with Her, and taking the best of us, leaves the world desolate . . ."

SOR JUANA: I was wrong, so wrong! The world is never desolate! (*Picks up flute.*) Now, I shall play the song without missing a note . . . (*The* SISTERS *laugh.* SOR JUANA *begins to play.*)

CURTAIN

Father Antonio Núñez de Miranda died February 17, 1695. Sor Juana Inés de la Cruz died April 17, 1695, two months to the day after the death of her beloved confessor.